Z 678.9 .A4 U61~~93 199~~

Y0-BED-527

Boss, Richard W.

The library administrator's
automation handbook

DATE DUE

DE 2 2003			

DEMCO 38-297

NEW ENGLAND INSTITUTE
OF TECHNOLOGY
LEARNING RESOURCES CENTER

THE LIBRARY
ADMINISTRATOR'S
AUTOMATION HANDBOOK

THE LIBRARY ADMINISTRATOR'S AUTOMATION HANDBOOK

By Richard W. Boss

NEW ENGLAND INSTITUTE
OF TECHNOLOGY
LEARNING RESOURCES CENTER

Information Today, Inc.
Medford, NJ
1997

9/98

36083687

Copyright© 1997 by   Information Today, Inc.
                            143 Old Marlton Pike
                            Medford, NJ 08055

All rights reserved. No part of this book may be reproduced in any form without the written permission of the publisher.

Printed in the United States of America.

Library of Congress Cataloging-in-Publication Data

Boss, Richard W.
    The library administrator's automation handbook / by Richard W. Boss.
        p.   cm.
    Includes bibliographical references and index.
    ISBN 1-57387-038-2 (hardcover)
    1. Libraries—United States—Data Processing. 2. Libraries—United States—Automation.   I. Title.
    Z678.9.A4U6193   1997
    025' .00285—dc21
                                                            96-52791
                                                                 CIP

Price: $39.50

Book Editor: Diane Zelley
Cover Design: Jeanne Wachter

Table of Contents

Introduction

One of the most significant decisions in a library administrator's career is the decision to automate one or more of a library's operations. This book describes the present state of local library automation; the planning, selection, and implementation process; and the library administrator's role in that process.

The author believes that a basic understanding of hardware, system architectures, software, standards, and data communication is essential for an administrator to make intelligent decisions. The bulk of the text, therefore, attempts to put down a foundation on which automation decisions can be based.

While the emphasis is on automated library systems, a chapter is devoted to related technologies, including CD-ROM, remote database services, and the Internet—including the World Wide Web.

Automation is not solely a technological problem. Throughout this book, emphasis is placed on the context in which the technical decisions must be made. All of the steps in the process of making and carrying out the decision are covered.

Chapter 1 is an overview of library automation today, including a discussion of the potential benefits of fully automating a library. Chapter 2 describes the variety of computer hardware available in library automation, while Chapter 3 discusses system architectures—particularly important in light of the fact that a shift from hierarchical to client/server architecture is underway. Chapters 4 and 5 discuss system and applications software. Chapter 6 describes the functionality of contemporary automated library systems.

Chapter 7 identifies and discusses bibliographic and networking standards, with the emphasis on the Z39.50 standard for the linking of automated library systems. Chapter 8 details CD-ROM, remote database services, and the Internet. Chapters 9 and 10 discuss data communication, with the first focusing on data cabling and local area networks and the second on remote data communication.

Chapter 11 discusses planning and procurement, and Chapter 12 discusses the costs of automation and related technologies.

A bibliography and a glossary have been included; terms in bold face throughout the text are defined in the glossary.

Chapter 1

Library Automation Today

By late 1996, over 14,000 commercially developed integrated, multifunction, multiuser automated library systems had been installed in libraries worldwide. Almost all of the systems supported local cataloging, an online cataloging support system interface, authority control, circulation, and an online patron access catalog. A majority also supported acquisitions and serials control. A smaller number of libraries had implemented inventorying, information and referral, media booking, and journal citation files modules. Approximately 40 percent of the systems served more than one location, with 5 percent of the total supporting multiple libraries.

There were at least 120,000 micro-based (PC and Mac) integrated, multifunction systems installed, with at least one-fourth of the systems mounted on a LAN (local area network). Most of the micro-based systems supported local cataloging, circulation, and an online patron access catalog, but fewer than one-third supported other applications such as acquisitions, serials control, and an online cataloging support system interface. Authority control was utilized in only 20 percent of the systems.

EVOLUTION OF LIBRARY AUTOMATION

Library automation dates back to the 1940s, but the first period of significant activity was not until the mid-1960s when **batch processing** began to give way to **interactive** operations, and manufacturers began to incorporate telecommunications capability into their computers. While batch processing systems provided fast, reliable data collection, elimination of filing, and automatic printing of purchase orders or overdue notices, they did not provide the highly current information that libraries required. Also, since most of the early libraries that automated had one or more branches, data communication was vital.

By the mid-1960s, the benefits of applying automation to library operations—directly as in circulation control, or indirectly as in the production of catalog cards—were sufficiently clear for the Library of Congress to begin work on developing formats that would allow the distribution

1

of machine-readable cataloging records to libraries and library service organizations.

Toward the end of the 1960s, interactive systems offering immediate access to all files by a variety of approaches became common. These systems were configured around **mainframe** (IBM 360 or equivalent) computers, with software usually developed and maintained in-house. Because of the high cost of hardware and the substantial time and expense of software development, these early efforts took place in large organizations with substantial financial and human resources—large academic and public libraries, and libraries serving corporations and governmental agencies.

The Library of Congress's initiatives with regard to data formats facilitated the creation of OCLC and other bibliographic utilities—organizations which do for libraries much what service bureaus do for businesses. OCLC's initial objective was to provide libraries with shared, and hence affordable, access to automation for cataloging and the production of catalog cards. While this is still a significant activity, today over 75 percent of OCLC's nearly 7,000 full cataloging participants download cataloging records into their local library systems rather than obtaining cards, and nearly 80 percent use the interlibrary loan subsystem for resource sharing.

As computer technology developed and the cost of computing power dropped through the late 1960s and early 1970s, more libraries could afford the computer hardware for automation of their internal operations. However, hardware represented only the tip of the iceberg in automation expenditures. Software design, development, and maintenance typically represented 80 percent of the cost of implementing a system. Few libraries had the resources or interest to establish large in-house programming departments, nor the money to contract for custom software development by a commercial firm.

Cooperation and entrepreneurship filled the software gap by focusing development efforts on commonality in basic library functions, rather than differences among local implementation of these functions in individual libraries. Libraries that had already developed automation software began making it available for use by other libraries, and individual entrepreneurs recognized business opportunities in developing off-the-shelf systems and marketing them to multiple library clients. The library-developed shared software was generally mainframe dependent. Commercial systems took advantage of the emergence of cost-effective **minicomputers** (Digital PDP series and equivalent) with capabilities particularly suited to library automation.

Minicomputers came in a wide variety of sizes and capabilities, and were particularly well-suited for interactive applications—those in which the computer gives immediate response to the users of terminals linked directly to it. Minicomputers were also inexpensive compared to mainframe computers, with prices in the tens-of-thousands rather than in the hundreds-of-thousands of dollars for the computer itself. The interactive capability that is common to all minicomputers made them particularly easy to use by those who had little computer experience. If users entered the wrong commands, the computer could prompt them back on the right course. Software development for minicomputers also was faster and substantially less expensive. In the cost of computer power, or the number of instructions executed per dollar, minis were generally less expensive than mainframes. The cost of **peripheral equipment** was also less for minis. The mainframe continued to be important for very large libraries, however, because only it could support hundreds of users.

The roots of these origins are still visible in today's library automation vendors: the mainframe-based software packages which were developed by Northwestern University (NOTIS) and Mankato State University (PALS) are still being used and continue to be supported by Ameritech Library Services, and the minicomputer-based systems developed by CLSI are still being used and continue to be supported by Geac Computers, Inc.

The introduction of **microcomputers** in 1981 led to a further expansion of library automation opportunities. Just as minicomputer technology had expanded the horizon to mid-sized libraries, microcomputer technology, from PCs and Macs (beginning in 1985) to multiuser supermicros, extended the promise of affordable automation to small libraries. Not only was the hardware affordable, there were a number of avenues for software development, including inexpensive specialized library applications software, powerful generic software such as database management systems, and custom software developed in-house by dedicated hobbyists.

Despite the impressive developments in microcomputer technology, the indisputable utility of much of the available library automation software for microcomputers, and the increasing use of PCs and Macs as components in larger systems—with the exception of school libraries—PCs and Macs did not have the impact on library automation in the 1980s that minicomputers did. The two major reasons were that the operating systems used on PCs and Macs, which were widely used in all sizes and types of libraries for office automation, were a limitation; and the market focus of most of the companies selling PC- and Mac-based library applications software was school libraries. Nevertheless, PCs and Macs did much to demystify automation and contribute to broader expectations of system functionality and ease of use.

The real impact in the microcomputer revolution was brought about by **supermicros: multiuser, multitasking** systems which could use the **operating system** and **applications software** developed for minicomputers, but could bring sophisticated library automation to libraries with less than $100,000 to spend for a complete system.

The three reasons for the success of supermicros were the use of true multiuser, multitasking operating systems; the use of multiple processor boards to handle high-volume processing; and the broad market focus of the vendors selling the software: libraries of all sizes and types.

CURRENT AUTOMATED LIBRARY SYSTEMS

By late 1996, there were at least 60 vendors worldwide marketing integrated multiuser, multifunction automated library systems or library applications software packages for minis and supermicros, more than half of them active in the United States. All of the systems supported the core software applications, including acquisitions, serials control, circulation, and online patron access catalog modules; and a majority supported at least eight additional modules.

There were also at least 40 vendors of PC- and Mac-based products, with at least 20 of them active in the United States market. All of the systems supported circulation and online patron access catalog modules, and several of them also supported acquisitions and serials control. A few systems included additional modules.

All multiuser minis, supermicros, and PC- and Mac-based micros available in the last decade were designed to capture records from a cataloging support system—either a bibliographic utility or a CD-ROM-based cataloging support system—although most purchasers of PC- and Mac-based systems have continued to rely on local keying of records. There were three major bibliographic utilities in the United States (OCLC, RLIN, and WLN) and a dozen more elsewhere in the world: each supporting online cataloging by scores, hundreds, or thousands of participating libraries by late 1996. OCLC, the largest, had nearly 7,000 members and another 14,000 participants. Several companies were offering stand-alone cataloging support systems configured around PCs and CD-ROM drives. The largest of these, The Library Corporation, had nearly 10,000 installed systems.

The vendors of automated library systems and bibliographic services range from small companies generating less than $5 million a year in sales, through mid-size companies with revenues of $5 to $75 million, to large companies such as Ameritech Library Services and OCLC, with revenues of $110 million and $140 million per year, respectively. Interestingly, multi-billion dollar corporations, such as IBM and UNISYS, which had offered library systems as part of full automation product lines, have dropped out of the market in the past five years, although their products continue to be supported by other companies.

DIFFERENTIATING SYSTEMS

Now that most systems are using the same microprocessor boards (Intel and Motorola) regardless of system size, it is far more difficult to differentiate among systems than it was in the past. The most common distinction is to describe one group of systems as integrated, multifunction, multiuser systems and the other as PC- or Mac-based systems.

An **integrated** system is one in which all modules share a single bibliographic database, a single command language, and changes in one module are immediately reflected in all other modules that use that information. In a fully integrated system, a change from one module to another requires only one or two keystrokes.

A **multifunction** system is one which includes at least two major modules: usually at least circulation and an online patron access catalog. Some systems support as many as 14 modules.

A **multiuser** system is one which is capable of supporting more than one terminal or other remote peripheral, and allowing multiple users to access different system modules at the same time, supporting all operations and remote peripherals simultaneously.

Integrated, multifunction, multiuser automation systems are almost always configured on a mainframe, mini, or supermicro. All use a multiuser **operating system**, such as UNIX, VMS, or MVS. The products are marketed in two ways: as turnkey systems or as supported software packages. A **turnkey system** is one in which all hardware, software, installation, training, documentation, and ongoing hardware and software maintenance are provided by a single vendor. For as long as the purchaser subscribes to the vendor's maintenance program, the vendor assumes responsibility for all aspects of system performance (hardware reliability, system response times, software functionality) and development.

A library purchasing a turnkey system normally does not need to employ or retain systems analysts or programmers, nor specialist computer operators. Day-to-day operation of the system can be performed by clerical staff, with vendor personnel responsible for hardware and software maintenance. However, it is necessary for a library to appoint a system manager to work with the system vendor, undertake changes in system parameters, and coordinate staff training. Systems which are configured with a large number of PCs also require a PC configuration specialist and those utilizing a LAN (**local area network**) may require a network specialist.

Vendors of **supported software** packages offer similar services, but in relation to software only. They provide software, documentation, training, and software maintenance and development. While they may offer assistance in hardware selection and configuration, supported software vendors will not usually guarantee system performance even when the hardware has been configured and installed in accordance with their guidelines. Software-only products vary widely in the extent of their requirements for specialized support staff. Some are configured on the same hardware as the turnkey systems; with software maintenance, operational documentation and training provided by the supported software vendor, and hardware maintenance handled by the computer manufacturer, they require no more specialized staff than do turnkey systems. Other supported software products require that a library have access to systems analysts, programmers, and full-time operators. In these situations, vendors limit their activities to development, training, and documentation of generalized applications software. Fine-tuning and coordination of the system and applications software with the hardware, and implementation of the system are responsibilities of the purchasing library or its parent organization.

PC- and Mac-based systems differ from integrated, multifunction, multiuser systems in several respects. Many are not truly integrated, lacking a single file shared by all modules, using different command languages for different modules, and requiring that a user log-off and log-on again to change modules. However, given the increasing power of PCs and Macs, and the demands of the marketplace, an increasing number of PC- and Mac-based systems are becoming integrated. They also are multifunction, although the range of functionality usually is somewhat narrow—for market reasons rather than technical ones. They also can be multiuser since the software can be mounted on a network server allowing several devices to access it at what appears to be the same time. They are not **multitasking**, in the sense that a micro-based system doesn't do several things at once; instead it supports switching very quickly from task to task.

Because these historic differences are becoming less and less clear, it is necessary to develop a new basis for differentiating systems. There are four options: one which uses the most common configuration—multiuser or single-user; one which uses the number of processor boards in the computer; one which uses the operating system; and one which uses the vendor's target market as the basis for differentiation.

Multiuser supermicros and single-user micros often use the same Intel or Motorola processor boards. These may be 486, Pentium, or Pentium Pro-type processor boards; the critical difference is in their number. A PC or Mac uses a single processor board; a more powerful supermicro system may use as few as two and as many as twenty; and a very few machines use hundreds. The use of multiple boards allow the software to divide a task among several processors, thus making it possible to support a large number of users performing a variety of complex tasks without adversely affecting response time. While single processor systems are often called micro-based, and the multiprocessor systems are sometimes called supermicro-based, the use of the terms is not yet well-established. The key is that supermicros are designed by manufacturers to be **multiuser**, and micros are designed to be **single-user**.

Operating systems have been an excellent way of differentiating systems in the past. The more powerful systems used operating systems such as UNIX, VMS, and MVS, while most PC-based systems used DOS, and Mac-based systems used Mac/OS. That too is changing. UNIX is becoming a popular operating system for use on a single PC or a PC-LAN, and Windows NT is beginning to be used on all sizes of machines. The only thing that is clear is that there is a gradual trend away from DOS for library applications—an operating system that cannot effectively utilize the memory and speed of today's PCs.

The **target market** has also been an excellent way of differentiating systems in the past, but that may not be true in the future. While the leaders in the PC-based system market, among them Follett and Winnebago, still focus on small libraries, especially school libraries, companies such as Ameritech Library Services and DRA are now actively selling systems to school districts for use as district-wide systems and consortia of small public libraries.

While none of the four options for differentiating systems is ideal, the most appropriate would appear to be the first: the most common configuration. The author will, therefore, refer to multiuser and single-user systems throughout the book.

RELATED INFORMATION TECHNOLOGIES

There are several related information technologies which interact with library automation: **CD-ROM, online database services**, and the **Internet**. CD-ROM has become the most popular form of access to electronic publications in the past five years. There were over 6,000 titles commercially available in 1996, with some 2,000 of them marketed by companies which specialize in sales to libraries. While the majority of titles purchased by libraries in 1990 were indexes and abstracts, the emphasis in 1996 was on reference and educational titles. CD-ROM has not displaced the much longer established online database services, although it has changed their use. In the mid-1980s, almost all searching done in libraries was done by librarians accessing databases stored on remote systems such as Dialog; in the mid-1990s, most searching done in libraries was by patrons accessing titles on CD-ROM, and searching for highly current information was done by both librarians and patrons accessing databases stored on remote online database service systems.

The improvement of user interfaces and changes in pricing made it possible for libraries to make available access to online database services by patrons. OCLC's *FirstSearch*, the fastest growing of the patron-oriented remote database services, increasingly called **online reference services**, saw the number of searches against its databases increase from 7 million in 1993–94 to over 12 million in 1995. Ebsco, Information Access Corporation, SilverPlatter, and Vista also reported dramatic increases in the use of their databases. The companies, most with revenues of under $10 million per year, continued to be dwarfed by Dialog—a company which realized most of its $300 million in revenues from expert searchers in corporations.

As the amount of money spent for access to electronic publications becomes a significant part of library budgets, libraries have begun to develop strategies for optimizing service and cost. They do this by analyzing ease of use, currency, and pricing for a specific title mounted on a single CD-ROM drive, on a **CD-ROM tower** attached to a **CD-ROM server** supporting multiple users, and on an online reference service's computer. An infrequently accessed title is usually more economical to access on an online reference service. A moderately used title may be less expensive to purchase in multiple copies for stand-alone PCs than licensed for use on a network. A single approach may not work. While a search might begin with in-house CD-ROM products, searching for highly current information involves access to an online reference service which loads updates as frequently as daily or weekly.

Many libraries have begun to pull together automated library systems, CD-ROM servers, and online reference services so that they can be accessed from a single PC- or Mac-based workstation. The user selects the information source to be accessed from a menu on the opening screen, and is connected to the information source—which may be within or outside the library.

TRENDS

There were several distinct trends in library automation in the mid-1990s: the increasing use of PCs and Macs as remote peripherals on multiuser systems; the use of **graphical user interfaces (GUIs)**, including Web-based online patron access catalogs; a gradual move toward **client/server architecture**; the **linking** of automated library systems; and the expansion of the type of information included in automated library system databases. Each of these trends is discussed in the following pages.

Remote Peripherals: Throughout the first 30 years of library automation the remote peripherals were almost always **dumb terminals**. A "dumb" terminal is a device which consists of a keyboard and monitor; it lacks memory and disk storage, therefore, it can display only characters, not images. A computer can identify a "dumb" terminal only by the port to which it is connected. PCs and Macs were initially used as remote peripherals to avoid having someone who used a micro for office applications move to a separate device when s/he wanted to access the library's automated library system. The **intelligence** of the micro was not used in accessing the automated library system; **terminal emulation** software was loaded on the micro to make it possible for it to appear as a dumb terminal to the computer to which it was attached.

As libraries increased the menu options available to staff and patrons—including access to the automated library system, a CD-ROM server, and online reference services—they began to use micros in lieu of dumb terminals throughout the library. A typical system sold in 1996 was typically configured with a mix of dumb terminals and micros, and a minority of all systems were configured exclusively with micros.

There are significant financial implications when a library substitutes micros for dumb terminals. The cost of a typical automated library system may increase by 15 percent or more when half of the remote peripherals are micros, costing an average of $2,500, instead of dumb terminals costing an average of $500. Considerable attention was, therefore, being directed toward **network PCs**, low-cost ($700–900) devices with limited capacity, but with the capability of downloading software as needed from a host or server. The first of these network PCs were introduced in the third quarter of 1996.

Graphical user interfaces (GUI) are Windows-type displays with pictorial **icons** to help the inexperienced searcher and the capacity to pull down related information in a separate window while retaining the existing display—a boon to productivity. Vendors of automated library systems focused their initial efforts on developing GUIs for online patron access catalog devices but saw demand build for GUIs on staff devices in technical services after a series of reports documented dramatically increased productivity in the libraries which developed their own GUIs.

Client/server is a computer **architecture** which divides functions into client (requestor) and server (provider) subsystems using standard communications methods. A client may connect to one or more servers; a server may connect to multiple clients concurrently. Client/server makes it possible to tailor clients to specific types of users and to provide those users with a single-user interface to access a variety of information sources, including the automated library system.

As of mid-1996, approximately 200 client/server systems had been installed in libraries, the majority of them Ameritech Horizon systems. At least a score of the other vendors in the industry were developing client/server systems. The most common pattern was not to create a brand new system, but to evolve existing products. A common approach was to begin with the implementation of GUIs and then gradually move the presentation software from the host computer to the desktop. The next step was the exporting of raw data from the host computer to the desktop, with the formatting being done at the desktop. At that point the architecture would become client/server.

With client/server systems, appropriate software must be mounted on each user's PC to supported the distributed processing. As new software releases are issued, each PC has to have it loaded. Even in relatively small libraries, this can be time consuming.

Linking automated library systems has been pursued by libraries for more than two decades, but early efforts offered no more than a physical connection. One had to know the **command language** of the target system in order to use it. Few library staff, and almost no patrons, were able to become proficient in the searching of several different automated library systems in an area. Efforts to make the linkage **transparent** initially focused on proprietary solutions, but it soon became obvious that a **standard** was needed to reduce the costs to affordable levels. **Z39.50**, the linking standard, provides that each system conform to the standard without regard to changes in other automated library systems. Z39.50 is based on the concept of client/server, with the target system acting as the server. A system need not have client/server as its internal architecture to function as a server. The client portion of Z39.50 can be mounted on a searcher's PC or Mac, or it can be a multiuser application on the automated library system in the searcher's library.

Web-based online patron access catalogs began to become available in 1996. Rather than using the vendor's proprietary user interface, they offer Netscape or another Web browser as a single-user interface for the online patron access catalog, online reference services, and the World Wide Web, thus providing a single familiar user interface to all information resources. As attractive as they are, Web browsers do not offer as wide a range of searching capabilities as a vendor's proprietary software. For that reason, an increasing number of vendors are expected to offer proprietary, Web, and Z39.50 options in a single bundled user interface package, thus providing a choice to the user.

Broadening of scope of functionality has been a phenomenon of the 1990s. During the first three decades of library automation the database on a system consisted almost entirely of that which had previously been in the card catalog. In the past five years the scope has been broadened to include **journal citation files**. Most commonly these have been periodical indexes. By loading magnetic tapes of periodical indexes onto the automated library system, it has become possible for staff and patrons searching by author or subject to identify periodical articles as well as monographs. With a link to local holdings, a library's periodicals collection became as accessible as its monographs. However, the time and expertise required to load and index the tapes prompted a number of libraries to choose online reference services over locally mounted files.

As of 1996, **information and referral files** were a popular choice among public libraries. Such files typically contain the names, addresses, and service descriptions for agencies which provide services to the community. A community calendar also is often included. The latest broadening of scope has been the inclusion of **image files**. An image of a newspaper clipping, photograph, or manuscript is stored and retrievable with just one or two keystrokes if the **address** of the image is linked to a field in the bibliographic record.

All of these trends are discussed at greater length elsewhere in this book.

Chapter 2

Hardware Basics

Every library administrator should understand a few basics about computer hardware. Choosing hardware, or evaluating that offered by a vendor, is important because it may affect a library's ability to expand its system to accommodate growth in activities, the addition of other functions, or the extension of the system to serve other libraries.

A **computer** is a device capable of performing systematic sequences of operations on data at high speeds without a human operator intervening during the time the data is being run. A **mainframe** or full-size computer is a digital device that has a **central processing unit** (CPU), multiple input-output (**I/0**) devices, and a primary memory or **RAM** (random access memory) capacity of many hundreds-of-millions or billions of **characters** (letters and numbers). Historically mainframes have been used when hundreds or thousands of terminals and other remote peripherals had to be supported. Now that other computer types can support hundreds of terminals at less cost, mainframes are only rarely selected for use by libraries. There are still several score in use in large libraries, however, and thousands in large businesses.

While little used in library automation today, mainframes continue to be available in many sizes. At the top are the supercomputers manufactured by companies such as Cray. Supercomputers are very powerful, special-purpose machines designed for scientific or other research applications requiring extremely rapid execution of a high volume of complex calculations. Operating speeds are measured in billionth of a second (nanoseconds).

Below the supercomputers, most mainframe computers are properly characterized as large-scale or medium-scale machines designed to perform common scientific and data processing tasks. IBM is the dominant company in this segment of the market. Although large-scale computers are generally smaller than super-computers, they also have operating speeds measured in nanoseconds. Large-scale computers have a great amount of parallel circuitry as well, so that multiple bits can be processed simultaneously. Medium-scale computers are somewhat smaller and slower. Relatively small mainframe computers are now available, priced as low as $20,000. They are called mainframe computers primarily because they share the **architecture** and operating systems of larger mainframes.

A **minicomputer** is a compact digital device that has a CPU, at least one input-output (I/O) device, and normally a primary memory of 32 to hundreds-of-millions of characters. Historically minicomputers have been used when scores to a few hundred terminals or other remote peripherals had to be supported. The choice of a minicomputer over a mainframe usually has been made when the smaller, more cost-effective machine could support the number of terminals planned. When a library could use either type machine, the hardware requirements of the most attractive applications software usually determined the choice of computer type. Until the late 1970s, most vendors of automated library systems used **proprietary operating systems** which would work only on the hardware platforms for which they were written, therefore, dictating the hardware choice. However, beginning in the late 1970s, the introduction of **open operating systems** such as UNIX and Pick—which are not machine-dependent—for automated library systems gave libraries and vendors much more latitude in hardware choice.

A **microcomputer** is a complete computer processor manufactured on a single integrated circuit chip with a memory measured in the hundreds-of-thousands to a few million characters, and a related input-output capability. The vast majority of microcomputers are PCs or Macs. PCs and Macs are single-user devices which support a single function at a time. While they can be multifunction, the limitations of operating systems—most commonly DOS or Mac/OS—result in rapid switching from task to task, rather than the **multitasking** common to other types of computers. As Windows 95 and WindowsNT are installed on millions of micros, and library applications are rewritten to utilize these much more robust operating systems, true multitasking will become available to users of micros, and it may become common for inexpensive slave terminals or PCs to share access to the applications software on a micro.

A **supermicro** is a somewhat more powerful micro which uses the same microprocessor board as a PC or a Mac, but it has multiple microprocessor boards. A microprocessor is a single-chip, integrated circuit device capable of performing the operations typically associated with the control and arithmetic/logic sections of a CPU. Powerful, inexpensive microprocessors have been made possible by large-scale integration, a manufacturing technique whereby thousands of highly miniaturized circuits can be consolidated in a very small space.

Supermicros usually have a primary memory measured in many millions of characters (now commonly as high as 512 million and sometimes even more than one billion) and use an operating system other than DOS or Mac/OS, thus giving it the capability of supporting multiple users performing different functions at the same time—true multitasking. A supermicro often uses the same software as was developed for minicomputers.

FROM MAINFRAMES TO SUPERMICROS

From the late 1940s through the early 1970s, computer automation specialists emphasized the economies of scale to be realized by using large capacity computing equipment that would serve many users from a centralized facility. This argument was based on **Grosch's Law**, a principle articulated in the late 1940s by the computer scientist Herbert R. J. Grosch. The law states that larger—and consequently more expensive—computers provide significantly greater processing power per dollar than smaller, less expensive machines. Assuming that the additional processing power was required, Grosch's Law implies that the consolidation of computer capabilities in a single, large CPU, rather than in several smaller ones, results in a lower unit cost of computer automation. By the mid-1960s, the development of time-sharing operating systems and telecommunications technology made such consolidation of computer resources feasible.

Minicomputers were introduced in the 1950s but were used only in limited applications until nearly twenty years later. Then, in the early 1970s, many computer users began to complain about the difficulties of dealing with seemingly unresponsive computer centers. They expressed a strong preference for more direct control over computer resources. Coincidentally, the replacement of transistors with integrated circuits containing many miniaturized components on a single silicon chip resulted in drastic reductions in the cost of minicomputers.

By the mid-1970s, many business and government agencies were using minicomputers to decentralize or distribute their computer resources and placing computers under the control of operating divisions or departments. A number of studies documented that Grosch's Law was no longer valid. Computing began to be decentralized, with machines being placed as close as possible to the end users.

While tens-of-thousands of minicomputers continue to be used, including hundreds in libraries, very few are now being purchased. For all practical purposes the supermicro has taken its place. This fact is somewhat obscured because many companies label their supermicros as minicomputers.

Today the range of machine options is the greatest ever, with hundreds of models available, including supermicros priced at as little as $5,000 and as much as $500,000. Even libraries requiring a system supporting as few as 30 concurrent users can cost-effectively automate independently. Unfortunately, smaller libraries have a more limited range of choices: sharing a multiuser system or using PCs or Macs.

PCs and Macs incorporate a microprocessor, random access memory circuits, and a keyboard in a single unit designed to be attached to a monitor. The more complex may have multiple input-output devices. These systems are rarely suitable for use in an integrated, multifunction, multiuser automated library system, however, because they are designed to be used with an operating system which is designed to support a single user performing one task at a time.

All computers have at least the following components as diagrammed here:

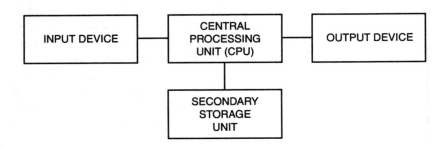

Each will be discussed in depth.

THE CPU

The **Central Processing Unit** (CPU) is the heart of the system, where the work of the computer is done. It contains the silicon chips that control and coordinate the system and perform the arithmetic and logical operations. These chips are not the only chips in a computer, but they are the most vital because they issue instructions to the other components of a system, such as copying the data from a disk, adding a column of figures, or searching a database housed in an external storage device.

Computer scientists refer to the CPU as that portion of the system that is described above. Many laymen, including librarians, occasionally use the term to describe the physical box that houses the processing functions. However, this box also houses additional chips that make up the primary or main storage chips and communication channels among these chips. This book uses the term CPU to describe the broader concept.

The CPU chips also contain the instruction sets of the computer. These are the chips that give the computer its identity. Some chips will do arithmetic functions, some will compare the bits in cells to determine if they are alike. It should be remembered that a chip is like a brain—some are better at math, some better at English—depending on the information that has been programmed into the brain.

The CPU can be conceptualized as having three components: **control unit**, **arithmetic/logic**, and **primary memory** or **RAM** (Random Access Memory).

- The control unit section directs the operation of the other sections, as well as the relationship between the CPU and its peripheral devices.

- The arithmetic/logic section contains the specialized electronic circuitry essential to computation. The CPU performs repetitive logical operations involving the testing of specified conditions or the comparison of data. In most information storage and retrieval applications, these logical operations are more important than the arithmetic operations for which computers were originally developed. Most mainframes, minicomputers, and supermicros have multiple processors in the arithmetic/logic section.
- The primary memory or storage section provides storage for data and programs within the CPU. CPU memory is often described as primary storage to distinguish it from auxiliary or secondary storage devices, such as disks. The information stored in the primary memory is recorded in an encoded, machine-readable form that is essential for computer processing. Primary memory can be accessed more quickly than secondary storage because it is kept inside the CPU. Since it is substantially more expensive, it is generally not used for long-term data storage.

In summary, the CPU controls all activities of the system, performs all calculations, stores and executes the instructions in the computer program, and holds the data while it is being processed.

Some cells in the CPU are designated as **registers**. Registers, of which there may be many, are parts of the CPU which hold small amounts of information. They are used for many functions, e.g., when two numbers are added together a register holds one number while the other is being fetched. In this discussion the registers that are of primary importance are those that hold **addresses**; the CPU locates instructions and data through the use of address registers.

There are two register functions that assure that programs are location independent. A relocation register allows the programs to be relocated dynamically and keeps track of their locations. The programmer may always assume that a new program starts at point zero and the register will assign the addresses necessary and keep track of which program is at which address. The computer also limits the addresses that can be used by one program, a necessary function in order to keep programs from interfering with each other in a multiprogram atmosphere.

Pipelining is another important concept in CPU design. Pipelining is a hardware concept or technique that permits the execution of instructions in stages and thus several instructions may be acted upon by the CPU at one time, each at a different stage of the pipeline. The instruction moves along the pipeline from one stage to the next, a different operation being performed at each stage. Pipelining requires multiple processors in the arithmetic/logic section of the CPU.

RISC (Reduced Instruction Set Computing) has become a popular CPU design among library automation vendors in recent years. The IBM RS/6000 platform is particularly widely used. RISC is distinguished from the traditional **CISC** (Complex Instruction Set Computing) in that it does not use microcode, is register rich (uses many registers), and implements simple instructions concurrently (through the use of pipelining).

RISC architecture takes advantage of compilers (programs that translate high level languages into machine language) which break down processes into simple or single tasks (reduced instruction sets). The technology uses registers to temporarily hold code or instructions that are generated by the compilers. This cuts down on the transfer of instructions between registers and primary memory. The RISC programs tend to be longer than CISC but contain instructions that are simple and execute faster because there is usually one machine cycle per instruction.

Some kind of pipelining is implemented in virtually all recent models of mainframes, minicomputers, and supermicros, but one of the major reasons RISC systems deliver higher performance is the increased efficiency of RISC pipelining techniques. RISC machines can reorganize the instructions during processing for maximum pipeline efficiency. The number of processes which can run concurrently depends on the number of stages in the pipeline. If the pipeline has four stages then four processes may run at a time, all in different stages.

In late 1996, most of the machines offered by vendors of turnkey multi-user systems were RISC-based.

PRIMARY MEMORY AND SECONDARY STORAGE

The **primary memory** of the CPU—the storage capacity within the CPU itself—is limited. It is, therefore, necessary to store much of the data used in processing outside it in one or more **secondary storage** or **mass storage devices**. Before distinguishing memory and secondary storage, it is necessary to discuss how the capacity of a computer is measured:

Bits and Bytes

In computer terminology, a "character" is any letter, numeral, punctuation mark, or other symbol encountered in data or software programs. A unique coding pattern is established to represent each of the characters to be recognized by the computer. While various coding schemes have been developed, most automated library systems are now supermicro, PC, or Mac-based and use the American Standard Code for Information Interchange (**ASCII** code). In contrast, mainframes generally use the Extended Binary Coded Decimal Interchange Code (**EBCDIC**), a code developed by IBM. Both codes employ binary digits, abbreviated as "**bits**," to note the pattern for each character. The bit can represent "1" or "0," or "on" or "off," with the different combinations of the two symbols representing the various characters. The bits usually are represented by a timed electrical impulse. The combination of bits that encode a given character is termed a "**byte**." Although the ASCII code uses seven bits to represent each character, an extra bit usually is added to each character string for error control, bringing the number of bits per byte to eight. Regardless of the number of bits involved, a byte represents a character in the computer system—whether a letter, number, or another symbol.

Computer capacity—both that of primary memory and secondary storage devices—is measured in bytes and expressed as a number followed by the symbol K or KB, or in larger systems as MB or GB. While 1 KB should be 1,000, the convention of using K to represent a count of 1,024 units became common in discussions of computer capacity when systems were small. This coding is not limited to the description of bytes, although these are usually intended when the notation of K is used. A computer described as having 512 K of main memory can store 512 times 1,024 bytes or characters. In practice, the value of K is rounded to the nearest 1,000 and the memory capacity is described in kilobytes or thousands of characters. It is, therefore, common to hear the expressions 512 KB. Very few systems today are sized in KB, however, because virtually all have measured in millions of bytes or MB, or even billions of bytes or GB.

While the byte is the most commonly used expression of memory and storage capacity, computer capacity is sometimes described in **words**, a measure that denotes the number of bits the control unit can retrieve from the primary memory at one time. An 8-bit word computer can access eight bits, or one byte (one character), at a time. The word lengths of most available computing devices range from eight to 64 bits, although most of the older machines installed in libraries have 16-bit or 32-bit word-length capacities, and the newer machines are 64-bit. When capacity is expressed in words, the same convention of using K for 1,024 (words in this case) is followed. Word length is a major factor is a computer's throughput: the more the computer can process at a time, the faster the work gets done.

To convert a statement of primary memory capacity that has been expressed in words to one expressed in bytes, multiply the number of words by the number of bits in each and divide by eight. Thus a computer with 64 K, 16 bit words of main memory can store $64 \times 1,024 \times 16$ bits, or 1,048,576 bits in primary memory. Dividing 1,048,576 by eight, the equivalent character capacity is 131,072 bytes (nominally 128 KB).

Primary Memory

The capacity of today's CPUs is usually quoted in millions of bytes (megabytes or MB), although some CPUs, including some supermicros, have capacities measured in billions of bytes (gigabytes or GB). The computers most commonly used in libraries have from 32 to 512 MB of primary memory. The greater the primary memory, the more programs can be held in the machine and the more data can be accommodated at one time. However, the operating system or applications software can limit the amount of usable primary memory.

Secondary Storage

The central processing unit can automatically move data back and forth between the primary memory section within the CPU and the secondary storage devices. The secondary storage devices usually consist of one or more magnetic or optical disks and at least one magnetic tape drive. Although the secondary storage device offers less expensive storage than primary memory, access is considerably slower. The ability, however, to move data back and forth between the primary memory and secondary storage device makes it possible to handle larger programs and greater quantities of data on a small computer having a limited primary memory section. The concept is called **virtual memory**.

Virtual Memory

The purpose of virtual memory is to allow running large programs in a relatively small physical memory space. It works by bringing segments of a program into a computer's primary memory from secondary storage as needed. When the program segments have been run, new program segments can be brought into the same memory space and overlaid on those previously brought into primary memory. The concept is used with computers of all sizes.

The type of computer system determines not only the maximum primary memory but also the maximum secondary storage. A large mainframe computer can accommodate billions of characters of primary memory. The disk drives often have capacities of 7.5 GB or more each, with up to a score or more possible on a single computer; therefore, virtual memory is almost unlimited. During the 1980s, minicomputer systems often were limited to less than 1.0 GB of primary memory and four to eight disk drives, each with a capacity of 600 to 900 MB; but some of today's minicomputers support several GB of primary memory and a score or more of drives rated at 2–5 GB each. The first supermicros often were limited to 128 MB of primary memory and two or four disk drives, usually with capacities of 300 to 700 MB each, but some of today's supermicros accommodate up to 2.0 GB of primary memory and ten or more drives rated at 2–5 GB each. In fact, a few multiprocessor supermicros can be expanded to 100 GB of secondary storage. Until the past few years PCs and Macs had only 1.0–4.0 MB of primary memory and an internal hard disk drive of 100 to 500 MB. In the past few years there have been dramatic advances in design and manufacturing, resulting in primary memories of 32 MB and 1.0 GB internal hard disk drives on PCs and Macs.

Input and Output (I/O)

Data is input to the CPU from peripherals and output from the CPU to peripherals. The term **peripherals** is used to describe various hardware components: disk drives, tape drives, terminals, laser scanners, and lightpens. Disk and tape drives are part of the central site hardware, but they are still "peripheral" to the CPU. Terminals, laser scanners, and lightpens typically are removed from the central site and, therefore, are often called **remote peripherals**.

The CPU prompts a **channel** when it wants an I/O operation initiated and signals it again when completed. Channels connected to secondary storage may be selector channels or multiplexor channels. Selector channels have only one subchannel, can be connected to only one device at a time, and are used to provide high speed transfer of information between secondary storage devices and memory. Multiplexor channels have many subchannels and are used to connect lower speed peripherals to memory.

There are also communication channels in the CPU which connect the CPU and primary memory and **cache**. This is the area of the data bus and the physical connection among the chips is through circuits on the board which holds the chips. The communication speed along the data bus is significantly faster than the communication speed between primary memory and the secondary storage media.

A Direct Memory Access (DMA) chip in the CPU handles the transfer of information between secondary storage media and primary memory without the use of the CPU. This allows the CPU to continue processing; it is not necessary for the CPU to stop and supervise I/O action when more instruction or data are needed in primary memory.

Data is fed into the CPU through an **input** device, usually a terminal, PC, or Mac. Other input devices include magnetic tapes, CD-ROMs, lightpens, optical character recognition (OCR) wands, and laser scanners. The last three types of input devices are used to scan a label on a book or patron card. The bars or machine-readable symbols are read into the computer electronically.

The **output** device, which displays completed data, may be a terminal, PCs, or Mac, a printer, or a magnetic tape unit. Until recently, a PC or Mac connected to an automated library system used terminal emulation software, thus making it appear to the computer as a terminal. With the advent of client/server architecture, the functionality of a PC or Mac configured as part of an automated library system is dramatically increased. This topic will be discussed in the chapter on system architectures.

Online and Off-line

A peripheral device that is electronically linked to the CPU and that is using this linkage in a particular operation is described as operating **online**. If a device is not connected to the CPU, or is not utilizing the connection in a particular task, it is said to be **off-line**. Thus, when a keyboard is being used to enter data into a storage device under the control of the CPU, it is operating online. If the same keyboard is used to enter data onto a diskette or tape cartridge that will later be loaded into storage that is under the control of the CPU, it is operating off-line.

Batch and Real-time Processing

The terms **batch processing** and **real-time processing** are commonly used to describe modes of data processing. A system operating in batch mode stockpiles data and passes it to the CPU for processing and output at a later time. In a real-time system, data is processed immediately upon entry and all machine-readable files are simultaneously updated, often as part of the processing operation itself. Real-time systems thus maintain data files that reflect the current status of a particular application. When a user enters instructions or data, gets back results in real-time, and uses the results to enter in more instructions or data, the system is said to be **interactive**. Batch systems, on the other hand, do not provide such up-to-the-minute tracking because there is a lag ranging from minutes to hours between the recording of a transaction and the processing of data relevant to the transaction.

All real-time systems are online systems, but an online system may be operated in either batch or real-time mode. Online terminals may be used to enter data that becomes immediately available, or data may be loaded in batch mode using a diskette or tape cartridge and then maintained on disks for online retrieval via terminals.

Data is recorded in the central processing unit by setting the physical components of the memory device so that the CPU can "read" or detect the data. In the earliest computers, vacuum tubes were selectively switched on and off to represent the combinations of conditions that represent individual characters. During the 1960s and early 1970s, the memory sections of CPUs consisted of small, circular metal cores that could be magnetized in either of two directions and individual characters were represented by the pattern of magnetization. This system is reflected in the term **core memory** which is still occasionally used as a synonym of a computer's primary memory. The memory sections of contemporary computers generally store information electronically rather than magnetically: sections are composed of large numbers of highly miniaturized, random access memory circuits integrated on chips of silicon or other semi-conductor material. Each circuit is capable of being in one of two states, conducting electricity or not conducting electricity. Thus, in a manner similar to that employed by magnetic cores, individual characters are represented by the presence or absence of electrical current in a specified combination of circuits.

STORAGE TYPES

"Storage" is the term used to describe the components of a computer system in which programs and data are stored. Storage in a computer system is on three levels: primary, cache, and secondary. Primary and cache storage are usually referred to as "memory," with primary storage often distinguished from cache by referring to it as **primary memory** or as **Random Access Memory** (RAM).

Primary Memory

Primary memory, the term the author prefers, is that area of the system composed of memory chips that temporarily hold processes immediately before action by the CPU. In order to pass control of the CPU to a process it must be in primary memory or in cache. Access from the CPU to the information in primary memory or cache is through an internal data bus. A **bus** is a communication channel which goes directly from the CPU to the primary memory or cache without the need of an I/O action such as is used with a peripheral.

Cache Memory

Cache memory is a group of cells interposed between the primary memory and the CPU to improve memory transfer rates by storing that which has recently been used by the CPU and is expected to be reused in the very near future. Because of its location between the CPU and primary memory and the use of a high speed bus or communication channel, information stored here is available to the CPU faster than that in primary memory or secondary storage.

Buffers

Buffers are areas of primary memory cells which hold data waiting for I/O transfer. Buffers are used to compensate for the inequality of timing of the high speed CPU and the relatively low speed I/O devices. Timing is an essential design of all hardware platforms, and buffers provide a means of temporarily storing information until the receiving component of the system is ready.

Read Only Memory

Read Only Memory (ROM) is an extension of primary memory. It contains information that is not directly accessible to the user; information that may not be altered. Information in ROM may be commonly used machine language code or microcode. It frequently contains part of the operating system.

Secondary Storage

Because the memory of a CPU is limited, it is necessary to store not only data, but also much of each of the programs in one or more secondary storage or mass storage media, such as disk or tape. These media are mounted on devices called drives and are connected to primary memory by I/O channels which provide a link for the passage of data in and out of the computer box. Secondary storage makes virtual memory possible.

SECONDARY STORAGE MEDIA

Secondary or mass storage media are designed to retain information in machine-readable form while awaiting computer processing. They supplement the necessarily limited capacity of the CPU's primary memory, which is reserved for the storage of programs and the data that the computer is processing at a given moment. In the absence of secondary storage, information would have to be reentered prior to each incident of computer processing, and applications involving large amounts of data could not be computerized at all.

Magnetic Disk

A magnetic disk, commonly called a **disk pack** when the disk can be removed from the **disk drive** on which it is mounted, consists of several rigid layers, or platters, each with several hundred tracks of information. The tracks are subdivided into sectors. Now that most disk drives are sealed and the disk packs nonremovable (so-called **Winchester drives**), the term disk drive is more common than disk pack. The capacity of a disk drive varies based on the number of platters or layers and the density of recording. At the present time, capacity typically ranges from 1.0 GB to 9.0 GB, although the 2.0–9.0 GB drive is most common in supermicro-based systems and 1.0 GB in PC or Mac-based systems.

When information needs to be moved off a disk drive, an access arm with a read/write head moves over the surface of the platter to locate the track, find the sector in which the information is stored, and transfer the data to the CPU. The access arm is guided by a controller. The access arms and disk controller move less slowly than the CPU; therefore, the queries may stack up. In human time, only fractions of seconds are involved, but they can add up to several seconds of response time in the course of a complete search. While the electromechanical nature of the device makes it slower than retrieving information from the primary memory, the performance for properly configured disk drives is suitable for patron access catalogs and active circulation files.

Until recently, the total cost of the secondary storage represented a larger percentage of the total system cost than the CPU; but in the past few years, costs have dropped dramatically so that secondary storage usually represents less than 5 percent of the cost of a system.

Winchester Disk Drives

Most multiuser systems, including supermicro-based systems, are now configured with Winchester disk drives. The Winchester drive features a sealed head-to-disk assembly that need not be removed and is free of contaminants. Thin film technology makes it possible to get 2.0 GB or more on a single disk drive smaller than a microwave oven. The read-write head moves only 50 micro-inches from the surface balanced by a column of air to facilitate rapid scanning. The sealed conditions of Winchester disks make them twice as reliable for secondary storage as regular magnetic disks.

Magnetic Tape

Although early computer systems used paper media—such as punched cards or punched tape—for recording and storing machine-readable data, magnetic tape storage devices have been the most widely used means of complementing disk storage for the last two decades. Newer technologies have been introduced, including bubble memories and optical disks, but none has displaced magnetic tape because it is the most economical of the several types of storage media. Magnetic tape is actually the secondary storage **medium**. The peripheral device is the **tape drive**, which includes a take-up reel and a motorized mechanism designed to move the tape past read/write heads. These heads use electricity to record bits by magnetizing the tracks in a predetermined pattern or by sensing a previously magnetized pattern of bits. The most expensive tape drives will accept various types of tapes; others are limited to tapes recorded in a particular coding pattern or at particular densities. Although tape drives operate online, the tapes themselves may be stored off-line, hanging from racks, when not in use.

The typical magnetic tape employed in installed mainframe and minicomputer systems is wound on an open plastic reel. The tape is divided across its width in parallel tracks, most commonly nine, with each track intended to record one bit. The accumulation of eight parallel bits represents a single character. The ninth bit, called a parity bit, is used for error detection. Successive characters are recorded down the length of the tape in groups called blocks. The most common recording densities are 1,600 and 6,250 bits per inch (bpi). The characters themselves are typically represented in either the ASCII or EBCDIC code.

Supermicro-based systems usually include a magnetic tape drive inside a plastic cartridge similar to the cartridge used in audio tape recorders. There are two common cartridge formats: 4 mm DAT and 8 mm helical scan. Because the tape in most cartridge tape drives is constantly moving, the devices are called **streamer** tape drives.

The recording or reading of data onto or from a particular portion of a tape requires that preceding portions also be moved past the read/write heads; therefore, magnetic tape is typically reserved for applications where data will be processed serially in the same order in which it is recorded.

Open reel magnetic tape drives generally have been used for database loading and for dumping the entire contents of a database. Streamer tape drives, which have widths of four or eight millimeters, and are sealed in cartridges, cannot only be used for database loading and database dumps, but also as **logging tapes**. The streamer tape is constantly moving, thus making it possible for the data to be written to tape more quickly. Therefore, each transaction written to the disk can also be written to the tape drive, thus providing continuous back-up. If the capacity of the cartridge is equal to or greater than the total magnetic disk storage, the entire database can be backed-up unattended.

Even though streamer tape drives operate at speeds of several million characters per second, it may take several minutes to access and retrieve a particular record. Magnetic tape is, therefore, not a suitable storage medium for interactive computer applications in which data must be accessed rapidly and in more or less random order with respect to its recorded sequence. Such applications must use more expensive direct access storage media. Of these, magnetic disks are the most common.

Open reel tape drives are expensive, generally in excess of $20,000 each; streamer tape drives of up to 8.0 GB generally are priced at less than $5,000.

Diskette and CD-ROM Drives

The diskette remains the most common secondary storage medium for micros. While the 5.25-inch diskette, popularly known as a floppy, has almost disappeared, the 3.5-inch diskette, a relatively rigid and higher capacity medium, has been configured with nearly all PCs and Macs sold in the last several years. The typical high-density diskette accommodates 1.25 MB of information. While very economical, data transfer from and to a diskette is slow. While a supermicro can be configured with a diskette drive, it rarely is because there are faster media available.

CD-ROM discs, which generally are not erasable, are increasingly being configured on PCs and Macs. Their low cost and high storage capacity (600 MB) make them ideal for electronic publications. In the last year CD-ROM recorders have dropped in price to as low as $1,500. That makes it possible for a small publisher or a library to create a CD-ROM without using a service bureau. Supermicro systems are often configured with a CD-ROM drive because a great deal of system **documentation** is now supplied in that format.

Other Storage Devices

The magnetic disk offers considerable storage capacity with very good retrieval speed. Optical disks—such as WORM (write-once-read-many), erasable optical, and CD-ROM—offer greater storage capacity and lower cost, but at considerable sacrifice in access speed. The storage capacity of an optical disk usually is 600 MB (CD-ROM) to 4 GB (WORM), with storage costs a fraction of that for magnetic media. Access speed is usually half or less than that for magnetic media.

While most libraries now use magnetic disk storage, in the future storage systems may combine magnetic and optical devices, with the storage location determined by the access speed required and the frequency of use of the data.

TYPES OF REMOTE PERIPHERALS

A remote peripheral may handle both input and output, or only one or the other. All of the remote peripherals discussed in the following paragraphs do both, except as noted.

Terminals

The most widely used remote peripheral is the **terminal**, a device consisting of a keyboard and a monitor. Data can be input via the keyboard and output onto the monitor. Most monitors incorporate a television-like **cathode ray tube** (CRT) mounted in a plastic or metal case measuring 12 or more inches in width. The CRT has a phosphorescent screen, typically measuring 13 to 17 inches diagonally across the screen, on which characters are displayed as light images on a dark background. Some devices allow the user to display dark characters on a light background—a screen display described as reverse video. A filter in front of the screen reduces the glare that has contributed to complaints of operator eye-fatigue. In most cases, dials or other controls permit a user to further adjust the contrast and intensity of the display to suit personal preference.

Monitors are changing rapidly, with color displacing monochrome and 15 to 17-inch screens replacing 13-inch screens. While 21-inch color monitors are available, they cost up to three times as much as 13-inch monitors.

Keyboard-oriented input is an error-prone activity. It is probable that two to five percent of the finished work will be incorrect, even if care has been taken to look for and correct errors on the screen during data entry. Common data-entry error-detection techniques include double-entry and editing the information on the screen. The former method entails retyping the material so that computer can electronically compare, character for character, the second version with the previous version. Double-entry is a highly effective method of detecting errors since it is unlikely that the same keystroking errors will be made during both initial entry and rekeying (especially if a different operator types the second entry). But such verification virtually doubles the already high cost of labor to enter the information. Editing the information on the screen is, therefore, more common. A **spell-check** program can be of some value in looking for errors in common words.

Scanners

Electronic scanning—solely an input technology—uses reflected light to determine the content of material. Once identified, the data is encoded and recorded on magnetic media, or transmitted directly to a computer. Several types of electronic scanning devices are designed for special applications. One, bar code recognition, is well known in libraries and retail stores. **Bar codes** represent numbers by using the height, width, and distance between marks to express characters. They cannot be read by humans, so the characters represented by the bar codes are usually printed next to the bars in numbers and letters. Several different bar codes are in use; the best known are Monarch's Codabar, the Universal Product Code (UPC), and Intermec's Code 39. Because it was offered by CLSI—the oldest, and for many years the largest, vendor in the industry—**Codabar** is the one most widely used by libraries. A **check digit** is used as one of the characters to detect incorrect scans.

Bar code technology is suitable only for scanning a limited amount of information, typically no more than 18 characters. The label (with the codes) may be affixed to library materials, patron cards, laptop PCs, or anything else, and is typically scanned by a pencil-shaped wand equipped with a photocell. In high-volume environments a laser scanner on a stand can speed scanning because the laser moves across the label several times at a rate much faster than a manual rescan when the first pass was incorrect.

Used both for identification labels and for extended data entry, optical character recognition (**OCR**) is another type of electronic scanning technology. As the name implies, OCR uses reflected light to identify the individual character content of input documents (e.g., letters, numbers, punctuation marks, or special symbols). Since these characters vary in size and shape, each will mirror light differently. An input device called an OCR reader scans the material and identifies individual characters by comparing their light reflectance properties with prestored definitions. The identified characters are then encoded in machine-readable form. Keystroking labor is eliminated. In theory, catalog cards, patron registration cards, and other typed documents could be scanned. In practice, however, the range of acceptable input is quite narrow and varies considerably depending upon the particular OCR reader being used. Most of the available devices will only accept input documents prepared according to rigid format specifications and in type fonts specifically designed for optical recognition. Since most existing library documents were not prepared in a font designed to be read by machines, it may be several years before omnifont OCR equipment will make it possible to reformat material without keystroking. Most libraries now using OCR limit their application to scanning patron-and item-identification labels.

Almost all libraries place their labels inside the front or back covers of permanent library materials. Some libraries have placed the labels on the outside of all books, on the upper left-hand corner of the front of the book and have protected them with strips of clear tape. Many libraries put labels on the front covers of paperback collections. The labels last for at least a year, even on very heavily circulated books, and replacement is simple and inexpensive. Handling time is significantly reduced, during first labeling, when a portable scanner is used to do inventory, and each time the item is circulated, because the book does not have to be opened (assuming that the date due slip is also on the outside of the book).

Printers

Paper printers—solely an output technology—vary considerably in technology, output characteristics, operating speed, and intended application. Historically, **line printers** have been the dominant output device in installations with mainframe and minicomputers. The typical line printer features a "printing chain," consisting of chains of characters represented on embossed metal slugs linked in an endless loop. Multiple hammers are activated simultaneously so that the device appears to print entire lines at one time. Other line printers employ drums rather than printing chains, but their output characteristics are similar to those of chain printers.

The most common print chains have 60 to 64 characters, including the upper-case Roman alphabet, numerals, and the most widely used punctuation symbols. Special extended print chains have been developed for printing bibliographic data. Line printers accept continuous, fan-folded paper stock.

The rated speeds of available line printers range from several hundred to several thousand lines per minute, with mainframe computers generally supporting the faster models and minicomputer and supermicro-computer installations using slower devices with printing speeds of 300 or fewer lines per minute.

Variables like line lengths, page lengths, and the size of the character set typically reduce a printer's rated speed. Thus, a machine capable of printing 1,000 lines per minute with an upper-case print chain, will operate at half that speed if it must produce both upper and lower-case characters. Operating speeds will be even further slowed by adding foreign characters or special symbols. Although line printers are many times faster than typewriters, they process data at a much slower rate than computers.

Line printers are usually configured as **system printers**, devices directly connected to the CPU for the production of notices and reports. They are infrequently deployed as remote peripherals. Most libraries need consider only 150 and 300 lpm (lines per minute) printers. Line printer prices range from $4,000 to $30,000.

Several categories of lower cost impact printers are also suitable for use as system printers. These machines—generally priced under $4,000—are slower than line printers, but the fastest are comparable to 150 lpm line printers.

Laser printers usually are used as system printers only in local library systems configured with more than one system printer because they cannot print multipart forms.

Side printers are output only devices which are connected to terminals or PCs, rather than to the CPU. They tend to be slower in speed than system printers. Typically they produce four **inkjet printers**. Until recently less reliable than other types, inkjets are becoming popular because of their low cost and quiet operation. Color inkjets have become so good that most manufacturers no longer produce black-only models. The drawbacks of inkjets are the small paper tray capacity, their relatively short life expectancy when used in high-volume applications (more than 1,000 copies per month), and the higher per-page cost than laser printers. Their speed is acceptable: typically four pages per minute. Ink jet printers generally cost $300 to $600 in late 1996.

Laser printers are ideal side printers: they are relatively fast (4–16 pages per minute), reliable, durable, and offer a low cost per page. The major drawback has been cost. However, prices for low-end laser printers had come down to $400 in late 1996. The 16-page-per-minute units had come down to $1,500 each.

Dot matrix printers had almost completely disappeared from the side printer market by mid-1996. These printers create individual characters from a matrix of closely spaced dots. Each character is printed by a series of needles that are selectively driven into an inked ribbon. They tend to be noisy and slow.

COM

Computer output microfilm (COM) is a variant form of nonimpact output technology in which information is recorded on microfilm rather than on paper. A typical COM unit is capable of recording document images at rates ranging from slightly less than 10,000 to more than 40,000 lines per minute. However, because of their expense—COM recorders usually cost more than $50,000—most libraries use COM recorders operated by computer or micrographics service bureaus. Most multiuser library systems are able to format information so that it is ready for COM production.

The image capacity of COM varies with the type of microform and the reduction employed. For example, if a 48 to 1 reduction is used, a single microfiche can contain as much information as 270 computer printout pages. At the same reduction, a 100-foot roll of 16-mm microfilm can accommodate the equivalent of 7,200 computer printout pages. Some COM equipment uses such formatting strategies as the elimination of frame borders, to pack even more information onto the microform. Although earlier models were limited to the upper-case alphabet, numeric digits, and frequently-used punctuation marks, most newer COM recorders can accommodate both upper-and lower-case alphabets, accented characters, and other symbols encountered in bibliographic data.

COM is often employed to create back-up or to store historical data from a computer system. In another typical application, the COM recorder is used to produce a master from which a duplicator makes multiple copies. These copies are then distributed and accessed, using COM readers.

EXPANDABILITY OF HARDWARE

In the late 1970s, the largest CPU installed in a minicomputer-based turnkey system had only 128 KB of primary memory even though machines with eight times that amount of memory were already available. By 1985, hundreds of libraries had "swapped out" or exchanged their small CPUs for larger ones at an additional cost of $20,000 to $100,000 per machine. The major reason why systems were initially installed with small CPUs was the limited range of models available and the significant price differences among them. In the past few years, computer lines have become much more modular in design and highly expandable; therefore, there is no reason to outgrow a machine. The important thing is to insist on a unit which can accommodate current needs using only half or less of the CPU's maximum capacity.

The central processing unit (CPU) of a multiuser system installed by a small library should have a primary memory of at least 32 MB, and a mid-size library or consortium ideally should have a machine which has a memory of at least 256 MB. A good rule-of-thumb is 1.5 MB per concurrent user to be supported. The initial hardware configuration should have a spare capacity of at least 30 percent, thus avoiding upgrades for normal growth. A library also should require that its CPU have the capability of having the memory upgraded to double the initial memory.

Secondary storage expandability needs to be much greater than 100 percent. When a library loads journal citation files, disk storage often is tripled or quadrupled. As libraries begin to add image files, it is possible that they will increase disk storage by even greater multiples. Most libraries purchasing a multiuser system should not consider one which cannot accommodated at least 25 GB of secondary storage.

Micro-based systems should normally be configured on PCs or Macs with at least 8 MB of memory and 1.0 GB of disk storage expandable by at least 100 percent.

Chapter 3

System Architectures

Computer architecture embraces the science of assembling logical elements into a computer device. A computer architect puts the components of a computer system (control, processing, storage, input/output, etc.) together so they form a computer system and then turns them over to a system programmer, who then constructs or selects an operating system for the machine.

For the purposes of this chapter the major architectures are **hierarchical** and **client/server**. The former is the architecture which has characterized library automation for the past three decades. All of the processes are controlled by the **host** and all remote peripherals are **slaves** which are limited to entering and retrieving information. The latter is an architecture which has become a hot topic in library automation in the mid-1990s. It shifts a considerable amount of control from the computer room to the desktop.

There are a number of hierarchical architectures. The greatest differences are among mainframes, minis and superminis, and micros. Until UNIX came along, most applications software could be run on only a single hierarchical architecture. UNIX is the first **open operating system** available for all types of machines, regardless of the architecture.

Client/server architecture is most easily differentiated from hierarchical architecture by how a PC or Mac functions within a system. In client/server architecture, the PC or Mac-based client communicates with the server as a computer; in hierarchical processing, the PC or Mac emulates a "dumb" terminal to communicate with the host. In client/server the client controls part of the activity; but in hierarchical processing the host controls all activity. A client PC or Mac almost always does the following in a client/server environment: screen handling, menu or command interpretation, data entry, help processing, and error recovery.

As the library automation industry is moving toward client/server architecture, this discussion will focus on that architecture.

CLIENT/SERVER DEFINED

The simple definition of *client/server* is:

> *A computer architecture which divides functions into client (requestor) and server (provider) subsystems, using standard communication methods (such as TCP/IP and Z39.50) to facilitate the sharing of information between them. In contrast, hierarchical systems concern functions, including control of the presentation on a host computer. The remote peripherals are either "dumb" terminals or micros (PCs or Macs) operating in terminal emulation mode.*

Characteristics of Client/Server

Among the characteristics of a client/server architecture are the following:

- The client and server can be distinguished from one another by the differences in the tasks they perform.
- The client and server usually operate on different computer platforms.
- Either the client or server may be upgraded without affecting the other.
- Clients may connect to one or more servers; servers may connect to multiple clients concurrently.
- Clients always initiate the dialogue by requesting a service.

The Dividing Line

The dividing line between the client and a server can be anywhere along a broad continuum: at one end only the user interface has been moved onto the client; at the other, almost all applications have been moved onto the client and the database may be distributed among clients. Client/server architecture does not presuppose that client and server are on separate machines, although that is the more common approach.

The Gartner Group, a market research firm, has identified five points along the client/server continuum which typify alternate "styles" or approaches: distributed presentation, remote presentation, distributed logic, remote data management, and distributed database. They can be characterized as follows:

Distributed presentation: The presentation is handled partly by the server and partly by the client.

Remote presentation: The presentation is controlled and handled entirely by the client.

Distributed logic: The application logic is handled partly by the server and partly by the client.

Remote data management: Database management is controlled and handled entirely by the server.

Distributed database: Database management is handled partly by the server and partly by the client.

The illustration on the next page (Figure 3.1) graphically depicts the five styles. A vendor's product could fit more than one style. That usually occurs when a vendor decides to use remote presentation for patron access catalog clients but designs staff clients per the distributed logic or remote data management style.

While a client usually is configured on a 486 or Pentium-based PC and a server on a supermicro, mini, or mainframe; a single machine can act as both client and server on a network. For example, two automated library systems in different libraries which are linked for resource sharing are functioning as client when requesting information, and as server when providing it.

One client may be used to communicate with several different servers. An example of that would be a PC-based client which can access not only a local library system, but also a CD-ROM server, a remote local library system, or a remote online database service.

Open Systems and Client/Server

An important computer industry development which has facilitated client/server architecture is referred to as **open systems**—a concept which features standardized connectivity so that components from several vendors may be combined. The trend to open systems began in the 1970s as a reaction against proprietary systems which required that all hardware and system software come from a single source, and gained momentum in the 1980s as networking became common. While various parts of an organization might not hesitate to purchase proprietary systems to meet their own needs, the desire to provide access from other parts of the organization, or to exchange information, would be an incentive to select an open system. For client/server, open systems are essential.

Operating Systems and Client/Server

It is often said—incorrectly—that one must use an open operating system (such as UNIX, Pick, or OS/2) to achieve an open system. While the use of an operating system supported by scores of computer manufacturers facilitates interconnectivity, it is not essential. Digital and Hewlett-Packard both have designed their proprietary operating systems so that they comply with POSIX, a standard which makes the system look to a network like a UNIX-based system. To emphasize this fact, Digital has designated its proprietary operating system OpenVMS.

UNIX is the most popular operating system for servers because of the large range of platform sizes available. The most popular client operating systems are Windows (including Windows 95), DOS, OS/2, UNIX, Macintosh, and Windows NT—in order of popularity. The availability of multiple client operating systems makes it possible to fit a client/server library system into the desktop environment with which the people in an organization are already familiar.

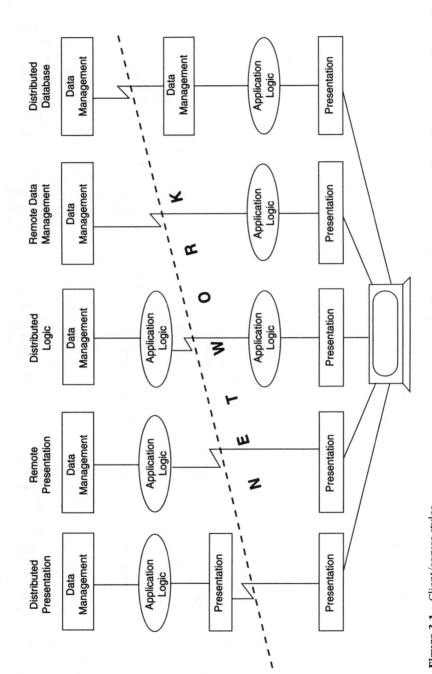

Figure 3.1 Client/server styles

RDBMS, SQL, and Client/Server

Most client/server systems use a **relational database management system** (RDBMS), software that handles the storage and retrieval of records in a database using a series of tables of values. While there has been a great deal written about **object oriented databases**, very few vendors of automated library systems were using them in late 1996. Their value is in their ability to handle images as well as text.

There is a common misconception that client/server is synonymous with networked SQL (Structured Query Language) databases. SQL, a popular industry-standard data definition and access language for relational databases, is only one approach—albeit the one selected by almost all automated library system vendors. While one can reasonably expect the use of an RDBMS and SQL, the absence of either does not mean that a system is not client/server.

RISC and Client/Server

RISC (Reduced Instruction Set Computing) machines are not necessary for client/server, although most multifunction, multiuser automated library systems now use them. They are a popular choice because of their excellent price performance, their use of a standard **SCSI** interface for connecting to a wide variety of disk and tape drives, and ease of connection to LANs and WANs.

Mainframes and Client/Server

Mainframe computers, such as an IBM 3090 or comparable machine from another manufacturer, can be used in a client/server environment. Despite all predictions that mainframes would disappear with the implementation of client/server, over half the client/server implementations of Fortune 500 companies use a mainframe as the server. However, a majority of the organizations have used a mainframe because they already owned the equipment; they plan a gradual migration to smaller servers.

The most popular first choice for implementing client/server on a mainframe is a high-volume online transaction processing system (OLTP); the next is very large database applications. For many of these applications a mainframe will be selected for the server, although not one as large as necessary in a hierarchical environment.

PCs, Macs, and Client/Server

Client/server requires **intelligence** (e.g., memory) on the client. A "dumb" terminal won't work, but an "x-terminal"—basically a PC without a disk drive—will. The dividing line between client and server determines how much memory is needed—usually a minimum of 8 MB. Some projections anticipate a minimum PC memory requirement of 16 MB by 1997.

Now that today's $2,000 PC is as powerful as the $25,000 engineering workstations of five years ago, it is common to refer to PCs as **workstations** when used as clients. The term actually refers to a powerful supermicro used as a single-user device.

Graphical User Interfaces and Client/Server

A GUI (graphical user interface)—a presentation of information to the user using icons and other graphics—is often called client/server, but unless information moves from the server to the client in machine-readable (raw) form, and the client does the formatting to make it human-readable, it is not true client/server. Further, there is nothing in the client/server architecture that requires a GUI.

While a GUI may make a system easier to use for the novice, it is equally valuable for the expert because it can support multiple concurrent sessions, with multiple windows available for displaying information.

It is possible to tailor a client to provide a personalized interface which meets the needs of any particular user based on an analysis of tasks performed or on an individual's expressed preferences. Most vendors working on client/server plan at least three different client types: OPAC, technical services, and circulation.

The following illustration presents a typical GUI:

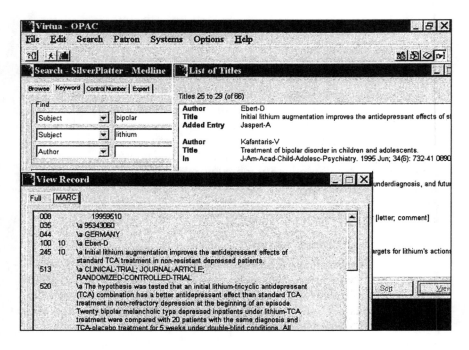

Figure 3.2   A GUI from VTLS Inc.

HOW CLIENT/SERVER WORKS

A library staff member or patron formulates a request in the command (or query) language of his/her PC or x-terminal (the client); this is then translated into an information request in standard format (e.g., Z39.50) or a proprietary format understood by the information source (the server). The link between the client and the server may be a LAN (local area network) within the building, an organization-wide LAN, or a WAN (wide area network) which links several LANs together using telco circuits. Upon receiving the standardized request, the information source (server) retrieves the appropriate data, packages it into a standard form, and ships it back to the PC or x-terminal (client).

The server does not need to know the command language of the client to respond to the request. That is why a client can be used to access many different servers.

Major Applications

There are two major applications for client/server in a library environment: as the architecture for an automated library system and as an approach to linking heterogeneous systems. In the first application, a vendor designs a system using client/server architecture to facilitate use of that system to access multiple servers in an organizational environment in which clients are already in use, to facilitate bringing together multiple product lines (DRA and Geac, for example), and/or to improve staff/patron productivity. In the second application, a vendor designs a client to facilitate transparent access to systems of other vendors, and a server to facilitate transparent access to its system from others. While the underlying principles are the same, the vendor has considerable latitude in the design of its own client/server system, but must strictly conform to standards when using client/server to link its system with those of other libraries.

Client/Server on a Single Machine

Some vendors claim that they use a client/server architecture on a single machine even though the presentation is not controlled at the desktop. The claim is legitimate if one thinks of client/server as a logical concept, not a hardware configuration. However, the author has chosen to define client/server in a way that is more responsive to the intent of libraries considering the purchase of client/server systems. They wish to be able to connect multiple clients and multiple servers on a network. While a vendor with a client and server on a single platform can move toward client/server as defined herein more quickly than one with a traditional hierarchical design, it should not claim client/server in a marketplace which does not share its definition of client/server.

TCP/IP, OSI, Z39.50, and Client/Server

When client and server are on the same machine, communication between them may be proprietary—*yet one more reason why this is not true client/server under the definition posed by the author*; when they are on separate machines, the common practice is to conform to a standard—called a **protocol** when the standard applies to communication. The most widely used set of protocols is **TCP/IP** (Transmission Control Protocol/Internet Protocol). TCP/IP functions at the "transport" and "network" layers of the International Organization for Standardization's **Open System Interconnection (OSI) Reference Model**, and is used by most organization-wide LANs and virtually all WANs. The Internet also uses TCP/IP as its communication protocols.

While the United States government has been pressing for a migration from TCP/IP to the complete OSI Reference Model, it now appears that change will be evolutionary, with protocols developed for a specific industry or activity (such as interlibrary loan between two libraries) written to work at the highest layer, level seven, with either TCP/IP or OSI.

TCP/IP is not a single protocol, but a suite of more than 100 protocols. The most important of these are telnet, FTP, and SMTP. **Telnet** is a program that allows interactive sessions between host computers on a network, as well as allowing users at remote geographical locations to log onto the other network hosts. **FTP** (file transfer protocol) supports interactive sessions between computers for the transfer of (a) data file(s) to the requestor's computer. **SMTP** (simple mail transmission protocol) is the electronic mail protocol.

Among the other standards or protocols which may be used in a client/server environment, are NetBIOS, SPX/IPX, and Named Pipes. These protocols are similar to TCP/IP, but less complex and usually used with smaller networks. For example, no LAN support currently exists for Named Pipes. In some organizations, a simpler protocol may be combined with TCP/IP. However, when interfacing with a variety of systems, it usually is necessary to support multiple protocols; it is not enough that a client/server system support only TCP/IP.

Z39.50, a standard developed in 1988 by NISO (National Information Standards Organization), is the official designation of a protocol for communication between client and server in a bibliographic context. Z39.50 is defined as a common set of procedures and formats connecting two information processes: the originating system where requests are made and the target system where the database resides. Z39.50 functions in the upper three levels of TCP/IP (or OSI), and Z39.50 is "wrapped" in a TCP/IP message when moved over a LAN or WAN.

The ISO (International Organization for Standardization) 10162 and 10163 international standards are closely related; Z39.50, Version 2 (1992) was specifically designed to bring national and international standards into agreement. Internationally, the standard is commonly called "SR" for search and retrieval. As of late 1996, the ISO was expected to replace 10162 and 10163 with 23950, an international adoption of NISO's Z39.50 version 3.

Z39.50 is discussed at greater length in the chapter on standards.

Bandwidth Requirements

Client/server architecture, if the client/server interface is properly designed, does not demand much more **bandwidth** than host/slave architecture. The minimum requirement for a terminal or micro (PC or Mac) to access an automated library system is 9600 bps (bits per second). However, as systems move beyond bibliographic records pointing to information to the information itself (full-text, images, and multimedia), the requirements will increase. For example, a color image of a typical journal page would require 18 minutes to retrieve unless compressed. Even compressed, it would take nearly one minute. The minimum bandwidth requirement for images, therefore, is 56 Kbps.

Costs

Client/server is generally represented as more cost-effective than hierarchical computing. That may be the case for organizations which have been using mainframe computers supporting many hundreds of concurrent users (including research libraries using Classic NOTIS), but it usually is not the case in organizations which have been using minis and supermicros supporting 10 to 500 concurrent users—which accounts for some 97 percent of the libraries using multiuser, multifunction automated library systems. One can purchase a great deal more processing power when using a large number of PCs or Macs in a client/server environment instead of a mainframe in a hierarchical environment, but when the comparison is with a machine of the type used in most automated library systems, the higher network and labor costs of client/server usually more than offset the modest savings in CPU processing power.

In several recent consultations undertaken by the author (unpublished), the following start-up costs were projected for client/server and hierarchical processing options, including hardware, software, installation, training, database load, remote peripherals (PCs and Macs), and network infrastructure within library facilities:

Number of users	Client/Server	Hierarchical
20	$ 193,000	$ 134,000
100	570,000	456,000
200	1,310,000	1,006,000
300	1,870,000	1,432,000

The remote peripherals and network infrastructure costs represented more than 80 percent of the difference in each case. Had network costs outside library facilities been included, the client/server cost would have been even higher.

Client/server architecture also was more expensive to operate in each of the studies, primarily because network expertise is needed. Automated library system vendors assume responsibility for total system performance for hierarchical systems by providing remote diagnostics, remote fixes, and field service. However, vendors will not assume responsibility for total system performance when there is a network between the server and clients. Diagnostics, remote fixes, and field service extend only as far as the server. The customer is responsible for the network and remote peripherals, except as a defect in the vendor-supplied client hardware or software is identified.

Interviews with organizations which have implemented client/server over the past five years have confirmed that system management costs are significantly higher in the client/server environment than in a hierarchical system environment. Every one of the score of interviewees stressed that an experienced network manager is a must, even when there are fewer than 50 concurrent users.

While comparative costs always should be examined, one should start with a skeptical frame of mind when approaching client/server. The key to the choice between computer architectures is likely to lie elsewhere. The benefits of client/server may well outweigh the costs associated with the architecture.

The comments on costs for client/server architectures do not apply to Z39.50 client/server used for linking heterogeneous systems. That cost is relatively modest: usually $11,000 to $25,000 for the server, and $2,000 to $8,000 for a multiuser client. Single Z39.50 clients for use on a PC cost under $200 each.

BENEFITS OF CLIENT/SERVER

The single most important benefit of client/server architecture in a library environment is the ability to access a wide variety of information sources using a single workstation and a single user interface. As client/server is widely implemented, it should be possible for a staff member or patron to access the database on the local library system, a CD-ROM server, an automated library system in another library, or a remote database service from a desktop device using the query language (a.k.a., command language) of the system to which s/he is accustomed. Search results could be merged and edited, or used to formulate yet another search.

The type of research described herein can be done without the benefit of client/server, but only at the cost of time—a great deal of it. But the client/server benefit is more than just being able to access a wide variety of information sources, it is also improved productivity. Key to this improved productivity is the client design. Most vendors have developed, or are developing, different clients for technical services, circulation, and online patron access catalog applications. In addition, there are provisions for tailoring each client, not only to the size and type of library, but also to particular user needs.

Chapter 4

System Software

System software consists of the software programs which manage general computer operations. It is distinguishable from **applications software** which addresses the specific uses to which the computer is tasked. The most important components of system software are the operating system, the utility programs, and the database management system (DBMS).

OPERATING SYSTEMS

The **operating system** is the set of interrelated programs designed to facilitate the use of the computer in developing and executing application programs. In early computer systems, a human operator monitored operations and determined the priorities of input, processing, and output. By the mid-1960s, computers were being slowed by the need for human intervention. Operating systems were, therefore, developed to let the computer manage its own operations.

An operating system accepts and responds to the commands submitted, sets up jobs, schedules, and handles related tasks that would otherwise have to be undertaken by the system's human operator. The operating system also identifies users and determines whether, and to what extent, they are to be given access to computer resources. It then responds to user-entered commands that initiate the execution of specified programs and also allocates required hardware and software resources to the programs and controls their progress and termination. It must also act on errors or other exceptional conditions that occur during the execution of a program and alert the user with appropriate messages.

Until the past decade most operating systems were developed by computer equipment manufacturers specifically for use with their equipment. In the mid-1980s, the move to **open operating systems**—those which can be used with a wide range of machines—gained widespread support. Not only does an open operating system such as UNIX or Pick make a vendor and its customers less dependent on a single hardware line, but it also makes it easier to interface or link hardware from different manufacturers.

41

Library administrators' interest in automated library systems is motivated by a need for a solution to operational problems or better public service. Seldom is the role of the operating system examined as a factor in the effectiveness of the product selected. However, the operating system is actually the vital interface between the application software and the computer hardware that runs the programs; therefore, the operating system should be evaluated just as closely as any other part of a system.

In order to fully understand the workings of an operating system, it is helpful to have a more comprehensive knowledge of the hardware, software, and firmware components; and the computer language(s) that are used to implement the system.

While hardware was discussed in the previous chapter, it may be useful to reiterate the role of the CPU: it performs processes—parts of programs—that are dictated by the operating system or the applications software. When processes are to be carried out, they are transferred from secondary storage to primary memory. There are two types of processes: **batch** and **interactive**. Batch jobs are the processing of large amounts of data at one time, usually data that has been accumulated over a period of time, such as the loading into a system of a tape containing bibliographic records. Interactive processing involves an ongoing two-way communication between a user and the computer system.

There is communication during the processing and movement of data in and out of the CPU during the process—it can be illustrated as a search by a user for a particular title in the library's bibliographic database. Interactive processing through many ports—processing that appears concurrent to the users—is certainly one of the most important functions of the modern operating system.

COMPONENTS OF OPERATING SYSTEM SOFTWARE

The operating system has several major components which are discussed in the following sections: operating system processes, operating system structure, input/output controller, scheduling controller, multiprogramming, concurrent processing, deadlock, memory management, virtual memory, disk access, file systems, file security, and firmware. If the reader decides to skip the description of the operating system components, the author recommends that s/he resume reading with the section "Operating System Options."

Operating System Processes

As stated before, each set of instructions to the computer is composed of programs made up of processes. A **process** is a single task; the term implies action. It is a set of instructions being held or run by the computer system. Processes are either batch or interactive.

A process may be running, ready, or blocked. It is running if it has control of the CPU; it is ready if it is waiting for CPU control; it is blocked if it is waiting for some action such as **I/O** before it can access CPU control.

The operating system dispatches the CPU control to the first process in the queue when it becomes available. In order to keep a process from monopolizing the CPU, the operating system may issue interrupts. The process that has CPU control may maintain control for a specified time period. At the end of this time period, the operating system issues an interrupt and gives control to the next process in the queue, moving the process which has had CPU control to the end of the queue.

If the running process needs I/O action before its time period is up, it will issue an interrupt and the operating system will pass CPU control to the next process in the queue. The original process then enters the blocked state where it waits for the needed I/O.

Each process has a process control block (PCB) which is a data structure containing information about the process, including the state of the process, pointers to both the process that created it and processes that were created by it, the priority of the process, the process identification, pointers to the process resources, register information, and the processor on which the process is running if it is a multiprocessor system. The PCB is necessary for the operating system to locate all the information about the process, and the register area saves information necessary to find the proper PCB. The PCB for each process is stored in the operating system kernel.

An operating system is able to perform the following functions on processes: create (including assigning a name, assigning priority, creating a PCB, and allocating the process resources), delete, suspend, resume, change priority, block, dispatch, and enable interprocess communication.

Interrupts occur when a running process is stopped and are identified by classes. A supervisor interrupt may be initiated by the user. He or she requests the operating system to provide a service such as **I/O**. I/O interrupts are initiated by the I/O hardware and include the interrupt issued at the end of the transfer of information into primary memory. Restart interrupts are initiated by the user at a console. Program check interrupts may occur when there is a problem with an instruction in machine language to the computer. Machine check interrupts are caused by malfunctioning hardware.

Operating System Structure

Many operating systems use an hierarchical structure. At the base is the computer hardware, the next level is the kernel of the operating system, and above that the various other operating system processes. At the top of the hierarchy are the user processes or applications programs. The kernel section of the operating system resides in the primary memory or ROM. Other operating system programs are kept in online secondary storage media. The kernel calls up these other programs into primary memory when they are needed.

The **operating system kernel** supervises all other functions of the operating system. One of its most important functions is the managing of interrupts. At an interrupt it accepts control from the CPU and transfers it to the needed operating system function.

The kernel also contains that group of instructions which divide primary memory into memory units which temporarily house the other programs of the operating system, applications programs, and data. In addition to these functions the kernel also creates processes, synchronizes processing, handles communication between processes, stores and manipulates PCBs, supports I/O activities, and supports the file system and system accounting functions.

Input and Output Controller

Input/Output devices are peripherals and may include secondary storage, terminals, PCs, printers, lightpens, and laser scanners. The I/O controller provides for movement between these relatively slow devices and the high speed CPU. It also regulates buffers in primary memory to hold the data during the I/O process.

The I/O controller determines the status of each device, whether it is sending or receiving messages or accessing files. The I/O controller also reads the I/O device, ascertains its location, and returns replies to the proper device. It passes requests from the I/O device to the applications software for implementation and then takes the completed message back to the proper I/O.

Another aspect of the I/O controller is **spooling** (simultaneous peripheral operation online). Spooling allows data to be accumulated and stored on a secondary storage device which acts as a buffer. A spooler will accept and hold data temporarily until the destination peripheral is able to accept the output.

A spooler may accept input and output at the same time. It may send to the system printer a command to print a report on the use of monographs during the past month and accept a list of new monographs that are to be printed on an order form to a jobber. The spooler allows the computer to hold data without using valuable primary memory space.

Scheduling Controller

The simplest form of scheduling is that of the batch job. The CPU accepts input, does the job assigned, and outputs the results. A single interactive process is also simple because only one I/O device is used and the job is again solo in the CPU. However, in an integrated multiuser system, it is necessary to schedule the work done by the CPU. The CPU is capable of processing more requests than those supplied by a single I/O device. The scheduling controller assigns time and space in the CPU to utilize the computing power of the CPU most efficiently.

Multiprogramming

The object of **multiprogramming** is to increase the efficiency of the CPU by assuring that it is not idle, but in use at all times. It is kept busy doing jobs or processes that emanate either from the applications software or the operating system itself. There are several terms associated with multiprogramming: **multitasking** implies that several separate but interrelated computer tasks form a single program; **multiuser** indicates that the computer has multiple ports and can service them concurrently; and **time-sharing** is a term used to describe a method of using a computer system to allow a number of users to execute programs at the same time, with the system processing them in such rapid sequence that the users appear to be handled simultaneously.

Scheduling performance is judged by CPU utilization and measured in throughput, turnaround time, and response time. Throughput is based on the number of processes that are completed in a particular time frame. Of course, the type of process must be taken into account when judging the throughput. Turnaround time (usually used to judge the effectiveness of the servicing of batch jobs) is the amount of time it takes a process to go through the system, be processed, and arrive at its peripheral. **Response time**, which is so important to library applications, is the time lapse between the request and the response in an interactive setting. Response time is also limited by the speed of the I/O device.

In the multiprogramming environment, processes in primary memory gain CPU control and enter the running mode through different methods depending on the operating system. Processes are queued for use of the CPU. The choice of which process to select for activation is done through one of several algorithms: First In First Out (FIFO), Shortest Job First (SJF), Round Robin (RR), Shortest Remaining Time (SRT), Highest Response Ratio Next (HRN), Fair Share Scheduling (FSS), and multilevel queues. Each of these algorithms can be categorized as preemptive or nonpreemptive. A process that has control of the CPU while it is running is said to be nonpreemptive; the CPU cannot be taken away from the process until it relinquishes control. An algorithm is preemptive if it allows for the control of the CPU to be maintained by the operating system not the running process, so the operating system may assign a quantum or otherwise interrupt a running process.

Round robin (RR) scheduling is most popular in a timesharing environment and is preemptive. The first process in the queue is given a CPU burst of a predetermined amount of time, usually from 10 to 100 milliseconds. If the process is not completed in that time it is moved to the back of the queue. Each process is then moved through the CPU in this manner. No process is allocated more than one quantum in a row. Some processes may finish in less than the allotted quantum in which case an interrupt signal is sent to the operating system and the next process in the queue is activated.

Fair Share Scheduling (FSS), a system that is used in the UNIX environment, uses a RR concept but develops several queues with differing priorities.

Concurrent Processing

Until recently all computer programs were written with sequential instructions. However, there is now a trend toward **concurrent processing**. Operations can be performed out of sequence if the output of a previous instruction is not needed. Concurrent programs may be completely independent or they may be asynchronous; that is, needing occasional cooperation.

The problems of dealing with asynchronous processes is one that is faced in the world of library automation when several processes may be accessing the same database. If all the processes want to read the data at a given time, there is no problem. However, when some desire to write to the database while others are seeking to read data, the mutual exclusion algorithm applies. One of the processes must have exclusive access, but others must not be expected to wait too long for access. Mutual exclusion is an important aspect of a multiuser system and is handled by both hardware and software.

Many operating systems support communication between processes through the use of pipes and filters. The UNIX operating system uses that approach. A filter is a program that allows the processing of a stream to a single output—this output can be another process. Pipelining facilitates this by providing the communication link between processes. The output of one process may be the input to another.

Deadlock

Deadlock prevention and control are a major concern of an operating system. Deadlock may be defined as a process that is blocked waiting for some action that is not going to occur. More than one process may become deadlocked when one process holds resources needed by others. Sometimes, spooling buffers become deadlocked because they are filled to capacity and are waiting for a printer to become available.

The operating system may pull preemptive resources from a process; it may not remove nonpreemptive resources. Mutual exclusion may produce deadlock. Other conditions that may also produce it are holding resources while waiting for additional resources and a circular wait in which a series of processes are all waiting for resources held by each other.

Attempts to prevent deadlock require the operating system to prohibit actions that produce it. However, in an interactive environment this is not foolproof and there are also detection methods and procedures for recovery.

Memory Management

In order for the operating system to manage complex scheduling, especially in an integrated multiuser system, it must allocate the space in primary memory to accommodate more than one process at a time. Processes must be moved out of secondary storage to primary memory. In many systems there is also a cache. Programs that access the CPU from cache must be shuttled into this area from primary memory. Some hardware architectures provide direct access into the cache without routing through primary memory.

Once a process has been fetched from secondary storage there must be a decision as to where it should be placed in primary memory. Some operating systems divide the primary memory into fixed partitions of equal or unequal size for processes; others use variable partitions. In the former, processes may be placed in any partition in which they fit; in the latter, the processes are stored in partitions exactly the size of the process.

As processes leave primary memory, they leave holes. If there are adjacent holes, these can be combined to form another partition. This process of merging holes is called coalescing.

Another method of fitting programs in the primary memory is by compaction. At times the various processes that are occupying the memory partitions do not fill up the entire partitions thereby creating holes. Some operating systems make it possible to compact all partitions to one end of the CPU thus making available a large partition composed of the holes from each of the previous partitions. This method will permit another program to enter primary memory.

Virtual Memory

Virtual memory or virtual storage operating systems take multiprogramming systems one step further. They allow larger application programs to run on the CPU than can fit into primary memory. The operating system divides the program processes into pages or segments that can be swapped in and out of primary memory allowing the processing of very large programs without the addition of primary memory. Virtual storage implies a much larger set of addresses than those that are actually in primary memory. Addresses referenced by a process in the run mode are virtual addresses; addresses in primary memory are real addresses. As a process runs, the virtual addresses are mapped into real addresses.

Disk Access

Although it may appear that access to the information on disk would be serviced on a First Come First Served (FCFS) basis, this is not the basis of achieving the fastest response times. Since a multiuser system will generate more requests than can be serviced immediately, there is generally a queue for disk information. Service of requests in the queue may take several forms. Shortest Seek Time First (SSTF) dictates that the arm housing the read/write head go to the position of the data that is closest to its present position (it will move either inward or outward). A variation is the

Shortest Latency Time First (SLTF) strategy which will service requests for data closest to the head. The next request that is serviced will be the one which requires the least rotation of the disk.

SCAN implies that the disk arm swings back and forth across the disk; it will service any request that is in its path. In a C-SCAN strategy the arm moves from outer rim inward. It services all requests in its path and when it reaches the inner rim, it jumps back to the outer rim and begins the inward journey again. N-Step SCAN strategy is another variation of the SCAN strategy. All requests that are received while the arm is moving in one direction are batched and placed in order for optimal service on the return swing.

Most library systems use multiple disk storage. One disk controller is attached to the central unit through an I/O channel. The disk drives are connected to the disk controller.

In many systems there is a **disk cache**. A record is not written directly to a disk but rather held in a buffer in primary memory called a disk cache. The record is then available if needed again and can be accessed much faster than if it were in secondary storage. However, the writing of a record to cache implies that the modified record is not available on a disk. Some operating systems flush the disk cache periodically to keep the disk storage synchronized with what the system thinks is stored on disk.

A technique that is important in the disk system is the RAM disk. The RAM disk is an area of primary memory which simulates a disk. Since access to RAM is faster than disk access this technique improves system performance.

Another technology that may affect operating systems in the future is that of optical disk storage. These disks are made with a laser which burns microscopic holes in a metal or glass coating or a laser which causes bubbles on the coating. In either case the ability of these disks to store information at a capacity far greater than magnetic disks and provide faster search time has made them the potential alternatives for the storage of massive journal citations or full-text files.

File Systems

A **file** is a collection of data, usually stored in a secondary storage device. The file system of the operating system manages these files. File system functions include opening the file, closing the file after it has been referenced, creating a new file, deleting a file, copying a file, renaming a file, and listing or displaying the contents of a file. The operating system should allow the user to set up the structure of the files, e.g., MARC format using fixed and variable length fields.

Within a file are **records**. These records may have the following operations performed on them: read a record into a process, write a record from a process into a file, update existing records, insert new records into a file, and delete records from a file.

The file system of an operating system usually controls access methods, file management mechanisms, storage management of the files in secondary storage, and methods for maintaining the integrity of the files.

There are many files in an automated library system. Within the files are records composed of fields which are fixed or variable in length. Files are organized in several manners: sequential, indexed sequential, direct access, and partitioned.

In a sequential file, records are stored in the order in which they are entered into the file. In an indexed sequential file, the records are stored in a logical order according to some key contained in the record. They are indexed by certain fields and can be accessed through the index which has pointers to the records. Direct access files store records at positions relative to the beginning of the file, and access to the records is through the relative record number. Partitioned files are compilations of sequential subfiles; the starting address for the files is stored in a file directory.

The file system of the operating system is also concerned with the allocation of space in the secondary storage units and the method in which the data in these devices is accessed. There are two methods of accessing data: queued and basic. Queued methods are used when the sequence of records needed can be determined. Queued methods are used for sequential and indexed sequential (ISAM) file organizations. Queued methods attempt to have the next needed records available for referencing by using anticipatory buffering and I/O actions. Basic access requires the reading of records in a physical block and is used to access files that are stored randomly on a disk.

Allocation of space on secondary storage is somewhat like allocating space in primary memory using variable partitions. In paged systems the smallest amount of information that can be transferred from secondary storage to primary memory is a page. It is clear that the information blocks in secondary storage should be of this size and multiples of this size. Locality dictates that it is also helpful to store logically contiguous pages in addresses that are contiguous in secondary storage.

Files tend to grow and change, making noncontiguous allocation a necessity. Noncontiguous allocation is usually handled by a scheme called block allocation. Common ways to implement block allocation are block chaining, index block chaining, and block oriented file mapping.

Block allocation usually involves use of both contiguous and noncontiguous space which is divided into blocks; blocks are composed of sectors. The operating system assigns additional blocks to a file that is already stored on disk by locality, that is, by assigning blocks as close as possible to the other blocks of the file.

Block chaining is accomplished by implementing a user directory to point to the first block of a file. Each block contains both data and a pointer to the next block of the file. It is standard to assign one full rotation of the disk as a block. Sometimes the blocks have pointers in both directions, forward and backward.

If index blocking is used there are pointers in a separate index. The index contains both record identifiers and pointers to the records. The index block is of a fixed size, and if more than one is needed, they are chained together so that searching takes place in the index blocks. Some operating systems maintain these indexing blocks in primary memory. One drawback to this method is that additions of new records usually necessitate the reconstruction of the index blocks.

A block-oriented file mapping method is used by many systems. Instead of maintaining an index, the system maintains a file map. The map has one entry for each block on the disk, and each block is identified by a number which can be converted into an address. The user directory has a pointer to the first block of a file in the file map. Each block on the map has the block number of the next block in that file so that all the blocks in a file can be located through the file map. The last entry of the file is one that is set to "nil" indicating that there are no more blocks in the file. This method permits searching to be confined to the file map and access to the blocks needed on a disk may be accomplished through direct access.

Each file has a file descriptor or file control block which contains information about the file. The file control block may contain the file name, the location on secondary storage, organization (sequential, indexed sequential, etc.), access control data, type of file (data, program, etc.), creation date, date of last modification, and access activity. File descriptors are maintained on secondary storage and are moved to primary memory when the file is opened.

File Security

One of the main problems of maintaining the integrity of a library database is that of security. File protection is shared between the operating system and the applications software. There are several reasons for a user to access a file: read, write, delete, update, or append. All of these actions are controlled by the operating system.

The operating system can limit access to files by naming, passwords, and access control. A user may be unable to access a file because s/he cannot name the file or s/he may not be able to give the operating system a password that will unlock the file. **Access control** is somewhat more complex. It involves the categorization of users. Users are categorized by owner (creator of the file), specified user (user designated by the owner), group or project (members of a group that are working on a project that concerns the file), and public (any member of the community). The operating system maintains a list of those who have the right to access and the access level permitted. The user identification must be entered to obtain access.

Access control can be taken down to the segmentation or program level by the use of a matrix. There are three actions that allow access to segments: read, write, and execute. Read means that the user can simply look at a segment. Write gives the user permission to modify the segment. Execute gives the user permission to run the segment. Yes and no are attached to the three actions. Segments may be tagged as read only, read and execute, etc. If the segment has no access it is completely secure. A program which can be executed only is also secure because no user may modify it; read only implies information retrieval. A program that allows read and execute may be used for retrieval and copied but not changed. The read/write classification protects data files. Access to read/write/execute programs is usually controlled by the user access methods. In order to secure files to a greater degree many operating systems also use encryption methods.

Another important security control is **back-up**. Occasionally, systems do go down and power is interrupted so the integrity of the system is more secure if the library provides for periodic back-up. This may be difficult if the system must be shut down during back-up. It means scheduling a staff member when the library is closed. Another reason to do periodic back-up is to provide time to reorganize files.

The operating system usually provides for incremental back-ups also. The transactions from a remote peripheral are logged and copied to a backup disk as an invisible action to the user. The users may also designate files for backup. Backups are done as a batch process.

Firmware

Most operating systems functions are entirely in software; however, some operating systems are a combination of software and **firmware**. Firmware is the term used to denote microprogramming—instructions that reside in ROM. These instructions may be in machine language or microcode. Microcode is a level of programming that is below machine language instructions.

Although microcode corresponds to the machine language instructions that tell the CPU to perform these actions, the instruction sets of microcode are much simpler than machine language, and microcode has access to more of the hardware than machine language. These instructions are not only stored in ROM but also run in control storage, a high speed ROM. The negative side of microcode is that it occupies valuable ROM space.

Operating System Options

Available operating systems vary considerably in power and complexity. Although the simplest—primarily those designed for personal computers— handle one task at a time, most operating systems for larger computers are designed to support multiple users simultaneously. The more powerful operating systems are also capable of maintaining two or more programs in primary memory at the same time (multiprogramming) and executing two or more tasks at the same time (multitasking). Such systems are likewise time-sharing because they can support multiple remote peripherals. In addition, some operating systems are capable of multiprocessing, or committing the resources of two or more CPUs to a program.

Real-time operating systems are those that can deal with interruptions and requests from users at terminals at the moment they occur. They also are able to put lower priority work in the background and pull it into the processor when there is time available.

The most widely used proprietary operating systems are Digital's VMS and IBM's VM and MVS. VMS runs on all of the Digital machines and requires little data processing expertise. VM (or rather, VM/SP for Virtual Machine/System Product) is popular on IBM 4300 series machines because it is relatively easy to use. MVS is more complex and complete, but is labor intensive, requiring at least two systems analysts or programmers for even a relatively small system. Other popular proprietary operating systems are Hewlett-Packard's MPE/IX and IBM's AS/400.

There is a marked movement away from proprietary operating systems to ones which are independent of specific hardware lines. The two "open" operating systems which are supported by a score or more hardware platforms are UNIX and Pick. UNIX, an operating system developed by Bell Laboratories, is the more popular, primarily because it is an excellent tool for both scientific and general applications. Pick, developed by Richard Pick, is particularly well-suited to complex database applications. Either will make it possible for a vendor to develop software which can run on a wide variety of hardware platforms. While there is a common perception that a library can replace applications software without changing a UNIX operating system, that is usually not the case because there are several versions of UNIX.

At the end of 1997, most multiuser automated library system vendors were using UNIX as the operating system. Dynix (now Ameritech) had used Pick, but a few years ago began using it under UNIX in order to combine the advantages of using the most popular operating system and the sophisticated database features of Pick. The change facilitated the introduction of Dynix Scholar, a product which targets the school library market. UNIX is the only operating system widely available on all levels of machine, from PC to mainframe. CLSI (now part of Geac) moved from its own proprietary operating system to UNIX. Geac replaced its GLIS product, which had used its own proprietary operating system, with Advance—a UNIX-based system. DRA and Gaylord, both long-time users of Digital VMS, were developing UNIX-based products in late 1996. DRA's Classic had used Digital VMS (an operating system choice which was expected to remain available) and its Inlex had used HP MPE/IX; Gaylord had used Digital VMS. Two small vendors, Gateway and NSC, continued to use IBM's AS/400. While it might appear that UNIX has become dominant, there was speculation in late 1996 that Windows NT might gradually displace it.

Most PC-based system vendors focused on DOS, but in early 1995, Follett offered a Windows NT option. COMPanion and Chancery were the only vendors working exclusively in Mac/OS in 1996, while both Nichols and Winnebago had both DOS and Mac/OS offerings.

System Selection Implications

A library purchasing an automated library system should require that the operating system used by the vendor be "open," therefore, facilitating the connection of the system to a network. If a vendor with a proprietary operating system is considered, it should be an operating system which is "POSIX" compliant, meaning that the system conforms to open system standards and looks like an open system to a network. A library should also protect itself against a change in operating system by the vendor. The contract should provide that the vendor will continue to provide, for five years from installation, the same enhancements to the library that customers with the new operating system receive except as the enhancement can only be written using the new operating system. Alternately, the vendor shall provide the new operating system as part of the maintenance and enhancement program to which the customer subscribes, rather than at additional cost to the library.

UTILITY PROGRAMS

Utility programs, as opposed to operating systems, perform tasks that are routinely required by computer users. As with other types of system software, they are usually supplied by computer hardware manufacturers or by companies specializing in software development. Among the most important types are those that copy data from one medium to another, such as from disk to tape. Some utility programs are designed to sort data into a predefined sequence or to merge two or more sets of presorted data, and several kinds facilitate the software development process by simplifying the work of programmers. Other utility programs assist in detecting and correcting errors or "bugs" encountered during application program development. The support of editing and report generation also are functions of utility programs.

DATABASE MANAGEMENT SYSTEMS

In the past two decades, the **database management system** (DBMS) has become a popular way of handling large files of non-numeric data, including bibliographic information. This book uses a formal definition of database management systems: *A database management system allows multiple independent users to have concurrent access to a central repository of* *information.* A DBMS eliminates data redundancy. Each bibliographic record only has to be entered once, as a DBMS permits access to the entire record through any of its fields, even if the need for a particular access point was not foreseen when the database was created. Before the development of DBMS, one had to either create separate files for each required access approach—author, title, subject, call number, etc.—or to create multiple indexes to the bibliographic file at the time the database was being developed. A DBMS provides the ability to modify—and even restructure—the database, without affecting existing programs or creating new file structures. This facility is known as data independence.

Using a DBMS also strengthens the data's integrity by protecting it against hardware and software malfunctions and unauthorized access or modification.

The design and architecture of most DBMS software packages permit multiple-independent users to access common data. The term independent refers to people from different areas of an organization having access to the same information or data. When accessed by independent users, data is said to be shared. However, if information is specific to (only used by) a single person or group, or to a very small number of users, the data is called private.

When data is private, security features are built into a DBMS that prohibit independent users from accessing the data. "Shared data" and "private data" place different requirements on the functions provided by DBMS software; therefore, an organization must determine the needs of its users and how data flows throughout the organization. Suppose, for example, that budget data for each library of a consortium sharing a system is private. This would mean that a librarian at one library could not consult data about another library.

Shared data is desirable when all users are entitled to the information. For example, holdings information would normally be shared throughout a consortium. Shared data, however, has raised important issues, such as access rights and update privileges.

The need to share data may also change over time. When a needs assessment is being conducted, the investigator(s) may perceive the data as private, but once the data becomes machine-readable and is available through online terminals, other organizational units may find use for it. Again, some concept of the organization's data flow and wide consultation with prospective system users will help clarify whether data should be shared or private.

Concurrency, another important concept in building databases, is also provided by the DBMS. Concurrent access means that multiple-independent users create, maintain, and/or retrieve the same data. Concurrent access can apply to shared or private data. For example, data may be shared between acquisitions and cataloging but not concurrent. Acquisitions orders an item one month and cataloging processes it the next. Although the bibliographic data is shared in this case, access is serial. If the user requires current data and the system supports an interleaving of transactions from both acquisitions and cataloging, the access to common data is concurrent.

In the early days of computer automation, sharing tape and manual records data was serial: only one user could have access at any one time. The technical feasibility of concurrent processing came about with online systems. However, many vendors' operating systems did not provide the necessary support for concurrency until recently. Most DBMS, therefore, were developed to provide control for concurrent access because, at the time of their development, the operating systems did not contain the needed features. The requirement to provide users with concurrent access to the same data surfaced during the early implementations of online, terminal-based systems.

Database management systems have carried out security recovery, and other features supporting concurrent access, that are not needed when data is accessed serially. These features require executing many computer instructions but should be justified by exploring the benefits. Most database management systems have proved to provide the largest benefits in an online environment with large databases and a need for concurrency.

Concurrent access will require security controls in DBMS software for protecting data not commonly found in standard-access methods. If concurrent access is necessary, then a DBMS is highly desirable.

Centralizing data is another common reason for adopting a DBMS. The concept of building a central repository of data is key to the concept of a database. The design process to accomplish this requires determining the data fields required by the various applications and eliminating duplicate information, thus yielding an integrated database. Integrating data can be a complex process in itself, regardless of which DBMS software is chosen.

When an application does not include integrated data, using a DBMS is a high price to pay for the benefits received. Many of the design points of commercially available library software are based on the assumption that data integration is in fact a user's primary objective. Many noncommercial software packages available from other libraries do not assume the need for data integration.

If a database is to represent useful information about the real world, it must reflect data as it exists in the real world. Programmers have for years forced data to appear as needed for the convenience of the computers, not the users. Data does not exist in the real world as fixed field entities, and yet in the data processing world it often has. In order for a DBMS to provide information to dissimilar users, it must reflect data and its structure as the users require it.

Data about the same title repeats from one to several times, depending on how many editions and copies a library has. If there are several physical pieces, the identifying information should be consistent. Conventional physical file processing techniques offer two common solutions: they create variable length records and they separate the data into master and transaction files.

When library automation was in its infancy, record lengths were fixed, thus often causing unsatisfactory abbreviation or truncation of data elements, or wasted storage space. Variable length records were subsequently introduced to handle the variable characteristic of data. With rare exception, it is now possible to enter information without abbreviation or truncation.

Not all data is stored in variable length records. Separate master records and transaction records are often used. One variable length record may exist for each patron. The circulation transactions—which records the patron identification number, the book identification number, the loan date, and other information—appears on a transaction file which may consist of fixed length fields. To tie the patron and transaction records together, keys on the various records are repeated. For example, the key of the patron master record is repeated in each transaction record. This solution, however, causes replication of data.

One major drawback of repeated data is its inconsistency. Redundant data requires redundant input procedures, redundant maintenance, and is often reported on redundantly. This leads to the data being out of synchronization with other places in which it is recorded. Redundant and inconsistent data can hardly be used to generate information. Many features of database management systems have been designed to reduce redundant data and will aid the designers of the system in providing consistent data to users. If the data being studied does not repeat, is not redundant, inconsistent, or viewed as structurally different for different users, then one should use a DBMS. But it provides benefits only when data is required to serve the users as information and conventional file processing methods have not met this need in the past.

Any database management system must be used with a compatible operating system and programming language.

Relational Database Management Systems (RDBMS)

Many database management systems in the integrated library world are **relational databases**, more complicated than the traditional hierarchical DBMS. This type of database structure allows for faster searching, better security of sensitive information, and ease of modifying fields. Relational database structures conserve storage space and allow for faster searching by creating files that contain records with unique information. This file structure is transparent to the user. A MARC record that appears on a terminal screen is a compilation of information from several different files. The unique record in the bibliographic file will contain the name of the monograph, the ISBN number, bar code number, and any other information that is unique to it. The record will contain pointers to records in all other files that have information about this record, e.g., there will be a pointer to a record in the author file and one to a record in the publisher file, etc. The record for this author will contain pointers to all records in the bibliographic file which contain monographs by this author. This structure allows optimum use of storage space through an absence of repetition. It also permits quick location of information through a variety of fields. The pointers establish "relationships" between records.

Indexes provide fast searching for information. All fields in records are indexed in inverted files. These files are loaded with the terms most popular at the beginning of the file. If the patron searches the author, Hemingway, the inverted file for the author file will be searched. If the library owns more books by Hemingway than by Wolfe, Hemingway will be nearer the top of the file, therefore, requiring less search time. The Hemingway record in the author file will have pointers to the records in the title file that have books written by Hemingway, and the patron will see on the screen all the books that the library owns written by Hemingway.

The inverted index provides fast access to information because there is no need to search record by record. The operating system indexes the records at the time they are loaded into the system. At the same time it reconstructs the files.

Relational databases use relational languages which operate in a different manner than procedural languages. Procedural languages require that steps be outlined in order to perform a search of the database. Relational languages permit the software to figure out which steps to use in order to achieve the search result.

While DBMSs and RDBMSs are associated with specific operating systems, the most popular ones are available for several operating systems. While a vendor usually has a choice of several database management products, it usually selects the one that optimizes the application and operating system environment.

Object-Oriented Database Management Systems (ODBMS)

As libraries move from automated library systems controlling bibliographic records to automated library systems controlling all forms of information, including full-text, image, and multimedia files, the need for a different DBMS is being expressed. A few vendors have responded by employing an ODBMS.

While an RDBMS stores data in tables, an ODBMS stores information in arbitrary structures, nested structures, and dynamically varying structures. These structures make up software objects or sub-objects. A software object, like a physical object, is a self-contained unit that groups data structures with the methods that are used to process the data. This property of an object is called data encapsulation.

All objects belong to classes. A subclass of objects inherits all the properties of the superclass. For example, one may define an automobile as an object with four wheels, a means of transportation, and a shelter against the weather. Under this definition, one cannot call an object with three wheels an automobile as an automobile has been defined as an object having four wheels.

Bibliographic records are easily handled with an RDBMS because the information can be distributed over a relatively small number of tables—typically no more than 30. In contrast, objects, which can include full-text, still images, and motion images are difficult to distribute among tables. Imagine disassembling all of the attributes of an automobile to store the automobile in tables.

An RDBMS supports simple operations such as find, select, combine, and display while an ODBMS allows arbitrary operations, defined by users, with arbitrary complexity.

There are standards for RDBMS, but not for ODBMS. There is a de facto standard for the latter developed by a trade group calling itself the Object Management Group. The group has been seeking ANSI (American National Standards Institute) and ISO (International Organization for Standardization) approval of the draft standard it developed since 1993, but the process of review and approval is a slow one. There is, therefore, a risk that a product purchased today will not conform to the standard when it is published by NISO or the ISO.

As automated library systems evolve from bibliographic systems to information systems containing full-text, images, and multimedia, the value of using an object-oriented database management system increases. However, neither relational or object database management alone appears to be the ideal approach for libraries. The ideal would be a combination of the two so that bibliographic records utilize an RDBMS and other records an OBDMS—at least until such time as the features of the two are combined into a single database management system. There are predictions that object-oriented RDBMSs will be common in three to five years.

There is ample precedent for using both an RDBMS and an ODBMS on a single system. A number of Fortune 1000 companies have already done it. However, there is now an even easier way, the use of object/relational adapters which enable objects to be stored within an RDBMS.

Libraries should expect the systems they purchase to use RDBMS technology for the foreseeable future, but those concerned with accommodating substantial full-text, image, and multimedia files should determine what provision the vendor is making for such files, including the possible use of object/relational adapters.

Chapter 5

Applications Software and Programming Languages

Applications software consists of the programs that enable the computer to do the various jobs it was acquired by a library to do. These programs are sets of instructions to the computer to perform some action, e.g., check-out an item, check-in an issue of a periodical, provide online access to a library's materials, etc. It is the applications software which is usually compared when choosing among various options; however, each vendor's applications software operates within a complex environment which should also be evaluated.

Proper choice of applications software is crucial: it determines not only how well a library meets current needs but also its future needs, especially if the library seeks to change hardware or if the original software vendor discontinues its support.

While in use, software is stored in the central processing unit's primary memory; when not in use, it may remain in secondary storage. However, since most peripheral devices, such as secondary storage, operate under control of the CPU, they are not independently programmable with software.

PROGRAMMING A COMPUTER

In the earliest computer systems it was necessary to program a computer by setting the switches on the front panel. Each switch had only two settings, 1 (on) or 0 (off). Then, as now, "1"s and "0"s, designated as binary digits or **bits**, were entered into the computer usually arranged in groups of eight. For each sequence of eight there is a corresponding decimal number, e.g., 00000011 is 3, 01111110 is 126. There are numbering systems that make this simpler. The most used, called the hexadecimal (hex) system, is one that employs not only decimal numbers but six letters. In the hex system, the aforementioned sequence of zeros and ones would be coded as 03 and 7E, respectively. This is a far easier code for programmers to remember and use.

The way in which these numbers are stored in a computer is fairly straight-forward. The primary memory of the CPU contains silicon chips that have cells; each cell stores a specified number of binary numbers, the cells are connected by circuits. Most minicomputers and supermicros store 16 or 32 bits in a cell, although 64-bit machines are now becoming common. Most mainframes store 64; the first two generations of PCs stored eight, but the Intel 80386 and 80486 processors store 16; and Pentiums store 32. The numbers stored in the cells may represent real numbers, letters, or actual instructions in machine language. Each cell also has a unique address number to facilitate access.

Text on a computer is represented by a character set—the most used is **ASCII code** (American Standard Code for Information Interchange). ASCII code has numerical values for all letters and punctuation symbols. Most mini-computers, supermicros, and microcomputers (PCs and Macs) utilize ASCII. ASCII uses eight bits for each character or **byte** (letter, punctuation mark, or symbol).

Initially, programmers wrote programs in the machine's own language and then laboriously entered the "1"s and "0"s into the machine by manipulating the switches to create a series of electronic impulses. Today it is common to prepare a program on paper or at a terminal in a shorthand form that is human-readable. The instructions are subsequently converted to machine-readable form. The resulting machine-readable program is maintained on magnetic media from which it is loaded into the primary memory for execution. Programs that are frequently used in a variety of applications may be permanently recorded in electronic circuits, called **read only memories (ROM)**, which are located in the CPU's primary memory section. Such programs, which are typically written by the computer manufacturer, are called **firmware** to distinguish them from software that can be modified and transported from one machine to another. Most software is not permanently recorded in the computer because it would hinder the machine's versatility.

Bytes are arranged in a sequence and stored in cells in a sequence. The sequence is the order in which the computer is to execute the instructions. There is also a set of instructions that command the computer to step out of the sequence and jump or branch to a distant cell for the next instruction. Since the programmer does not know the exact location of the cells, a technique called **labeling** is used. Labels are given to specific instructions and the computer can be told to jump or branch to the cell that is represented by a particular label.

PROGRAMMING LANGUAGES

Technically, the term "**programming language**" encompasses the development of both systems and applications software, but in common usage, it describes the languages used to write programs which are to perform user-specified tasks or applications. **Applications programs** may be written in any one of several programming languages.

Computers can only process instructions that are encoded in machine-readable form. Programming manuals tell the programmer how to represent particular operations. If the code is written directly in binary form—now very rare—the program is said to be written in machine-level language, a programming language that can be executed immediately by the computer.

The individual instructions comprising the program are typically key-boarded at an input terminal for storage on disk or tape pending loading and execution under the control of the computer's operating system. The entry, debugging, and modification of programs is facilitated by the utility programs and other system software.

Machine Language

In contrast with tremendous advances in machine speed, miniaturization, and versatility, the basic level at which most **machine languages** operate has changed relatively little over the past several decades. Instructions can be executed only if they are submitted to the processor's control unit as sequences of numerical codes. Moreover, with a small number of exceptions, the typical machine language instruction represents an activity that is trivial by human standards, offering no direct correspondence with the idea of a "step" in an overall problem solution.

Even when support software is utilized, the writing of programs in machine-level language is a time-consuming, error-prone task. Today it is rarely used because there are now ways to bridge the gap between what the programmer wants to say and what the computer is designed to recognize. The solutions are two levels of languages besides machine-language: assembly language and higher-level languages.

Assembly Language

Assembly language is similar to machine language, but it has been designed to facilitate human understanding. The software development process has been made more efficient by writing programs using mnemonic commands instead of binary codes. Symbols and abbreviations, rather than "0"s and "1"s, are used to write programs. In assembly language, the most common application of mnemonic codes, the programming uses commands such as MOV, ADD, and STO. These commands are much easier for a programmer to remember than the machine-level counterparts, and the resulting program is obviously easier to read and correct. Frequently used instruction sequences can be combined into a single mnemonic code so that they can be invoked with a single command.

While they are easier to write, the individual instructions comprising assembly language programs must eventually be translated into the binary-coded, machine-level language that the computer requires. This translation is performed automatically by the computer using a special program called an **assembler**, also part of the system software. The assembler program, which is typically obtained from the manufacturer of the CPU, is usually written in machine-level language. All computers support an assembler program of some type, although the assemblers of different machines are usually incompatible.

Assembly language is most often used in those situations where the programmer requires very close control over the internal operation of the CPU, such as when writing operating systems, sort/merge programs, and other system software. While it is suitable for writing applications programs because of its efficient use of computer resources, assembly language is relatively slow to use from the standpoint of the programmer. Since hardware costs are dropping and programming costs are rising, programmer productivity is becoming more important than efficient program execution. As a result, application software is now usually written in one of the so-called higher-level programming languages.

Higher-level Languages

Higher-level languages are further removed from machine language than assembly. Whereas one assembly language instruction is usually the equivalent of one machine language instruction, a single higher-level language instruction may trigger a dozen or more machine language instructions. Many higher-level languages allow the use of English language commands. In short, higher-level language programs are easier, faster, and less expensive to develop than those written in machine or assembly language. The resulting programs, however, must be translated into machine-readable language prior to execution. This translation is performed by the computer itself, using a special program called a **compiler**—as distinguished from the assembler used when an assembly language program is translated into machine language.

Prior to its initial execution, a higher-level language program—called a source program—is translated by the compiler into a machine level object program. A variant form of the compiler, called an **interpreter**, avoids this step and translates individual instructions into their machine-level equivalents as they are encountered during the execution of a higher-level language program. As a rule, higher-level languages which utilize interpreters execute more slowly than those which utilize compilers, since instructions which initiate repetitive operations must be retranslated by the computer each time they are encountered. The economic advantage lies in the greater programmer efficiency. Like assemblers, both compilers and interpreters are examples of system software and, as such, often are obtained from computer equipment manufacturers or third party suppliers which support a particular hardware line.

While machine and assembly languages are normally written for a particular computer, higher-level languages can be transported or transferred from one computer to another with a minimum amount of rewriting. While assembly language programs do not have to be retained in the CPU's primary memory, higher-level languages do. Thus, as a language becomes more user-oriented, it becomes less machine-oriented. It is a trade-off of human time against the cost of using additional machine capacity. Because programmers' wages have risen dramatically while the cost of CPUs has dropped sharply, this trade-off has become very attractive in the last few years.

There are hundreds of higher-level programming languages currently in use, each designed with a particular set of objectives in mind. Some are intended for use over a wide range of applications; others address themselves to a more limited spectrum of problem types that are characteristic of a specific discipline. Regardless of basic orientation, there is a common property that is reflected in any higher-level program: the elemental vehicle for expressing the programmer's intention is constructed to convey a level of complexity consistent with the nature of the procedure being represented. This means that the activity which can be described in a single "instruction" or "command" bears no direct resemblance to a single machine operation. Instead, there has been substantial effort to provide some similarity between a higher-level language statement and its counterpart in the notation appropriate to the area of application.

FORTRAN

Since their introduction in the late 1950s, the higher-level languages have tended to be identified with particular types of applications. The earliest higher-level languages were designed for technical applications. FORTRAN (an acronym for "FORmula TRANslator") is the best known. FORTRAN instructions are written in an algebraic notation that is well-suited to the mathematical problems encountered in the physical sciences, engineering, and statistical analysis. FORTRAN compilers are available for computers of all types, although programs written for execution on a given computer system will not necessarily execute well on other systems. Although FORTRAN standards have been developed by the American National Standards Institute (ANSI), most compilers deviate from the standard by offering additional features designed to enhance the language's utility. FORTRAN compilers developed for microcomputers usually cannot accommodate all of the instructions available with compilers designed for mainframe or minicomputer installations. FORTRAN was used by Cincinnati Electronics in its CLASSIC circulation control system, but the company withdrew from the market after only a few years. Gaylord used a combination of FORTRAN and an assembly language in its first integrated, multifunction, multiuser automated library system.

COBOL

COBOL (COmmon Business Oriented Language) is the most widely used higher-level programming language in applications involving business data processing. Unlike scientific computing with its complex mathematical calculations, business applications are typically characterized by the repetitive performance of fairly simple computations involving large amounts of data. As a result, COBOL instructions emphasize data handling and report production. COBOL instructions are written in an English-like notation designed for simplified reading. As originally developed by a committee of computer manufacturers and users, COBOL was intended to be as machine-independent as possible. However, it has usually not been used on small mini-and microcomputers because the large number of instructions in COBOL means that the computer, in turn, must have a large primary memory.

COBOL standards have been adopted by ANSI, but some versions offer enhancements not included in the standards. As a result, though COBOL compilers are available for virtually all mainframe and minicomputers, a COBOL program written for a particular computer system cannot always be executed on others. Again, as with FORTRAN, COBOL compilers developed for microcomputers typically respond to only a subset of the instructions included in the mainframe or minicomputer implementations. COBOL was used by Sigma Data, a vendor that was active in the market during the late 1970s and early 1980s with corporate and federal libraries its primary target. VTLS also began with COBOL, but now uses a combination of "C" and COBOL. International Computers Limited's CADMUS—a turnkey system briefly offered by a major British computer manufacturer—also used COBOL.

While library automation applications share many of the characteristics of business data processing, bibliographic processing often requires the complex manipulation of character strings which may have no numeric values. The conventional higher-level languages (such as FORTRAN and COBOL) were designed to handle numeric information and brief records. Where more complex bibliographic records are to be manipulated, a group of string-processing programming languages (such as SNOBOL4, COMIT, or LISP) can be used. Unfortunately, most programmers are not familiar with these and few computer manufacturers support them. Finally, most string-processing languages use interpreters rather than compilers to translate the instructions into machine-language. As previously noted, programs written in interpreted languages tend to execute slowly and can prove costly because computer efficiency is poor.

MIIS/MUMPS

There is an exception to the general rule that the use of interpretive languages leads to inefficiencies in processing. Systems analysts working with medical records developed an approach that minimizes the sacrifice of processing speed. Meditech Interpretive Information System, generally known as MIIS, is an interactive, general-purpose operating system that contains an interpretive programming language (MUMPS—an ANSI standard language) and a complete set of database management and programmer-aid utilities. It is, therefore, a combination operating and programming language geared to working with character strings, such as those common in bibliographic records. OCLC's LS/2000 used MIIS/MUMPS, as did DataPhase (a vendor no longer active in the library automation industry).

PL/1

Although the higher-level programming languages discussed to this point have been developed for specific types of applications, PL/1 was designed with generality in mind. This programming language combines FORTRAN-like mathematic capabilities with COBOL-like data handling facilities. Some string-processing capabilities are also included. The resulting broad applicability has proven attractive to organizations that have to support a variety of operations. Originally implemented on the IBM System 360 and 370 series of mainframe computers, PL/1 compilers have since been developed for the mainframe computers of other manufacturers. Some minicomputer systems offer subsets of PL/1 or proprietary languages patterned after PL/1. Proprietary languages are unique to the developer and not generally available for use by others. DOBIS/LEUVEN, a library applications software package sold by IBM for nearly two decades, used a combination of PL/1 and an assembler.

BASIC

All of the programming languages discussed up to this point were originally developed for preparing programs off-line—the programmer wrote the program, put it on the machine, ran it, and then made corrections. With the development of online systems during the 1970s, programmers began working at terminals, and programming languages were introduced that returned results immediately. BASIC (the Beginner's All-Purpose Symbolic Instruction Code) is the best known and most widely used of these "online" languages.

BASIC is easy to learn and, although employing a FORTRAN-like algebraic notation, it can be used for both scientific computerization and business data processing. Some versions also include very rudimentary string-processing capabilities. BASIC has been used on a wide range of mini- and microcomputers. However, there are many versions. Record handling capabilities in BASIC are often more limited than in other higher-level languages; therefore, access to records is slower. As an interpreted language, BASIC also tends toward slow execution. With some computer systems, however, BASIC is available in faster compiler versions known as BASIC Plus and BASIC Plus 2. Ameritech's Dynix is written in BASIC, as are Ringgold's Nonesuch acquisitions and catalog control systems.

PASCAL

PASCAL is a language developed in the 1970s to overcome deficiencies in older languages. It was designed to serve as a language for teaching computer programming as a systematic discipline. Its greatest strength as an actual programming language is that it allows the programmer to find errors quickly. Chancery, which offers Mac-based systems, uses PASCAL; and COMPanion, which also offers Mac-based systems, uses a mix of C and PASCAL.

C

C is a highly structured high-level programming language developed specifically for multiuser, multitasking applications. It is machine-independent and was developed by the Bell Laboratory personnel, who also developed the UNIX operating system, which explains why UNIX was the first operating system to be written in C. It is particularly well-suited to systems programming. CLSI and Innovative Interfaces were the first to use the C language; and Data Research Associates was one of the first to undertake a major rewrite in order to take advantage of C.

A new version of C—C++—is now being used. C++ is an object-oriented language, one that does not tell the machine what to do but merely states what the end result should be and lets the CPU perform processes that will achieve the results desired. C++ is now the most widely used language for the writing of library automation applications, including both multiuser and micro-based systems.

A computer is not as efficient when running programs written in C++ as when running programs written in a language closer to machine language. Given the great power and relatively low cost of today's computers, coupled with the relatively high salaries of programmers, it is better to use a language which optimizes programmer productivity.

Java

Java is one of the newest programming languages. Introduced in mid-1995 by Sun Microsystems Inc., Java is a cousin to C++. The unusual feature of Java is that it allows programmers to create little virtual machines—known as "applets"—that can be temporarily downloaded from a network to a low-end computer and used to carry out a task. In mid-1996, IBM announced that it would begin marketing a network PC priced under $1,000 to provide system purchasers an option in addition to $500 "dumb" terminals and $2,500 PCs. Equally important, applets can be safely swapped among people via the Internet without fear of spreading hard-disk wrecking viruses.

Java offers software developers a way to create relatively small, self-contained programs that introduce "interactivity"—change, motion, responsiveness—to the information shared on networks, including the graphics-rich portion of the Internet, called the World Wide Web. All a user needs to run any Java applet is Web software that speaks Java. Clicking on the applet will start the program. There is no need for an additional complex program, such as a word processing package.

Among the trends that are behind the Java surge are the emergence of powerful computer networks, with information shuttling at increasingly higher speeds, therefore allowing the transfer of large text-based documents, detailed diagrams, color illustrations, and snatches of audio and video clips; the increased ease of sharing among machines on a network, including PCs, Macs, and more powerful machines; and the availability of low-cost, custom-made chips narrowly designed for specific tasks.

Because Java applets are independent software objects, they can be plugged together like so many Lego blocks. Unlike a current word processing package, which must be designed to work with a specific computer operating system, applets will run on any machine. What's more, such tools would not require large amounts of memory on the desktop, therefore making possible the use of low-end PCs.

Innovative Interfaces was the first automated library system vendor to introduce Java applets in its applications software in mid-1996. It limited the initial effort to administrative reports. VTLS introduced a new generation system designated "Virtua" in late-1996 which made extensive use of Java throughout the various modules.

System Selection Implications

When selecting an automated library system, the two criteria to keep in mind with regard to programming languages are (1) is it a higher-level language? and (2) is it a language for which there is an ANSI standard? If the answer to both questions is yes, there is less risk that a library will not be able to continue software maintenance and enhancement should the vendor cease to support the product.

Another issue which should be considered is a possible change in programming language by the vendor. Those not using "C" or "C++" may well change programming languages. A library should protect itself by stipulating that a change in programming language will not adversely affect the ability of the library to load product enhancements.

APPLICATIONS SOFTWARE

Most organizations no longer write their own software because it is too time-consuming and expensive. Instead, they rely on packaged or prewritten software that has been purchased. Most applications software is written and sold by firms that specialize in software development. Many hardware manufacturers still consider the creation of applications software the user's responsibility, or the responsibility of a specialized applications software company. It has only been in the last few years that IBM began to develop and market applications software; yet it now leads the industry in that regard.

Of the major hardware manufacturers, only IBM and UNISYS actively marketed multiuser library software packages in the 1970s and 1980s, but both sold off their products to other companies in the early 1990s. No general software houses offered multiuser library software packages during this period, but several library-produced software packages were available, among them NOTIS (from Northwestern University Library), and VTLS (from Virginia Tech), both subsequently spun off as separate companies.

Beginning in 1973, a number of commercial companies entered the library automation market. Initially, they were called "niche" market vendors, those which targeted a narrow market with a very specific product. Niche markets exist in banking, legal support systems, pharmaceuticals, and a score of other areas. A characteristic of niche market vendors is that they often "bundle" hardware, software, installation, and training, thus offering a so-called "**turnkey**" solution.

A comprehensive multiuser library automation software package developed by a commercial vendor may represent an investment of $2 to $5 million or more. In order to make it affordable, it is necessary to sell hundreds of packages. A score of companies have managed to do that, among them Ameritech Library Services, Data Research Associates, Geac Computers, Innovative Interfaces, Sirsi, and Gaylord in North America; IME, Siemens, and OPSYS in Europe; and Ex Libris in Israel.

Library packages for PCs and Macs became available beginning in the mid-1980s. Initially, they were single-function circulation or acquisitions systems. It was not until the 386-based microcomputer became common that vendors began offering library automation software packages with several modules. While the sales leaders continue to be Follett and Winnebago, there are now a dozen vendors with multifunction packages.

Library Applications Packages

Most library applications packages for multiuser automated library systems are sold by the module. The widely available modules are acquisitions, serials control, cataloging, circulation, and online patron access catalog. Other modules offered by several vendors include reserve book room, inventorying, information & referral, journal citation files, media booking, newspaper indexing, interlibrary loan, and imaging. A module may have submodules which include expanded functionality for those purchasers which wish to spend the additional money. Among the most widely available submodules are a cataloging support system interface for the cataloging module, a binding submodule for serials control, and a link to OCLC for the interlibrary loan module.

Most vendors of PC and Mac-based systems offer more limited range of functionality, but almost all offer cataloging, circulation, and online patron access catalog modules. For further explanation Chapter 6 deals with the functionality available as of late 1996 in greater detail.

SOFTWARE DOCUMENTATION

When packaged software is obtained from any source other than a turnkey vendor, it is usually necessary for the purchaser to assume some responsibility for ongoing software maintenance and enhancement. In order to be able to do this, the purchaser needs documentation or written information recorded during the development of the software that explains pertinent aspects of the system.

Documentation—the preparation of a detailed record of what has been done in developing a set of computer programs—should be an integral part of defining and programming a computer system. However, a commitment to good documentation is costly. In some environments, as much as 20 to 40 percent of the total development effort goes into documenting a new system—detailing how it is to work and how it was developed.

During the development of a computer program, documentation of how the program was designed is essential so that all people involved in a project will know what has been done and can pass information from one person to another, should staff changes occur. In addition, documentation may be important to prospective purchasers of the software because it facilitates evaluation and provides a basis for making subsequent changes in the software.

Not only is documentation essential to software design but to its subsequent maintenance as well. Effective continuing maintenance of the software demands that when testing of the system is completed, documentation be brought up to date, to reflect the changes made as a result of the tests.

Systems analysts and programmers involved in a given software development effort are normally responsible for preparing appropriate documentation. Although most programmers recognize the value of documentation, under the pressure of a tight schedule, many programmers neglect to fully document software development activities. This particularly occurs when a software development effort is "over-budget." Unfortunately, limiting the amount of documenting is often viewed as a way to achieve greater economy in program writing, but a software buyer may discover this only after beginning work on purchased software. Poor documentation then leads to significant increases in the time and costs associated with program maintenance and use. At a minimum, documentation should include the following:

System Specifications indicate the capabilities of the system and may be developed by the end user when a custom-developed system is being planned. More commonly they are prepared by the developer of a software package as the first step in the software design.

Programming Documentation describes exactly how the system works. Without such documentation, making changes to the programs may be difficult, prohibitively expensive, or impossible.

Documentation of Testing serves as both (a) evidence of the tests that the system has already passed, and (b) a good starting point for testing after any future modifications. This documentation proves that the system at one time performed properly. When later modifications are made, it is important to know that the system still performs the original functions accurately.

Operator's Manual contains complete instructions for loading and running each program within the system, as well as instructions on how to set up all equipment, how to process each type of transaction, the meaning of the error messages, and the appropriate action to be taken when an error message is received.

The manual should also specify appropriate back-up procedures including when the suggested frequency with which data should be copied for back-up. The manual should incorporate sample input and output for each type of transaction.

Procedures Manuals are usually written by the end user, since it integrates the computer system into an organization's internal procedures. However, many turnkey vendors provide such manuals for customers to adapt to their needs. This documentation comprises such things as data entry instructions, schedules of when output is due, how frequently to perform the back-up routine, etc.

Software documentation is particularly important when purchasing a software package developed by another organization for its own use. Good quality, commercially produced software is usually generalized and provides tables that permit users to tailor the system to their own requirements. Software developed by an organization for itself is often less flexible and will have to be modified by the buyer. Unfortunately, many software packages developed without future sale to others in mind are seriously deficient in documentation. It may, therefore, take the new owner a great deal of time to develop the documentation itself.

Even with inexpensive software packages for micros, adequate documentation is needed in order to make modifications; yet more often than with larger system packages, it is lacking.

If software is purchased as part of a turnkey system, the vendor is required to maintain and enhance the software. When application software is purchased from a computer manufacturer, software house, or another library, the buyer is usually responsible for continued maintenance and enhancement. However, ongoing support is available for some software packages. Since maintenance programming accounts for more than half the software development workload in many organizations, there is distinct advantage in selecting the software for which ongoing support is available.

Furthermore, given the changing requirements of users and the rising programmer turnover rate, "maintainability" has become a major factor in most software developers' decision to abandon assembly-language programming and use higher-level languages that employ readable English-like instructions, which are more readily understood by programmers.

While programming documentation is less important when purchasing a turnkey system, both operators' manuals and procedures manuals are important and should be evaluated as part of a procurement decision.

Chapter 6

System Functionality

The first successful multiuser automated library system vendors offered single function systems to support the automation of circulation control beginning in the early 1970s. As necessary adjuncts, the systems also provided capabilities for database creation and maintenance, and limited, staff-only, bibliographic database inquiry capabilities. As the oldest function, circulation control is generally fully developed in all vendors' product lines. Vendors that joined the market later, or those that began their systems with a different functional module, draw on knowledge of the capabilities of established systems to rapidly establish competency in this function. Other functionality began to be added in the 1980s, as hardware costs came down and increased system sales provided funds for development. By the mid-1990s, most multifunction systems included a dozen or more modules.

Single-function PC and Mac-based systems began to be offered in the mid-1980s. Most of those were single function circulation control systems. As PCs and Macs became more powerful, other modules were added, although the majority of such systems were still limited in the mid-1990s to cataloging, circulation, and online patron access catalog modules. A minority also included acquisitions and serials control.

The current emphasis on patron access capabilities represents a shift in the focus of local library automation. Previously, system development was aimed at providing support for staff, reducing tedious manual routines, such as typing and filing. As system capabilities removed these functions from cataloging and circulation, attention was directed to other labor-intensive technical services operations, such as acquisitions and serials control. The patron access concern has now reinforced interest in these functions as librarians and users realize the benefits of having access to information on items on order and in process, and resources other than monographs.

The core modules of automated library systems are considered to be acquisitions, serials control, cataloging, circulation, and online patron access catalog. Most mature multifunction integrated automated library systems now offer all of these core modules and the following general characteristics:

- a high degree of **parameterization** to enable individual libraries to implement their own preferences for variables, such as: loan periods, fines, material claim cycles, definition of the fields to be included in the various access indexes, screen displays, and sort options
- the ability to accept, maintain, and output records in all **MARC formats**
- support for all **material types**: monographs, serials, maps, manuscripts, sound recordings, etc.
- **access security** features limiting certain functions to users with appropriate levels of password authorization and terminals in specific locations
- provision of detailed statistics and **management reports** on all aspects of system use, performance, and operation
- support for **electronic messaging** among terminals linked to the system
- provision of **dial access** to the system from remote sites
- provision for system terminals or PCs on the system to access **remote databases** through a gateway in the CPU
- support for multi-institutional installations in which each library can maintain policy and parameter files independent of the other libraries using the system.

Each of the core modules is briefly discussed in the following paragraphs:

ACQUISITIONS

Capabilities generally include these activities:

- downloading of acquisitions records from cataloging resource files and use of those records through all phases of selection, acquisition, and processing
- creation and maintenance of vendor files
- accounting and fund control, including: multilevel fund nesting, automatic warning of depletion of funds, tracking of expenditures and encumbrances, verification of invoice arithmetic, automatic calculation of vendor discounts, and monitoring of fulfillment performance
- creation and maintenance of selection, desiderata, and negative selection decision files
- assignment of default vendors
- automatic generation of orders in paper or electronic form
- automatic claiming of outstanding orders and invoice
- monitoring the progress of materials through internal library processing.
- EDI FAX online ordering (generally in Beta release in late-1996).

SERIALS CONTROL

Serial control modules typically share a number of acquisitions module features, such as fund accounting, invoice checking, vendor file maintenance, monitoring of vendor performance, and ordering. Capabilities specific to this module are as follows:

- check-in support that minimizes the amount of operator keying by predicting details such as issue number, date, and number of copies
- production of spine labels and routing slips
- automatic detection of missing issues for claiming
- claim generation in paper and electronic formats, and tracking of claim responses
- routing
- binding control
- automatic manipulation of holdings data to support display or output of summary level holdings information, including all copies of a title, latest issue received, etc.
- support for a variety of output products, included printed listings, machine-readable tapes for reporting to union lists, and subscription renewal lists.
- EDI FAX online claiming (generally in development in late-1996).

CATALOGING

While the term "cataloging" is not a very good name for a module which includes not only the ability to catalog a title, but all aspects of database creation and maintenance, it is the most widely used term.

The **bibliographic file** capabilities supported by most major system vendors include the following:

- support for the MARC formats for bibliographic records
- interfaces to support the loading of bibliographic records from tape
- interfaces to accomplish the online transfer of bibliographic records from bibliographic utilities and standalone cataloging support systems
- provision of formatted screens for the keying of bibliographic records
- ability to accommodate brief bibliographic records
- record editing capabilities that allow the addition, change, or deletion of data in a record without requiring record deletion and re-input

High level data input validation routines are less common, many systems rely upon external cataloging support systems for such functions. Systems that offer input validation include checks to ensure that bibliographic records contain mandatory fields, single occurrences of nonrepeatable fields, valid fixed field codes, etc. Not all extend this support to the revalidation of records that have updated or changed. Such factors were not of great significance in older circulation-only systems and were accommodated to varying extents by the bibliographic utilities from which most libraries interested in bibliographic record quality control obtained their input. Now that correctly formatted bibliographic records are assuming increased importance in patron access catalog applications, enhanced bibliographic record validation capabilities are becoming more common. Support for the full ALA character set and non-Roman scripts is gradually becoming available.

The relatively short history of commercial library automation applications suggests that the development and maintenance of detailed, high-quality, bibliographic and authority databases may be the most important element in the long term utility of a library automation program. The hardware in any system configuration becomes obsolete and is replaced to take advantage of technological developments and declining prices, and software is continuously upgraded to provide new capabilities and improved functionality. A carefully constructed database can outlive several generations of hardware and software. The costs of creating minimal records and upgrading them little by little each time improvements in software capabilities reveal the utility of a data element previously thought to be superfluous soon outstrip the expense of creating full-length records in the first place.

In the absence of a standard format for **patron file** data, most systems allow for a wide range of library-defined patron record fields and category types. Keying is the most common form of patron record creation, but most vendors will provide facilities for tape loading of machine-readable patron records from other nonlibrary institutional files. Such loads are usually performed on a one-time custom basis, as an extra cost item. The provision of formatted screens for the keying of patron records is an industry norm, as is the ability to circulate materials to a patron immediately once the patron record is keyed into the system. Recognizing the importance of providing support for rapid system implementation, some vendors provide PC-based patron data entry systems that enable a library to begin patron registration well in advance of the delivery of system hardware, and to load the records into the automated system without further processing.

Not all systems can accommodate authority records and some that do retain only preferred forms of a heading, not notes, cross references, and related terms. Systems with full authority record capabilities generally provide for tape loading and keyed input, and support the MARC authorities format. Authority record interfaces to bibliographic utility files and the emerging CD-ROM-based authority files are less common. Basic **authority file** creation and maintenance capabilities include

- support for the MARC authorities format
- interfaces for tape loading of MARC formatted authority records
- support for keying of authority records, including provision of MARC formatted input screens
- interfaces for the online transfer of authority records from bibliographic utility systems and CD-ROM-based authority resource files
- maintenance of separate subject, name, and title authority files
- authority file record editing capabilities

- support for the automatic updating of authority records as replacement records are added from authorized sources

Not all systems that accommodate authority records have integrated them into the appropriate functional modules (bibliographic record creation and maintenance, and online catalog functions). The **authority control** capabilities commonly available include

- library-defined bibliographic records fields subject to authority control
- matching the defined fields in new or changed bibliographic records against the appropriate authority files, with automatic detection of nonmatches and linkage of matches to the related authority records
- copying of nonmatching headings into temporary files for online review and validation, with bibliographic record linkage retained to facilitate review and automatic addition of the records to the system after review
- support for multiple authority files from different sources, and linkage of bibliographic records to specified authority files
- global change capabilities, whereby a change in an authority file record is automatically reflected in all bibliographic records linked to that authority
- explosion of authority records and the integration of "see" and "see also" references into the online patron access catalog module. (Systems offer a variety of approaches to such integration, some displaying the exploded references in the "see" and "see also" format of traditional catalogs; others using them as user transparent support for other directional messages, for example, "This library uses Beijing as the subject heading for works about Peking cataloged since 1978. Select 1 if you wish to expand the search to include both Peking and Beijing, 2 to search only for entries cataloged under Peking, 3 to search only for works cataloged under Beijing, 4 to reformat the search, 5 to start another search.")
- suppression of user displays of blind references, but provision for staff display
- staff display of "see from" and "see also from" relationships

CIRCULATION

A library seeking **circulation control** can expect to find support for the following:

- check-in and check-out for all types of materials
- generation of overdue notices and billings
- fine calculation and payment
- detection of patron delinquency status
- placement of holds and issuance of recall notices
- support for multiple, flexible library-defined loan periods, fine levels, and patron- and material-type action options

- inventory capabilities that support an inventory of material on the shelves by collecting data on a portable bar code scanner and identifying missing items by comparing the information about items on the shelves with circulation records and the library's database
- reserve room/secondary collection circulation control
- micro-based backup charging devices to handle check-out when the main system is unavailable
- deletion of the linkage between a patron and an item once the item has been checked in, but retention of generic information on the transaction in the item record
- collection composition and use statistics, including identification of heavily used and uncirculated materials

Vendors are increasingly augmenting these capabilities. Among the recent additions are patron self-charging and electronic notification.

ONLINE PATRON ACCESS CATALOG

The online patron access catalog usually requires more computer resources and remote peripherals than any other application; therefore, it is a high product development priority for vendors. Capabilities generally supported include

- keyword searching across all indexed fields
- Boolean searching
- adjacency searching and truncation capabilities
- limiting of searches to specified fields or groups of fields
- application of language, date, and format qualification to limit result sets
- stop word capabilities
- browsing access to bibliographic and authority records and indexes

System search capabilities are only one aspect of the patron access catalog. Of equal importance are the system supplied aids to facilitate patron use of the catalog. Features to assist patrons in use on the online catalog include

- menu-driven search templates to guide novice users
- provision of a command mode to allow experienced users to by-pass the guided inquiry approach
- multilevel help capabilities, including user-invoked help screens and system-supplied guidance or suggestions for unsuccessful or overly broad searches
- online instruction in system use
- multiple display options of varying levels of detail
- retention of search strategy for modification or application in another search

- provision of print capabilities
- local library control of screen displays and messages
- local library definition and modification of the selection of fields to be included in specific indexes
- local library control of display options and display sort sequences

Recently, **GUIs** (graphical user interfaces) have become available from almost all vendors. A GUI-based patron access catalog usually offers the following:

- pull-down menus
- a mouse and arrows to scroll through open windows
- point-and-click navigation to a wide assortment of features
- multiple windows open simultaneously

ADDITIONAL MODULES

Beyond these core capabilities, the systems vary in the range of additional functionality supported. Most multiuser systems include an **information & referral** module. Also called a community information module, this product provides the capability for a library to build a database of campus or community information and to make that database available to users of the on-line patron access catalog with the same types of indexes and displays. Typically, a record includes the name of an organization, whom it serves, when the service is available, on what terms the service is offered, and where to go or call. A campus or community calendar also is a common feature.

Many multiuser systems offer informal support for **interlibrary lending** through the circulation control module using pseudo-patron records and, when an installation is shared by more than one library, the system may use electronic messaging capabilities. A few vendors are developing interlibrary lending modules which include linkages with the OCLC interlibrary loan system, copyright clearance monitoring, support for the ALA interlibrary loan format, and full management of all interlibrary lending activities with libraries sharing the same automated system installation, libraries using other automated systems, and libraries with no local automation. With the expected publication of a revised Z39.63 standard for interlibrary lending in 1997, there might be increased emphasis on the development of complete interlibrary loan modules.

For a time, there was emphasis on the development of **journal citation** capabilities for multiuser systems that provide access to local files of indexes and abstracts of journal articles using search techniques that parallel those of the patron access catalog. Such files are generally mounted on the same magnetic media as support other files. File contents may be selected to correspond to the journals to which a library subscribes or more extensive collections may be mounted. Closely related to this capability is functionality that will support the searching of journal information from selected citations against the serials control and circulation files to determine whether a specific journal issue is held by the library, and its current location and availability. The approach also entails the ability to switch searches from the patron access catalog to the citation file, and vice versa; and linkage to the interlibrary loan function to obtain cited materials not held in the home library. The module has not been as successful as expected because of the emergence of **online reference services**—online services designed for end-user searching.

While not a rapidly developing area, there is a continued interest among some libraries in **media booking** capabilities for management and scheduling of audiovisual materials and equipment. Several multiuser system vendors offer support as part of their multifunction integrated systems; however, as fewer than five percent of libraries specify this module, the functionality is limited. For that reason, there were a number of stand-alone media booking systems installed in libraries in the mid-1990s—including both on PCs and on multiuser CPUs.

All systems produce management reports. The most frequently used are coded by the vendor as part of its applications software. Most vendors of multiuser systems also offer **report generators** that permit a library to readily define specific data elements for inspection, combination, and output as specialized reports. The capabilities extend to custom formatting of output reports. Reports may be set up for one-time or ongoing production.

Most multiuser systems include a **CPU gateway** allowing any terminal, PC, or Mac on the system to go out through the gateway to a remote system. This makes it unnecessary for each remote peripheral to have its own modem. By 1995, the majority of such gateways had been augmented with **Z39.50** client software on the PCs connected to the automated library system or on the automated library system itself. Only some of the PC- and Mac-based automated library systems offered Z39.50 client software as of late-1996.

A majority of multiuser system vendors and a few micro-system vendors offer a **WebPAC**, a user interface which makes it possible to access not only the automated library system using Netscape or Microsoft's Explorer but also the World Wide Web.

Almost all vendors of multiuser automated library systems included **Z39.50 servers** at the end of 1996. The servers made it possible for the users of other automated library systems which had Z39.50 client software to access the server without knowing the command language of the system targeted. Only a few vendors of PC- and Mac-based systems were planning to support Z39.50 servers as of late-1996.

Web servers are generally available from vendors of multiuser systems. The software on the server converts a library's MARC records into HTML (Hypertext Markup Language) that can be read by Web client programs, such as Netscape or Microsoft Explorer, and accessed via the World Wide Web. The advantage for users is that they can interact with the library system using a graphical user interface which is familiar even though the person has no previous experience with the automated library system being accessed.

Imaging is available from several multiuser system vendors, but the offerings vary a great deal in their scope. While most systems can store an image and retrieve by linking a bibliographic record to the image using a tag in the MARC field, a minority of vendors offer scanners, software to edit and enhance images, and high-resolution workstations.

Newspaper indexing is perhaps the least common module, but it is possible to create newspaper indexes using the cataloging software of most systems.

Chapter 7

Content and Interfacing Standards

A successful automated library system requires adherence to a variety of standards: library-specific content standards for creating and formatting machine-readable records, and the structures for communicating them; and data communication standards for the transmission of information among systems.

The standards vary in their degree of formalization. Some have received formal approval from national and international standards bodies such as the American National Standards Institute (ANSI), the Institute of Electrical and Electronics Engineers (IEEE), or the International Organization for Standardization (ISO); others rely on informal adoption by associations and industry groups such as the American Library Association (ALA) and the Book Industry Systems Advisory Committee (BISAC). All share formal expression in detailed documentation, but the latter are de facto standards, rather than true standards.

Unlike some European countries, the United States does not mandate adherence to standards. Adoption is purely voluntary. Librarians have a tradition of cooperative adoption of standards that predates automation—witness the dimensions and paper content specifications for the "standard" catalog card. Increasingly adherence to standards by United States libraries is becoming a little more than voluntary. For example, a number of state library agencies make the funding of retrospective conversion contingent upon use of the MARC format.

CONTENT STANDARDS

Until recently, bibliographic records have been the primary concern of automated library system developers, but subject and name authority records are now assuming increased importance. A range of standards apply to the selection and presentation of information in these records.

In the English-speaking world, the *Anglo-American Cataloging Rules* are widely adopted as the de facto standard governing the selection and presentation of information in bibliographic and name authority records. The rules describe what information should be included, and how it is selected and presented. The objective is to foster uniformity in record content and consistency in presentation.

Recording of subject authorities and subject data in bibliographic records is guided by the use of standard subject heading and classification schemes such as the Library of Congress and MeSH subject headings and the Library of Congress and Dewey Decimal Classification Schemes. These de facto standards ensure consistency in subject indexing and in the subject authority records that describe the relationships between terms in subject listings or thesauri.

Such standards apply to all bibliographic and authority records, regardless of whether they are to be made available in machine-readable form. Content standards for other records of significance in automated library system linkage are discussed in the following section.

ENCODING STANDARDS—MARC

If bibliographic and authority records are to be encoded in machine-readable form, a second level of standardization—formats and guidelines for recording the data in machine-readable form—is essential for effective utilization and exchange.

The formats for encoding bibliographic and authority data in machine-readable form are based on a national standard developed by NISO (National Information Standards Organization) known as Z39.2, the *American National Standard for Bibliographic Interchange*. The MARC (MAchine Readable Cataloging) formats have been developed for the range of bibliographic material types, for authority records, and for holdings and locations data. Adherence to the formats make it possible for libraries to exchange records without extensive reformatting.

The acronym MARC has several meanings. It describes a computer record structure or format, a series of tags and indicators to identify parts of the record, the level of cataloging information contained in Library of Congress MARC Distribution Service (MDS) records, and the series of records distributed by MDS.

As a **record structure**, MARC was designed for the communication of information between computers. It specifies a record beginning with a fixed length leader, a directory or map of the location of various data elements in the record, and a series of data elements or fields—of both fixed and variable length-separated by field terminators. The record ends with a record terminator.

The **leader** is a fixed-length field which contains information about the record and the work described in it. The data includes information essential to manipulation of the record—record length, the starting position of variable data elements, and the number of character positions assigned to field and subfield identifiers—and general information about the record content—the status (new, changed, etc.), the type of record (bibliographic, authority, or holdings and location), and—for bibliographic records—the cataloging level represented in the record.

The **directory** contains one entry for each field in the record. It lists the field tag, the length of the field, and the starting position of the field. It enables rapid computer identification and processing of specific data elements.

The main body of the record is made up of a series of variable length **fields**, each of which is designated by a three digit numeric **tag**. The tag indicates the type of information in the field. Fields may contain a number of **subfields**, each identified by a specific code.

The MARC formats serve as **communication** formats—standard envelopes in which machine-readable data is transferred from system to system or application to application. Few automated library systems utilize MARC as an internal processing or storage format. The use of MARC as a communication format makes it essential that an automated library system be able to accept the input of MARC records, and produce MARC formatted output.

Not all systems which advertise **MARC compatibility** in fact have these capabilities. It is a relatively simple matter to program a system to accept MARC input and to convert the records to the internal processing format used in that system. It is significantly more complex to program a system to retain and output records in MARC. To accomplish this, all data elements must be coded with the appropriate MARC tags, *and* an accurate leader and directory must be constructed. If a record has been loaded to a system in MARC, retained in that format, and edited to add or change the data in any way, the system must make appropriate adjustments in the leader and directory to reflect the changes made in the record. Otherwise, the map that directs programs to specific data elements will be awry, and the record will be unusable. Some systems described as supporting MARC output are, in fact, outputting only copies of original, unchanged input records.

The second meaning of MARC is as a series of **tagging conventions**. The American Library Association's MARBI (MAchine Readable Bibliographic Interchange) group assists the Library of Congress in defining conventions for assigning of various elements of data to specific MARC fields. In a bibliographic record, the 100 tag or code means a personal author; 110 a corporate author; and 120 a uniform title entry. Each field is further subdivided using subfield codes to distinguish more specific elements of information, such as author's last name and forenames, book title and subtitle, etc.

This tagging structure is essential to the computer manipulation of machine-readable data. A computer cannot distinguish among author, title, and imprint data merely by inspecting the information. It requires that the data be coded using unique and consistently applied flags—tags, indicators, subfield codes, and delimiters—to identify each element of data.

Although in the past some librarians have considered that the **level of detail** supported by the tagging structure of the MARC formats to be too finely delineated, progress in automated library systems continuously reaffirms the wisdom of such a closely defined structure. Many libraries that began their automation efforts building databases that followed the MARC structure in broad approach but omitted detailed data specification (for instance, placing all imprint data in a single subfield in field 260 without applying subfield coding to distinguish publisher name data from place of publication and date of publication) have had to undertake costly and time-consuming upgrades of their records to take advantage of automation developments, such as the online patron access catalog.

MARC is sometimes used loosely to describe the **level of cataloging detail** in a particular record, full MARC indicating detailed bibliographic and subject cataloging adhering to all relevant national standards and encoded in the full level of detail supported by the MARC format.

Although the development and use of the MARC formats has made an overwhelming contribution to the development of library automation, and the distribution and sharing of records among libraries, life with MARC was not meant to be easy. For records distributed by LC since 1968, LC MARC is synonymous with **MARC II**, the formalization of the format after pilot testing using a first iteration of the format known as **MARC I**.

Many library professionals use the phrase **LC MARC** to distinguish records distributed by the Library of Congress from MARC records from other sources. The term is also used to distinguish the format in which LC distributes MARC records from those used by other distribution services. The term LC MARC is often used interchangeably with **USMARC**, a reflection of the fact that the basic tools for the definition of the MARC formats in the United States—the *USMARC format for Authority Data, . . . Bibliographic Data*, and *. . . Holdings and Locations*—represent technical standards established and maintained by the LC in cooperation with other agencies. The *USMARC Specifications for Record Structure, Character Sets, and Tapes*, published by the LC Network Development and MARC Standards Office, details implementation of the national level format used by LC in its record distribution services.

The different agencies that distribute MARC records have evolved their own implementations of the formats. The most common local interpretations of MARC are those used by the bibliographic utilities, particularly **OCLC MARC** and **RLIN MARC**. Usage of OCLC MARC is so widespread that many vendors and services utilize it as a standard distribution format in preference to USMARC. Local formats vary from USMARC in a number of ways. Some of the most significant are the way a file of records is output to tape, the inclusion of locally-defined fields in a record, and the interpretation of the meaning of specific fields in a record.

USMARC defines an output format designed to maximize the amount of data that can be recorded on a magnetic tape. Storage capacity on the tape is divided into physical blocks of 2,048 characters. Each block is packed with MARC data. A new record is not required to start in a new physical block. It begins immediately adjacent to the end of the previous record. OCLC and RLIN lay records to tape in an older format which, while also blocking tape capacity into 2,048 character sections, requires that each record begin at the beginning of a new tape block. Space between the end of one record and the beginning of the next block is not used. A system expecting to receive tapes in one format may have difficulty accepting those output in the other format. As with most MARC variations, vendors can accommodate such practices, provided that they are alerted to the need to do so.

USMARC provided for local definition of a number of fields. OCLC's use of the 049 field for holdings data is probably the most widely known. Many local automated library systems make extensive use of locally defined fields. An organization defining local field use needs to record its definitions and provide specific instructions for formatting data entered in these fields. Individual libraries need to document their practices to facilitate future uses of their records.

A third difference in variations of the formats is the data assigned to specific common fields. For instance, 001 is used to record the local system record control number. In records emanating from OCLC, this is the OCLC record number; in records distributed by LC, it is the LC control number, which is identical to the LC card number for which a specific field—010— is also defined. However, records distributed by LC do not repeat the LCCN in 010. If a system using LC records does not map the number in 001 to 010 before overwriting the contents of 001 with a local system number, a library will be left with no access to the LCCN—a significant unique control number for record matching applications. Some of the CD-ROM-based cataloging support systems that use records distributed by LC as the basis for their cataloging resource files do not perform such mapping before mastering the CD-ROM disks.

Despite the variations, use of the MARC formats is basic to the future of economic library automation and resource sharing locally, statewide, regionally, and nationally. Cost-effective operation and interchange are dependent on libraries subscribing to a single bibliographic format so that any system can output a record and receive a record in that format.

In addition to supporting the exchange of data among systems, adoption of a standard bibliographic format for encoding data in machine-readable form is cost-effective for libraries which have stand-alone integrated systems and do not plan to interface their systems with those of other libraries. Such a library may need to purchase machine-readable records, rather than undertaking local cataloging; generate a CD-ROM catalog from local machine-readable records; or move the database onto another computer. Every bibliographic utility, turnkey vendor, jobber, and commercial bibliographic service supports MARC and can provide output and accept input in this format. A library which uses MARC can, therefore, load records from any of these sources into its system and have tapes from its system loaded by these services without reformatting or extensive preprocessing. Reformatting to MARC from non-MARC records can be expensive. Service bureaus usually level a charge of $.05 to $.20 per record for reformatting when this is required.

The database is the most important part of an automated library system. While hardware may be replaced from time to time—the norm is every five to seven years—and software is periodically rewritten to transfer it to other hardware, to improve its performance, or to enhance it functionally; the bibliographic files, if well designed, will outlast several generations of hardware and software. The machine-readable bibliographic file is analogous to the 100 percent rag catalog cards which libraries use in their card catalogs. The cards are intended to last indefinitely and to be transferred to new card catalog cabinets when the old cabinets are replaced. Similarly, the bibliographic file represents a considerable investment and should be of high quality and transferable.

A few libraries have used the same database for more than a decade on as many as three different automated library systems, each time transporting it to the new computer system by outputting tape from the old system and loading it into the new. Files which conform to MARC have been transferred without reformatting, nonconforming files have required thousands of dollars worth of processing to support each transfer.

Holdings Statements

Closely related to standards for bibliographic records are standards for recording holdings. Linkages among systems require that holdings statements adhere to a uniform format so that both systems and users can recognize and combine records and holdings statements from one system with those from other systems. This is particularly important in the case of serial holdings because of their complexity. ANSI Z39.44 *Serial Holdings Statements*, adopted in 1986, defines the data elements to be used in recording serial holdings. It provides a list of data elements, informational codes and values, a description of how enumeration and chronology data is to be recorded, and definition of the sequence and formats of data area elements. The standard supplants ANSI Z39.42, a specification for serial holdings at the summary level, approved in 1980. A companion standard, Z39.57 *Non-Serial Holdings* was approved in 1989. A consolidated standard was in development in 1996; it will be known as Z39.71, *Holdings Statements for Bibliographic Items*. The Library of Congress has developed a MARC holdings format based on Z39.71. The format for encoding holdings statements in machine-readable form is defined in the *MARC Format for Holdings and Locations*.

INTERFACING STANDARDS

Library administrators and system designers establish interfaces among local automated library systems and between these and other automated library systems to accomplish a number of functions, including the following:

- transfer of records from a cataloging support system such as a bibliographic utility or a CD-ROM-based cataloging or authority control system
- linkage of limited or single function systems—such as acquisitions, serials control, or circulation control systems—to a multifunction automated library system that supports other functions
- linkage of multiple stand-alone, multifunction systems for resource sharing, particularly interlibrary lending and reciprocal borrowing
- implementation of automated ordering, claiming, and invoicing of library materials by linkage to the systems of book and serials jobbers
- transfer of financial or name/address data from a nonlibrary system to a local library system to avoid rekeying of information
- searching of the local library system from the terminals of nonlibrary systems
- accessing remote databases and services—bibliographic, fact, and citation files and messaging systems—from terminals on the local library system.

The interfaces fall into two groups: those capable of importing data into the local system files and those that support only look-up and display functions.

The most common interfaces in the 1980s were those between cataloging support systems—the bibliographic utilities (OCLC, RLIN, WLN, etc.) or stand-alone cataloging support systems (such as BiblioFile, LaserQuest, and SuperCAT)—and local library systems. Such interfaces were supported by virtually all major automated library system vendors. In contrast, only a small number of large public libraries and academic research libraries had implemented interfaces to the automated systems of book and serials jobbers to take advantage of the speed, data entry economies, and discounts available when customers supply order and claim information in machine-readable form and receive invoice and claim response information in the same form. The few automated library system vendors which did provide support for interfacing with jobbers tended to have a strong installed base in large public and academic research libraries, or had well-developed automated acquisitions and serials control capabilities.

Automated library system vendors generally offered facilities to link different installations of their systems but seldom provided support for linkage of automated library systems from different vendors. All such linkages usually offered only look-up and display access.

The main reason for the lack of support for interfacing systems before the 1990s was the lack of standards. Before discussing the standards which have been developed in the last few years, it is important to differentiate among various types of interfaces.

TYPES OF INTERFACES

There are three major methods of interfacing: magnetic tape transfer, terminal-to-computer interfaces, and computer-to-computer interfaces. Each has its own benefits and limitations. Terminal-to-computer and computer-to-computer interfaces both rely on the provision of a data communication medium to link the systems being interfaced. In library applications, the media most commonly used are dial access or leased telephone lines or **value added network (VAN)** services. The same interfacing considerations arise whatever the medium—satellite links, telephone lines, local area networks, etc.

Magnetic Tape Transfer

For a number of years the only available interface was magnetic tape transfer. A tape produced from one system was loaded into another system. Historically, interfacing in the library environment was facilitated by the development of the Z39.2 standard and the MARC (MAchine Readable Cataloging) format for bibliographic records, resulting in both a common format for encoding records and a standard for outputting those records to tape.

Tape transfer entails delays. It usually takes hours to output a tape of several thousand records, and hours to load them into another system. Organizations which rely on tape interfaces for ongoing data exchange usually schedule tape loading no more frequently than once a week or once a month. While some organizations find this an acceptable way of transferring information, those concerned with timeliness have sought to pursue other types of interfaces.

Magnetic tape transfer continues to be widely used. It offers a convenient method of outputting and storing data, and it is usually relatively simple and inexpensive to load data from tape. Most major vendors of multiuser library systems offer software to support the loading of records from tape, and hardware requirements are simple—a 1600 bps or 6250 bps tape drive or more recently, a 4mm DAT or 8mm helical scan cartridge tape drive. Micro-based systems usually require 3.5-inch diskettes.

Tape transfer is the usual method for undertaking the initial entry of bibliographic and authority records into a multiuser automated library system. Tape also provides the most common basis for the transfer of data that requires custom processing before being loaded into an automated library system—patron data from an external system, for instance. Provided that the local library system has a generic tape loading interface and the processed data is in the format it expects, a tape interface requires no alteration of the local system software.

Tape transfers are the usual method for transferring quantities of book and serial jobber data into a multiuser automated library system. The benefits of avoiding the keying of bibliographic data for approval plan materials and serial invoice data outweigh any delays inherent in the tape interface, and the jobber supplying the data can readily output it to tape in the format required by the local system. With tape transfers, the jobber is relieved of the complexities and expense of developing and maintaining the facilities to support an online interface.

Terminal-to-Computer Interfaces

Terminal-to-computer interfaces link the terminal of one system with the CPU of another. The operator must use the command language and search techniques of the remote system to interact with it. Three types of terminal-to-computer interfaces are common in the library environment: printer port interfaces, personal computer interfaces, and gateways.

The **printer port interface** is most commonly used to support the transfer of cataloging data from the terminal of a bibliographic utility into the local library system. A printer port interface permits the transfer of anything appearing on the terminal of the remote system into the local library system through a cable connected to the printer port of the remote system terminal. The more sophisticated interfaces use a PC or Mac and special software in the local library system to reformat data from the screen displays into the format required for the input of records to the local system. Screen images of bibliographic records do not contain the leader and directory elements required in a MARC record.

Printer port interfaces for the loading of bibliographic records support the transfer of only one record at a time, although, in some systems, the interface will simultaneously accept screen images from more than one bibliographic utility terminal. Once in the local system, records may be batched for addition to the database or they may be processed continuously as they are received. If a library obtains records from more than one bibliographic utility, it will need different software to handle the output from each utility.

Terminal-to-computer interfaces have also been achieved between local library system terminals and the CPUs of other systems, either by providing the terminal with a data switch and modem or by supporting a gateway in CPU of the local system. A data switch permits the terminal operator to access a remote system which shares the same communication protocols (asynchronous or synchronous) by dialing into the remote system and using the local system terminal as if it were directly connected to the remote system—searches are conducted using the terminology and formats of the remote system. Since terminals on local library systems often do not require modems to access their CPUs, it can be a costly process to configure all of the terminals on a local system to access remote systems.

An alternative is to install a **gateway** in the CPU of the local system, allowing all local system terminals to share one or more dial-out modems. Some gateways also provide software which facilitates searching of remote systems—automatic dial, automatic log-on, and searching aids. Access to remote databases, such as those brokered by Dialog, Mead Data Control, etc., can be achieved in the same way.

Terminal-to-computer interfaces have two major drawbacks: all interaction with the remote system(s) must be conducted using the format and commands of the remote system, and data cannot be transferred directly from the remote system into the files of the local system without special software such as that used in bibliographic utility printer port interfaces. (If the device used to access a remote system is a micro with hard or floppy disk storage, data from the remote system can be downloaded into the micro for later manipulation or printing by appropriate personal computer software.) These limitations are acceptable if a library needs to access only one or two systems, but can cause significant problems if multiple systems are to be searched on a regular basis.

Terminal-to-computer interfaces can be established between systems from the same vendor, or systems from different vendors. Although theoretically simple, such linkages can be difficult to sustain.

Even when a vendor links two systems at the hardware and software levels, the searching of multiple systems is complicated by difference in record and file structures. A library or consortium which automates today usually decides to use full-MARC records, while some of the earlier installations may have non-MARC records which cannot support many search features. The arrangement of system files may vary considerably even though the same vendor's system is used, different installations choosing to implement different index keys for accessing their databases. In most situations it will, therefore, be necessary to coordinate system practices before true computer-to-computer interfacing can be achieved.

Computer-to-Computer Interfaces

Computer-to-computer interfaces simplify the task of a terminal operator, as they are **transparent** to the user and allow the remote system to be searched using the same techniques that apply to the home system. An operator does not have to learn the search commands and other unique characteristics of the remote system.

Computer-to-computer interfaces can be established between two systems in the same room or at a distance from one another. The systems to be linked may be from the same or different vendors. Interfaces between identical (**homogeneous**) systems in the same computer room requires a high-speed cable or **bus** and special software. While common when computers were less modular, most libraries now merely add boards to an existing CPU when seeking to expand system capacity.

Linking homogeneous systems at a distance from one another facilitates resource sharing, but the proprietary vendor software used to achieve these linkages does nothing to make access to the systems of other vendors transparent.

Ad hoc or **custom interfaces** for computer-to-computer interfaces among heterogeneous systems can be written by a competent programmers with access to appropriate documentation. Depending on the complexity of the interface, the cost can be as high as $60,000 to $90,000. The interface has to be constantly adjusted to keep pace with dynamic changes in the systems being linked. If several interfaces are required, the initial cost can be hundreds-of-thousands of dollars, with annual maintenance costs up to half that. What is needed, therefore, is a standard interface—one which involves each system conforming to the same standard, thus not requiring vendors to write more than one interface.

OSI

The Open System Interconnection (OSI) Reference Model is the foundation on which most computer-to-computer interfacing standards have been built. The Reference Model was developed by the International Organization for Standardization (ISO) and has only had limited adoption in the United States, but it has influenced the evolution of **TCP/IP**, a parallel standard which is used to link systems on the Internet. Many of the standards developed under the OSI Reference Model also fit under TCP/IP; therefore, a discussion of OSI is appropriate.

Without standards, the fact that vendors A and B support an interface between certain functional capabilities is of no assistance if either wishes to link to the same function on a system from vendor C. Much of the development of an interface between vendors A and C or B and C would have to be undertaken *de novo*. In an OSI scenario, vendor A need only develop an interface between the threshold of its system and the appropriate protocol to be able to interface with any other system, B through Z, that supported that protocol.

OSI defines *what* a protocol should do; it does not define *how* it should be implemented. Some of the formal standards that implement functions defined in OSI predate the model, some have been developed with specific reference to the OSI architecture, and others are still being formalized.

OSI segments the process of systems linkage into seven functional layers arranged in a hierarchy (see Figure 7.1). Each layer defines discrete tasks that are essential for the linking of systems, and the layers build on each other to define operations of increasing complexity. A layer interacts only with the layer directly above or below it. Communication is accomplished when a request originating in the highest level of the framework in one

Open Systems Interconnection (OSI)

APPLICATION LAYER

ISO 8571	File Transfer, Access and Management (FTAM)
ISO 8649/8650	Association Control Service Element (ACSE)
ISO 9072	Remote Operating Service Element (ROSE)
ISO 10021	Message-Oriented Text Interchange (MOTIS)
CCITT X.400	Message Handling System (MHS)
ISO 9506	Manufacturing Message Specification (MMS)

PRESENTATION LAYER

ISO 8822/8823	Connection-Oriented Presentation
ISO 8824/8825	Abstract Syntax Notation One (ASN.1)

SESSION LAYER

ISO 8326/8327	Connection-Oriented Session

TRANSPORT LAYER

ISO 8072/8073	Transport Service

NETWORK LAYER

ISO 8348	Connection-Mode Network Service (CONS)
ISO 8348/AD2	Addressing Format
ISO 8348/AD1	Connectionless-Mode Network Services (CLNS)
ISO 8208	Packet Level Protocol (PLP)
ISO 8473	Internetwork Protocol
ISO 8878	X.25 to provide CONS
ISO 8880	OSI Network Service
ISO 8881	X.25 Packet Level Protocol in LANS
ISO 9542	ES-IS Routing
ISO 10589	IS-IS Routing

DATA LINK LAYER

ISO 4335	High-Level Data Link Control (HDLC)
ISO 7809	High-Level Data Link Control (HDLC)
ISO 8802-2	LAN Logical Link Control
IEEE 802.2	LAN Logical Link Control
ISO 9314-2	FDDI Medium Access Control (MAC)
ANS X3.T9.5/84-49	FDDI Station Management (SMT)

PHYSICAL LAYER

ISO 8802-3	Ethernet Standards
IEEE 802.3	Ethernet Standards
EIA RS-232C	Hardware Devices
EIA RS-422	Hardware Devices
EIA RS-423	Hardware Devices
ISO DIS 9314-1	FDDI Physical Layer Protocol (PHY)
ISO DIS 9314-3	FDDI Physical Layer Medium (PMD)
ANS X3.T9.5/84-49	FDDI Station Management (SMT)

Figure 7.1 Major standards included in the OSI reference mode

system is passed down the hierarchy within that system, across the physical linkage at the lowest level of the model to the remote system, and up through the layered structure of that system to the applications level. Responses take the same route in reverse.

Each layer has distinct boundaries that separate it from the layer above and the layer below, and each layer provides a specific set of services to the layer above it and draws on the services of the layer directly below it. The model allows great flexibility because each layer effectively isolates the layers above from the details of the layers below. So long as the group of services provided by a layer do not change, characteristics within the layer can be changed without affecting the rest of the system. Each layer adds to the services of its underlying layer until the total service is available to the application the system is designed to support.

The seven layers and their major functions are illustrated in the accompanying diagram and described in the following paragraphs. The layers are often described by their numerical position: the physical layer, the lowest level in the hierarchy, is Level 1; the applications layer, the highest level, is Level 7.

Although this account follows the traditional descriptive pattern working up the hierarchy from the lowest level to the highest, it is helpful to remember that in an actual implementation a request for service emanating from a system enters the network at the applications layer. As the request works its way down the structure in the originating system it is wrapped in the successive layers of protocols required to ensure its passage to the next lowest layer and across the link to the receiving system. As the bundle passes up through the hierarchy of the receiving system, each layer of wrapping is successively removed so that the request emerging from the applications layer of the receiving system is as naked as it was when issued by the originating system. The service response generated by the receiving system follows a similar procedure in passing back to the system that originated the request.

The lowest layer of the OSI architecture—the **physical layer**—provides services to the data link layer. The services are those required to establish the physical and electrical linkage between computer systems and communication channels. This layer focuses on physical aspects of the linkage such as electrical and mechanical compatibility. To the extent that higher level layer characteristics such as polling and handshaking depend on electrical or physical characteristics or linkages, these too are handled in the physical layer.

Physical layer services include acquiring, maintaining, and disconnecting the physical circuits that form the connecting communication path. The physical layer represents the traditional interface between data terminal equipment and data circuit terminating equipment.

The physical layer is responsible for bit synchronization and for identifying a signal element as a 1 or 0. However, it is concerned with data only at the level of the bit. It plays no role in determining bit patterns, not even the number of bits in a byte.

Typical physical layer protocols include the electrical and mechanical aspects of the RS-232C and RS-449 serial interface standards, the CCITT X.25 public packet network standard and its X.21 standard for synchronous transmission over digital data networks, other CCITT V or X series recommendations, and IEEE 802.3, 802.4, and 802.5 protocols for local area networks.

Data link layer services are concerned with the reliable transfer of data across the link established at the physical layer. Bit patterns acquire meaning at this level where the unit of data transfer is the block or frame—a group of data bits surrounded by system-supplied control bits used in data transfer, verification, and error control.

Link layer protocols manage operation of logical link connections such as the request to send and clear to send handshake exchanged between modems linked to computers wishing to transfer data, a logical (nonphysical) component of RS-232C; the specification of the way the data to be transferred is presented, in bit-oriented protocols such as IBM's Synchronous Data Link Control (SDLC) protocol or byte-or character-oriented formats such as IBM's Binary Synchronous (Bisync or BSC) protocol; and many other aspects of flow control, message sequencing, data acknowledgement, and error detection and recover procedures. This is the last level at which hardware considerations are relevant. All higher layers of the model deal with software only.

Data link control protocols include the character-oriented binary synchronous communication (BSC), ANSI X3.28, DDCMP, and the more recent bit-oriented ADCCP. IEEE 802.2 specifies link control for local area networks.

The **network layer** provides services for moving data through a network, including the assembly of frames of data into message packets (the data transfer unit at this level) which include additional control and identification data, routing the packets along the communication medium, and verifying packet receipt. The services include routing, switching, sequencing of data, flow control, and error recovery. Although some of these capabilities are duplicated at the link level, their use in the network layer is for network connections rather than data links.

Protocols in this layer select and control logical paths and connections between networks user end points. The upper levels of the layer include Internet protocols to control routing and recovery between network nodes, and gateway protocols which control data transfer between networks. The OSI model supports two levels of network layer service—Virtual Circuit and Datagram. Virtual Circuit service provides high quality, error-free channels which retain data in the sequence in which it was sent. It is more expensive to support and provides slower data transfer rates. Datagram service provides less expensive, high-speed data transfer with no sequencing or error control. Decisions on the level of service provided at the network level can affect the quantity and quality of services that need to be supported at the next highest level, the transport layer.

The CCITT X.25 packet layer is the most widely known network layer protocol for packet-switched networks and X.21 is used for circuit switched networks. Packet switching (X.25) is the basis for value added networks.

The **transport layer** is the highest layer directly associated with the movement of data through the communication network established by layers one through three. It is responsible for bridging any gaps between the services provided by the communication network and the requirements of the applications process the system is designed to support. In a specific situation, economics or lack of availability of service options may leave a user with no choice in the selection of the network used to link two computer systems, but the level of performance of that network may not be sufficient to support the application the user wishes to implement. The transport layer is responsible for providing services that compensate for any lack of quality in the network, resulting in a linkage sufficient to support the application. This layer has the ultimate responsibility for ensuring that all required telecommunications functions are performed. The transport layer implements these services only for those functions *not* performed by the network *and* required for the application.

For example, one of the effects of the X.25 protocols is to ensure that messages are delivered in the proper sequence. In systems using X.25, the transport layer is not required to support resequencing of messages that arrive out of order. Such support would be required if the communication system did not provide the service and the application required that messages be received in sequence.

OSI defines five sets of transport protocol classes, each representing a specific level of service requirement expressed in terms of the levels of error detection and correction supported; provision of flow control to regulate the flow of data from the sender so that messages will not arrive faster than the receiver can process them; and support for multiplexing—assigning several communication sessions to the same channel.

The transport levels of two communicating systems must communicate with protocols of the same class.

Services from levels one through four establish a raw transmission path. The **session layer** supports the elements required for the logical connection of the communicating systems. It includes two categories of services, administrative and dialogue, and again includes capabilities that may or may not be needed in a particular application. The layer's capabilities are described as functional units. Among them are choices governing the transmission mode selection—Duplex or Half-Duplex—and the type of data transfer required. Kernel or Expediated Data service are two of the service choices for data transfer. Kernel service entails session establishment, transfer of normal data, and session release. The Expediated

Data functional unit offers priority treatment for limited amounts of application data.

During the establishment of a communication session, the two systems being linked each propose a set of functional units to govern the session. If compatible, those elements included in the definitions advanced by both systems govern the communication session between them. If there are conflicting elements in the definitions—one system specifying duplex transmission, the other half-duplex, for instance—compatibility cannot be achieved and the session cannot proceed. Current session protocols include ECMA 75 and CCITT X.62, which is used in Teletex services.

The **presentation layer** ensures compatible syntax among the communicating processes by adjusting data structures, formats, and codes. Services in this layer include network security, code translations, and format conversions, and work closely with the protocols in the **applications layer**, the seventh and highest level of the hierarchy. The applications layer provides a window through which specific applications gain access to the services provided by the communication architecture.

The applications layer provides communication services that are most directly comprehensible to the user. These services include identifying the cooperating processes, authenticating the communicant, verifying authority, determining the availability of resources and ensuring agreement on syntax.

The applications layer can be visualized as a user-specific sublayer (e.g., libraries, banking, and airlines), an application-specific sublayer (e.g., file transfer, job transfer, and batch), and a common layer. The library-related communication standards approved by ANSI are application-level protocols, as are the CCITT X.400 electronic mail standards.

In systems using OSI, communication activity usually occurs in phases. A connect phase first establishes the connection, and then the data transfer phase begins to exchange user information. The user application information logically flows across the layer boundaries, while "request send" requests usually move data in queues or buffers. Each layer, in turn, adds any required protocol information and then passes the complete unit to the next layer. This process continues downward from layer 7 through 1 in the source system and upward from layer 1 through 7 in the target system until the data arrives at the required application. When data transfer is complete, a clearing phase ends the connection.

TCP/IP

The most widely used set of intersystem communications protocols is TCP/IP (Transmission Control Protocol/Internet Protocol). TCP/IP makes it possible to realize connectivity among equipment from many vendors over a wide variety of networking technologies. The TCP/IP suite of protocols governs the "transport" and "network" layers of the International Organization for Standardization's Open System Interconnection (OSI)

Reference Model, and it is used by most organization-wide LANs and virtually all WANs. TCP provides reliable transmission of data (OSI layer 4) and IP provides connection-less datagram service (OSI layer 3). The Internet also uses TCP/IP for its communication link.

While the U.S. Department of Defense, for which TCP/IP was first developed, has been pressing for a migration from TCP/IP to the complete OSI Reference Model, it now appears that change will be evolutionary, with protocols developed for a specific industry or activity (such as interlibrary loan between two libraries) written to work at the highest level, layer 7, within either TCP/IP or OSI.

TCP/IP consists of more than 100 protocols. The most important of these are telnet, FTP, and SMTP. Telnet is a program that allows interactive sessions between host computers on a network, as well as allowing users at remote geographical locations to log onto the other network hosts. FTP (file transfer protocol) supports interactive sessions between computers for the transfer of data files to the requestor's computer. SMTP (simple mail transmission protocol) is the electronic mail protocol.

Telnet

Telnet (terminal emulation link network) simply allows remote users to log onto systems connected to the Internet. It provides line-mode ASCII VT100 connection for UNIX, Digital VAX, and most other ASCII systems. If a remote user wants to access IBM systems which use EBCDIC instead of ASCII, there are special versions of telnet available.

FTP

Users usually want more than just an interactive session with a remote host; they also want to download files. FTP (file transfer protocol) enables a user to send or receive files to or from other computers on the Internet. If a user telnets to an Internet site and finds relevant information, it can be downloaded with FTP unless there are restrictions imposed by the organization controlling the remote host.

Electronic Mail

The most widespread Internet application is still electronic mail. SMTP (simple mail transfer protocol) is the protocol used for e-mail on the Internet. Networks that gateway to the Internet, such as CompuServe, use SMTP, a de facto standard, allowing an Internet user to send a message to just about any networked user.

A mass migration appears to be underway toward TCP/IP. An unpublished survey conducted by Austin, Texas-based First Market Research Corp. in 1996 established that the growing importance of connecting to various networking environments, especially the Internet, is causing all types of organizations to move away from proprietary protocols such as IBM's SNA (Systems

Network Architecture), Digital's DECnet, and Novell's IPX. Half of the interviewees said that their organizations had switched recently from a proprietary protocol to TCP/IP, especially SNA and DECnet. Most switches are gradual, with the old protocol continuing to be used as migration progresses.

A minority of organizations using TCP/IP—primarily those which communicate internationally—also are using OSI, especially for complex network management. TCP/IP and OSI are quite compatible.

The U.S. Department of Defense is no longer responsible for TCP/IP. A group known as the Internet Engineering Task Force (IETF), a body accredited by ANSI, has assumed that responsibility. ANSI handles the publication of the standards. In 1996, the IETF declared its intent to formulate strategies for the Internet to support both TCP/IP and OSI network protocols insofar as they might differ from one another.

As TCP/IP is more widely supported than OSI at this time, a library should specify TCP/IP conformity.

Z39.50-1995

Z39.50—Information Retrieval Application Service Definition and Protocol Specification for Open System—is the official designation of a standard for communication in a bibliographic context. Z39.50 is defined as a common set of procedures and formats connecting two information processes: the originating system where requests are made and the target system where the database resides. Z39.50 functions in the upper three levels of TCP/IP (or OSI), and Z39.50 is "wrapped" in a TCP/IP message when moved over a LAN or WAN.

The Z39.50 standard plays a similar role for text to the role played by SQL for relational databases. Z39.50 was developed by the library and information services communities. SQL, which was developed by IBM, became a de facto standard, and subsequently was elevated to an international standard by the ISO. SQL has not kept pace with object-oriented programming languages such as C++. Recent attempts to improve SQL have met with controversy in standards bodies. Developers are getting around this problem by using proprietary SQL extensions or by embedding the query methods directly in their programs.

Z39.50 is a protocol for information retrieval allowing a PC or terminal with access to a local computer to query the database of a remote computer using the procedures and formats of the local system. The protocol specifies the procedures and structures for the intersystem submission of a search request, a request for the transmission of records identified by a search, and the responses to this request. The responses supported include a count of the items found, and the option to transfer some items as part of the response. The standard allows a requestor to qualify a search after it has been executed, and to issue subsequent requests for transmission of one or more items from the set of those found.

Z39.50, Versions 1 and 2, specify the format and procedures governing message exchange between the requesting computer and the responding computer (the target), but does not address the interaction between the requesting computer and the user. (The standard also provides for a "private" query format which can be mutually agreed upon.) The Z39.50 client establishes the connection with the target utilizing OSI, TCP/IP or another appropriate protocol. Once a connection has been established, the search session with the target system is initialized, and the message and the maximum record sizes are established.

Once the session has been initiated, the client-created search will be translated from local syntax into an intersite syntax and transmitted to the target system. The data unit that contains the query (the search request) also contains additional instructions for the target system. Fields within the search request indicate the preferred record syntax (e.g., USMARC, UNIMARC, etc.) and whether brief or full records should be returned to the client. The search received by the target system will be converted from the intersite syntax into an equivalent search syntax for the target's local system. The local search then generates a result set in the target system. The target system responds to the client based on instructions received in the search request, such as reporting the number of records found, sending the complete result set, providing an error message, etc.

Z39.50, Version 3—completed in 1995—provides a number of improvements, including

- *Close, suspend, and resume dialogue*—allowing a search to be submitted, after which the connection is broken. At a later time, a new connection can be established to retrieve the search results. (Earlier versions required that all retrieval of search results be during the same session as the initial search.)
- *Periodic query facility*—allowing a client system to specify that a query be run by a server on a regular basis, with the query activated as needed.
- *Save result set service*—allowing a client to save a result set so that it is available after the current connection is broken.
- *Browse service*—allowing a client to scan database indexes and result sets.
- *Explain*—allowing a client to search a structured database to ascertain information about a server, for example, a list of the databases available on the server and the access points.
- *Item order*—allowing a client to order a copy or the loan of the bibliographic item identified. This capability supports the separate (Z39.63) ILL protocol.

Z39.50 is at the heart of today's automated bibliographic systems, making it possible for any library to reach beyond the four walls of its own collection to tap the resources of remote collections and databases. This standard is under continuous maintenance by the Z39.50 Implementors Group—or ZIG—so it is kept up-to-date and is responsive to users' needs.

Many vendors had not yet implemented Version 3 by the end of 1996, but V.2 and V.3 are designed to be compatible in order for their common features to be utilized even if a connected client and server are using different versions. A vendor's implementation of Z39.50 may be limited to interfaces with other systems, or may be the basis for its internal client/server communication. Most vendors still limit the use of Z39.50 to interfaces with other systems and use proprietary solutions for internal client/server communication because Z39.50 is a relatively new **protocol**; Z39.50-based products generally do not offer the richness of functionality that proprietary ones do.

All major automated library system vendors are expected to enhance their Z39.50 support to incorporate the features of this third version of the standard. When they have done so, Z39.50 will be an even more attractive solution for the linking of automated library systems. However, there continues to be a drawback to Z39.50 which is raised whenever several libraries in an area plan for the linking of systems: as implemented, the use of a Z39.50 client requires sequential searches of multiple databases and time-consuming merging of search results.

Every library should specify that its automated library system include a Z39.50 client, thus allowing it to access Z39.50 servers. The library may want to specify that the Z39.50 client software be mounted on the CPU so that it is available to all of the remote peripherals on the systems, or that it be included on each of the remote peripherals. The former is common if there are a large number of "dumb" terminals on the system; the latter if most of the remote peripherals are PCs. In a system which uses client/server architecture, the Z39.50 client software would always be on the clients.

Libraries should separately specify that the Z39.50 client should support multiple concurrent searches against several clients and the return of unified search results. This capability has only recently begun to become available.

Not all libraries may want to specify Z39.50 server capability. A small library which does not consider itself a resource to others may decide to limit its Z39.50 implementation to the client side so that it can access the holdings of larger libraries, but not incur the expense of facilitating access to its limited holdings. This does not mean they would not be available. They could be accessed via a dial-in modem. What would be missing is the transparency which Z39.50 provides.

Increasingly, Z39.50 client and Web browser support are being combined by vendors of automated library systems. This offers Web-based access to Z39.50 databases through a popular Web browser such as Netscape or Microsoft's Explorer.

COMPUTERIZED ORDERING AND CLAIMING

The Book Industry Systems Advisory Committee (BISAC) developed a format for the communication of book orders in machine-readable form. Adopted by ANSI as Z39.49: *Computerized Book Ordering*, the standard supports two formats: a fixed format and a variable-length format. It covers both formatting and content designation and applies to ordering by libraries and bookstores. Closely related is Z39.55, the standard developed by SISAC (the Serials Industry Standards Advisory Committee) for computerized serials ordering. Its full name is the *Computerized Serials Orders, Claims, Cancellations, and Acknowledgements*. A related standard, Z39.45 *Claims for Missing Issues of Serials*, defines the elements to be included in serials claims in any media, electronic or paper.

These standards are now giving way to **EDI** (electronic data interchange). There are three basic groups of accredited EDI standards. ANSI chartered Accredited Standards Committee X12 (ASC X12) in 1979. Its EDI standards have been widely adopted in the United States. The second group are the international standards developed by the ISO and the United Nations' Economic Commission for Europe (UN/ECE). Their standards are known as EDIFACT (EDI for Administration, Commerce, and Transport). The third set were developed in the United Kingdom as TRADACOMS.

EDIFACT grew out of a desire to bring together previous standards, including the previous United Nations standard (UN/GDTI) and the previous United States standard (ANSI X12, subsequently redesignated ASC X12 and frequently cited as EDI x12). Both the United Nations and ASC have committed to move towards EDIFACT, although the large installed user base means the previous standards will be around for quite some time.

A typical EDIFACT data stream consists of an outer envelope or interchange control delimited by tags, an inner envelope or functional group delimited by tags, and GE, and the actual transaction set defined by tags. The syntax for the International EDI Standard is contained within ISO 9735.

The EDI standards are designed to be generic and, with rare exceptions, only a subset of the standard is actually used between two trading partners. This subset is referred to as an EDI Implementation Convention or Implementation Guideline. Most commonly developed by industry groups, these implementations freeze a version and release of the standard and define exactly what data is required and where specific data is to be mapped in the standard. EDI Implementation Conventions are the life blood of EDI; they define what must, and what may, be included in an EDI message.

Security is an important issue in electronic communication. EDIFACT v3 is end-to-end at message level security, providing integrity (including sequence integrity), authentication, nonrepudiation of origin, and nonrepudiation of receipt. EDIFACT certificates may be conveyed in the security header, along with a message. EDIFACT v4 security is end-to-end at message, group and interchange level, providing integrity (including sequence integrity), authentication, nonrepudiation of origin, non-repudiation of receipt, and confidentiality. Confidentiality uses associated data, and can include compression before encryption.

Interlibrary Loan

Z39.63 *Interlibrary Loan Data Elements* describes data elements for use in transmitting requests for the loan or photocopy of library materials. The objective is to allow unambiguous identification of the items requested, responses to requests, and the requesting and lending organizations. The standard applies to requests and replies transmitted via any medium. While the standard was first published in 1989, a revised version was nearing completion at the end of 1996. The standard will be key to the development of interlibrary loan modules of automated library systems.

Common Command Language

There also is a standard for specifying the vocabulary, syntax, and semantics of a command language to facilitate the use of interactive information systems—ANSI Z39.58 *Common Command Language*. The standard is intended to apply to all online interactive information retrieval systems irrespective of the nature of the data or files involved—bibliographic, textual, numeric, etc. Most automated library system vendors are selectively incorporating elements of Z39.58 into their Z39.50 implementations. NISO plans to revise the standard beginning in 1997.

Patron Record Data Element

Z39.69, a pending standard as of late 1996, will describe the data elements for a library patron record to facilitate migration to future systems or to facilitate linking for libraries with reciprocal borrowing agreements.

Circulation System Data

Following a recommendation from the Automation Vendor Interface Advisory Committee (AVIAC), NISO established a committee to work on a standard for the exchange of circulation system data, including patron data. The charge is to identify common data elements involved in circulation transactions and to develop a format for the exchange of such data. Data elements to be considered include those relating to the circulation status of an item—on shelf, on loan-due back, not for loan, etc.—and those which reflect patron status. The objective is to augment the interlibrary loan standard—a successful search against another system can result either in an interlibrary loan request or a patron going to another library to borrow the material under a reciprocal borrowing agreement. When issued in 1997, the standard will be numbered Z39.70.

HYBRID SYSTEMS

As libraries become more experienced with library automation, there is an increased awareness that an institution's needs may not best be met by the functional components of any one vendor's system. Rather, administrators are beginning to consider the advantages of combining components from different vendors' systems into customized hybrid systems to meet local needs. A hybrid system might use the acquisitions module from Vendor A, the circulation module from Vendor B, and the online patron access catalog from Vendor C.

Among the advantages advanced for hybrid systems are improved functional performance in individual modules as vendors concentrate on the development of specialized functionality without the constraints of having to support all capabilities for all library situations; enhanced system responsiveness through the dedication of independent processors to specific functional modules; increased reliability as failure of a component would affect only a single group of functions rather than the system as a whole; simplified system development in terms of both overall capabilities, and the speed with which new technologies can be incorporated into specialized product lines; and simplified upgrade paths in which system modules could be upgraded one at a time.

It is unlikely that the standards will be developed to the level of detail necessary to facilitate the creation of hybrid systems. The emphasis is on setting the minimum criteria to facilitate the exchange of information among systems for specific purposes: online catalog search, interlibrary loan request, electronic order, or electronic claim.

Chapter 8

CD-ROM, Internet, and Other Related Technologies

There are a number of information technologies which can either be interfaced with automated library systems or be operated independently, including CD-ROM, the Internet, and online database services. Each is briefly discussed in this chapter and strategies for interfacing them with automated library systems are presented.

CD-ROM AND CD-LANS

The use of CD-ROM in libraries is now well established. Of the more than 6,000 CD-ROM titles available in 1996, more than one-third were regularly sold to libraries. While periodical indexes were generally the first electronic publications on CD-ROM sold to libraries, the coverage has now broadened to include a wide range of reference and research publications, including many government documents. There also are hundreds of educational and self-help titles.

While CD-ROM is generally regarded as a transitional medium, it is showing no signs of disappearing. The advantages of CD-ROM are its relatively great capacity (600 MB on one disk), speed of replication (seconds), low manufacturing cost (approximately $.50 each), and ease of shipping (a padded envelope or lightweight plastic case). Its principal disadvantage is the relatively slow data retrieval time (several seconds to a minute), especially when mounted on a network. Capacity is also becoming a problem as electronic publishers seek to publish large full-text, image, and multimedia files. **Multimedia**, which may include data, video, and audio on a single disk, needs several times as much capacity as is offered by CD-ROM. While Philips and Sony, the pioneers in the industry, are working on ways to expand the capacity of CD-ROM by encoding multiple layers of information on each disk (changing the focal length of the read head to get from one layer to another), the expectation is that CD-

ROM will be replaced by another optical digital disk technology around the year 2000.

Given the wide range of information available on CD-ROM, a library can't avoid investing in the technology. Fortunately, the investment is relatively modest when compared with that required for an automated library system. A stand-alone Pentium PC with internal CD-ROM drive could be purchased for as little as $1,500 in 1996, and prices were continuing to drop.

CD-ROM LOCAL AREA NETWORKS (CD-LANS)

As CD-ROM usage rises, libraries are faced with the purchase of additional PCs and multiple copies of some CD-ROM titles. In a search for alternatives, hundreds of libraries have implemented CD-LANs to provide access to electronic publications on CD-ROM to several staff and/or patrons at a time, rather than having each CD-ROM available only from the PC to which its CD-ROM drive is attached.

A CD-LAN typically consists of a CD-ROM server (usually a Pentium PC), a tower with several CD-ROM drives, server, a network operating system, and PCs with network interface cards. A minimum configuration of a Pentium 100 server with 32 MB of RAM, seven-drive tower, and ten networked PCs usually costs at least $30,000. The server, which is the most important component, can accommodate additional towers and PCs.

Early CD-LAN products were nothing more than simple switching devices, allowing the connection of any one of several workstations to any one of several disk drives. Since then, "caching" been introduced to make it possible for multiple users to access the same disk in rapid succession. The cache stores information which has just been accessed so that the CD-ROM will be freed for the next user. The content of the cache is constantly changing. Caching makes it possible for several users to access a single CD-ROM disk without degrading performance.

Five to seven persons can be working with the contents of the same CD-ROM at one time without a frustrating deterioration of response time (more than 15 seconds). The reason that is possible is because most users are inexpert and relatively slow. Therefore, the network doesn't really encounter concurrence for much of the time the five to seven users are active. The number of workstations on a LAN does not necessarily affect response time; the key is how many will seek access to the same CD-ROM, not how many are using the network.

Implementing a CD-LAN

Moving too quickly to implement a CD-LAN can be risky, however. The levels of use of CD-ROM titles may not warrant the higher cost of the licenses when mounted on a CD-LAN. In some cases, the network license fees are so high that no level of use warrants mounting the title on a CD-LAN. Some CD-ROM titles may not be networked at all. Some electronic publishers have complex licensing which prohibit networking or charge high license fees when a network covers more than one building or when dial-in access to the server is made available. Another potential problem is a level of use of a title that exceeds the capacity of the server.

Before implementing a CD-LAN, a library should estimate the level of use of each title and compare that with the license fee for mounting that title on the type of network (single building, multi-building, dial-in access, etc.) envisioned.

While a library may decide to continue to mount some CD-ROM titles on stand-alone PCs, in some cases, the best option is to access an electronic publication online using an online database service; in other cases it may be better to obtain a tape subscription to the publication and mount the file on a local library system using the journal citation capability of the system.

What is needed is a networking concept which provides access from anywhere to anything. Rather than starting with the concept that information should be obtained on a CD-ROM because that is generally perceived as the most cost-effective technology for information in machine-readable form, and demand for a CD-ROM title should be answered with a CD-LAN, the emphasis should be on determining the most effective way to meet the electronic information needs of library staff and users in light of the networking environment in the library and its parent organization.

CD-LANs

Early CD-LAN adopters often sought to use a PC-LAN product when creating a CD-LAN. This had to be done with care as some older PC-LANs didn't support devices with more than 250 MB of storage, less than half the capacity of a CD-ROM disk, and the MS-DOS limitation of 32 MB. The MS-DOS problem, however, was overcome with the Microsoft CD-ROM Extensions (MSCDEX). MSCDEX works around the MS-DOS limitation by functioning as a DOS redirector.

There were two inexpensive (a few hundred dollars) software products designed with CD-ROM in mind were introduced in the early 1990s: LANtastic and CD-Connection.

LANtastic, an offering of Artisoft, is "peer-to-peer" network software which allows users access to any device on the network, with each functioning as a server. There can be up to 300 CD-ROM drives and up to 300 users. LANtastic works with Ethernet or with Artisoft's proprietary topology. The uniqueness of LANtastic lies in the fact that it allows the network file server to share the CD-ROM disk as if it were just another network drive. The LANtastic network redirector redirects all DOS disk access requests to the server—including requests for CD-ROM data. Among other things, this avoids the need to pile LAN redirectors on top of CD-ROM drivers and extensions; LANtastic assumes DOS and MSCDEX compatibility. EBSCO's CD-ROM Network is based on the LANtastic Network Operating System.

CD-Connection is a relatively inexpensive server-based software product of CBIS. It can be used with any NetWare or NetBios-compatible operating system, including Novell's Advanced Netware. There also is a proprietary CBIS NOS. The software does not require Microsoft Extensions for the individual workstations; instead Extensions reside in the server. The major advantages of the server approach are security of the CD-ROM (they can be on a server not accessible to the users) and better performance since there is a device dedicated to the control of the CD-ROM drives.

In 1996, there was a definite movement toward CD-ROM products which used standard SCSI I/O interfaces and standards network operating systems.

CD-LANs in the Network Environment

A CD-LAN should never be planned without fitting it into the total networking environment of a library and its parent organization. Libraries which implemented CD-LANs—especially school, academic, and special libraries —will be pressed to provide access to the information on the CD-ROMs from throughout the organization, including from branch libraries, offices, student dormitories, and even from homes. This can be accomplished in two ways, implementing a **bridge** or **router** between the CD-LAN and the organization's general LAN or having the CD-LAN act as a self-contained node connected directly to the network like a workstation.

A bridge is a hardware/software product which connects two LANs with the same technology and a router is a hardware/software product which connects two LANs with different protocols. Increasingly, large organizations have many LANs which are tied together using an organization's backbone LAN.

Increasingly, CD-LAN products can act as self-contained nodes connecting directly to the network like a workstation, with the number of workstations depending on the capacity of the LAN used. Once a CD-LAN node is connected to the network, the library decides which workstations will have access to the CD-LAN node. A device driver and MSCDEX (Microsoft CD-ROM extensions) are then added to the CONFIG.SYS file of those specific workstations. The operating system will automatically assign drive letters to each CD-ROM drive. In the end, each CD-ROM drive appears as a logical device on the workstation. If a CD-ROM drive is assigned the letter "E," the user only types "E" to access that CD-ROM.

Interfacing a CD-LAN and a Local Library System

The simplest way of offering access to both an automated library system and a CD-LAN from a single workstation is to attach an A-B switch to each PC on the CD-LAN so that a user can switch from the CD-LAN to the local library system. Among the advantages of this approach are low cost and ease of installation; the work could be done by a library's own staff.

The second choice is having the CD-LAN accessible from the organization's general LAN. While this can be done in the two ways discussed in the previous section, having the CD-LAN act as a self-contained node on the LAN is preferable to a bridge or router because it is more straightforward. It may not be possible if the CD-LAN was not planned with that in mind.

When creating a network which combines access to both a CD-LAN server and an automated library system, a library should be careful not to have access to the automated library system from within the library go through the network server. When the connections from the PCs to the local library system are direct (i.e., without going through a LAN server), it is possible to negotiate response time guarantees for the automated library system with the vendor.

An option which an increasing number of libraries are pursuing is to make the vendor of the automated library system assume responsibility for interfacing the CD-ROM server and the automated library system on a single network. The automated library system would display a menu which includes not only the online patron access catalog, but also journal citation files mounted on the automated library system and CD-ROM products on the CD-ROM server. Not only does this make configuration and installation expertise available to the library which it may not otherwise have, but it usually makes training in the use of the CD-ROM server available which most vendors of CD-ROM hardware and software do not provide.

Terminal Access to CD-ROMs

It often is not practical to access a CD-ROM with the dumb terminals on a local library system or on interconnected LAN. The remote control software may have unexpected conflicts with certain CD-ROM search software. If a terminal or a PC running a terminal emulation program affects the remote access, keyboard remapping may be necessary. The function keys on the remote user's keyboard may not work in the same way as the keys on a standard microcomputer keyboard. Commands that require a combination of keystrokes such as <Ctrl>-<PgDn> become particularly tricky to remap.

Another problem with terminals concerns their display monitors; terminals have a 24-line display with the network connection or telecommunications status on the 25th line. In contrast, CD-ROM search software programs often utilize full the 25-line displays on a PC monitor. As a result, directions and function key assignments, displayed on that 25th line, may be overwritten by the telecommunications status. In other cases, the entire search software display may shift upward by one line and eliminate the first line altogether in order to accommodate the status line. There also is the potential problem if insufficient memory for use of the search software after installing the various device drivers *and* the remote control software. Thus, the most reliable approach is to use PCs, rather than dumb terminals.

Finally, there is the issue of printing: can the user direct output to the remote printer, or must he or she retrieve printouts from a central location? The remote control communications software may limit output to screen dumps only rather than printing or even downloading. If so, network administrators will have to forewarn remote users about output limitations.

Keeping the Goal in Mind

The goal should be to give anyone on the CD-LAN, local library system, or organization-wide LAN access to any electronic information from a single workstation.

THE INTERNET

The Internet is a worldwide network of networks connecting hundreds of thousands of computers in more than 60 countries with a common set of communications protocols. The Internet provides access to a vast library of state-of-the-art resources and fosters direct, immediate communication between people the world over. Among the resources available over the Internet are some 700 online patron access catalogs and thousands of specialized databases.

There are three major Internet capabilities: electronic mail, remote login (telnet), and file transfer.

Electronic Mail

By enabling the immediate exchange of information with colleagues and participation in online interest groups, electronic mail facilitates formal and information communication and enhances cooperation and collaboration in research and writing efforts. In addition to electronic correspondence capabilities, network users have access to hundreds of news and interest groups on most subjects. Network interest groups offer an outlet for ideas and opinions and serve as a resource for posing questions to others on the Internet. And an increasing number of journals exist only in electronic form and are accessible only with a network connection.

Remote Login (Telnet)

The Internet Telnet Protocol allows a network user to access a remote computer and use it interactively as if the local computer were a terminal of the remote host. Telnet provides access to online library catalogs, campus-wide information systems, online reference services, full-text databases, as well as other online resources. Census data, literary works, the Library of Congress federal legislation database, the Johns Hopkins Genetic Databases, and the Department of Commerce Economic Bulletin Board are just a few examples of electronic information resources available on the Internet.

File Transfer

The Internet File Transfer Protocol (FTP) allows network users to download files from databases residing at other sites. With any anonymous connection, users gain access to valuable data in "archives" on a wide variety of topics. Supreme Court decisions and opinions, public domain computer software, medical resources, and public polling data are examples of the sort of information that can be obtained via FTP.

Gophers

Navigating the Internet can be difficult for an inexperienced user. Therefore, an increasing number of institutions have developed "gophers," software packages which facilitate access by providing icons for making searching and retrieval easier.

One of the most popular gophers is Mosaic, originally developed by the National Center for Supercomputing Applications (NCSA) at the University of Illinois. Mosaic can be downloaded free by Internet users. The address is ftp.ncsa.uiuc.edu. Once available on a PC, the user can simply click a mouse on words or images to summon text, sound, and images from the databases which have been configured to work with Mosaic.

Enhanced Mosaic products may be purchased from a number of companies. Some automated library system vendors also support Mosaic in order for devices on the system to go out through a gateway in the CPU with the aid of Mosaic.

Free-Nets

A popular Internet application for libraries is the creation of a free-net. The first free-net was dedicated in Cleveland in 1986 to provide community information in such areas as law, government, medicine, the arts and sciences, and education. In addition, free e-mail services were provided for residents of northeastern Ohio. The following year the Youngstown (Ohio) free-net began operation, becoming the second free-net system. There were several hundred free-nets by the end of 1996.

In accessing a free-net, a user dials directly onto the system or through an Internet account. Registered users have electronic mail addresses and can send E-mail to users of the network and to addressees worldwide through Internet. Most free-nets are menu-driven so that new users can easily navigate through the network's offerings. Bulletin boards, forums or sessions where users can chat together, and file transfer functions are among the most frequent services offered.

A free-net is a computer-based electronic network that provides a wide range of community-based information and services to people in a community for little or no cost. Although not a requirement, these systems are generally administered by nonprofit groups or government agencies. Extra attention is paid to providing access to people who traditionally have little or no access to electronic information and services. Generally, community networks are activist-oriented—they have been established primarily to meet social needs rather than financial goals. Outreach to the community and feedback from the community are vital to the system.

WORLD WIDE WEB

The most significant aspect of the Internet in 1996 was the World Wide Web (WWW). The Web refers both to servers on the Internet and to a body of information—an abstract space of knowledge. The Web has been described as a wide-area hypermedia information retrieval initiative aiming to give unlimited access to a large universe of documents. Web operation relies on hypertext as its means of interacting with commercial users.

Hypertext is basically the same as regular text—it can be stored, read, searched, or edited—with one important exception: hypertext contains connections within the text to other documents. For instance, suppose one were to select the word "hypertext" in the sentence before this one. In a hypertext system, one could then retrieve one or more documents related to hypertext, such as a history of hypertext or Webster's definition of hypertext. These new texts would themselves have links and connections to other documents. Continually selecting text would take one on a free-associative tour of information. In this way, hypertext links, called "hyperlinks," creates a complex virtual web of connections.

Hypermedia is hypertext with one difference—hypermedia documents contain links not only to other pieces of text, but also to other forms of media—sound, image, and video. And images themselves can be selected to link to sounds or documents.

There were tens-of-thousands of Web servers in use throughout the world in late 1996. The number was growing at the rate of hundreds per month. Each server has a **home page** to which are linked other Web pages containing information.

Web Browsers and Search Engines

There are two major software products which facilitate access to the Web: Netscape's Navigator and Microsoft's Explorer. These **Web browsers** provide a common user interface for accessing the wide range of Web servers. These user interfaces have proved to be so popular that a number of vendors of automated library systems are offering Web user interfaces to their online patron access catalogs.

Navigating one's way through tens-of-millions of **Web pages** requires more than a browser. A number of products known as **search engines** facilitate identification of information on the Web. While mostly a software product, at the heart of a search engine is a powerful computer because it is necessary to search through billions of words (24 billion on 50 million

Web pages according to one estimate) to get all of the information on the Internet which matched the search terms which have been entered.

Of the nearly 250 search engines available in 1996, the best known is Yahoo—an Internet index which is among the easiest to use, but is not comprehensive. Its greatest value is its filtering software which results in the ranking of documents according to relevance. Alta Vista, a product of the Digital Equipment Corporation, offers the fastest software, but it tends to retrieve a great deal of irrelevant information. Other popular search engines are Infoseek and Lycos, both are more like Yahoo than like Alta Vista.

In 1996, some large organizations began to use Web browsers and search engines on their local networks, leading to the coining of the term "intranet." While this offered experienced Web users a familiar user interface, it also meant that frequently more powerful search software fell into disuse.

Decoding Web Addresses

If Internet addresses are off-putting, Web addresses are even more finger-twisting. It helps to know what the elements are because that reduces the chance of omission or other error.

A typical Web address will look somewhat like the following:

http://www.csua.berkeley.edu/-cdaveb/update.html

The first element, before the colon, is the HyperText Transfer Protocol which lets the browser know to expect a Web page. The second element, immediately following the colon, is the sub-domain which is an extension of the domain name. While www is the most common, other names such as web3 and w3 are also used. The third element, following the first dot (and in this case extending beyond the second dot), is the unique domain or the name which the organization which sponsors the net site has chosen to call it. The fourth element, which may follow the second or third dot, is the high-level domain which identifies the type of location of an organization, such as com for commercial, edu for education, gov for government. The fifth element is the directory where the Web page is stored. The sixth element, which follows the last dot, is the Hypertext Markup Language file that the browser uses to display the page. The net addresses are case sensitive, so avoid using caps; and avoid spaces within or between elements.

A library seeking to create a Web page should register its domain name with InterNIC at 703-742-4757.

ONLINE DATABASE SERVICES

Online database services are service bureaus which mount databases on their hardware for remote access by a wide variety of users, including persons acting for themselves or assisting end users in libraries, corporations, or other organizations. Billing is usually based on use. Among the measures of use are the number of citations retrieved, the number of minutes accessed, or the number of ports utilized.

The principal advantage of using an online database service, rather than mounting databases locally, is that one avoids purchasing or leasing databases which may be infrequently used. There also are potential savings in computer hardware and staff. The principal drawback of many online database services has been their complexity. Many require skilled intermediaries to search on behalf of end users. This adds considerably to the cost as well as frustrating some end users who would prefer to have complete control over the searches.

The online database services industry is highly fragmented. There are over 1,000 companies generating $10 billion annually in sales worldwide, including several which have annual revenues of over $100 million. Many of the companies—including America Online and CompuServe—target the consumer market. One of the giants—Dialog ($300 million per year)—targets professionals who search on behalf of end users in business, government, and universities. It offers over 200 databases (of some 5,060 available). A third group—including Dun & Bradstreet, I.P. Sharp, Mead Data Central (specifically its LEXIS product), and Westlaw—focus on specialized information for business, including special libraries. Mead and Westlaw have revenues comparable to Dialog's. A fourth group of companies is now emerging: ones which focus on online reference services which are designed to be used by end users in public and academic libraries. These services offer bibliographic, full-text, and image files. The user interfaces are similar to those available on CD-ROM products.

The major online reference services companies in 1996 were Ameritech Library Services (VISTA), DRA (Open DRAnet), Ebsco Electronic Publishing, H.W. Wilson, Information Access Corporation, OCLC (FirstSearch), Ovid, SilverPlatter, and UMI. OCLC's FirstSearch was the most used service in 1996, with some 25 million searches. This level of activity produced only $10.5 million in revenue, meaning that the average search cost well under $1.00. Most of the other online reference services companies are small, with revenues of under $10 million a year each from online reference services. Almost all realize considerable revenue from other products and services. UnCover has not been included in this group because it is more appropriately characterized as a document delivery company than as an online reference service. It lacks the online full-text reference files offered by each of the others.

DOCUMENT DELIVERY SERVICES

A document delivery service provides hard copies of articles and other publications in response to a submitted request, usually online. In the opinion of many, document delivery is nothing more than the copies in lieu of the lending aspect of traditional interlibrary loan. The term "document delivery" was popularized by commercial services offering rapid fulfillment of requests.

UnCover, the largest document delivery service in 1996, provides an extensive online index to more than 17,000 serial titles and rapid delivery of hard copies by fax or overnight courier service. As with most other document delivery services, UnCover assumes responsibility for handling the payment of royalties to copyright holders.

Chapter 9

Cabling and LANs

Data communication, once relatively simple, has become one of the fastest changing areas of information technology. In the 1970s, **bandwidth** requirements were only 300 baud (the same as 300 bits per second); in the 1980s, 1200 baud; and in the early 1990s, 9600 bits per second—the higher bit rates being achieved by encoding more than one bit in a baud. Given these requirements, libraries wired their buildings using telephone-type wiring which connected terminals directly to the computer in the computer room.

As libraries become concerned with transferring more than bibliographic information, it will become necessary to increase the bandwidth of data circuits even more. The following chart (see Figure 9.1) illustrates why increasing bandwidth beyond 9600 bps is so important. A single black and white image with a resolution equal to that of an economy mode fax transmission requires 50 seconds to transmit at 9600 bps (9.6 Kbps). By increasing the bandwidth to 1.54 million bps (1.54 Mbps), the time required is reduced to one-third of a second. As several devices usually share a single circuit, today's libraries need to accommodate a minimum of 10 million bps (10 Mbps) and must anticipate the time when 100 million bps (100 Mbps) of bandwidth will be required.

TRANSMISSION MEDIA

Data communication can be achieved via copper wires, coaxial cable, fiber-optic cable, microwave, or satellite. All have been successfully used by libraries. Each will be discussed in this chapter.

Copper Wires

Copper wires offer the lowest-cost transmission medium for short distances. Copper wires have been used for voice and data communication for decades, but not for video transmission as video requires a much greater bandwidth than copper wires have provided until very recently. Most of the copper wire installed by libraries over the past several years is **Category**

119

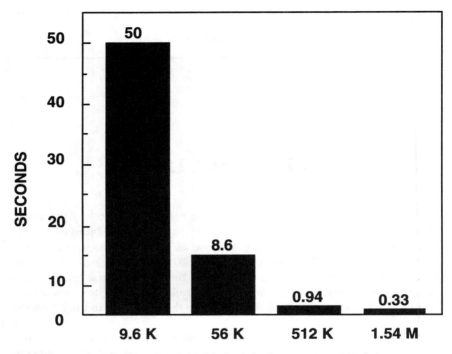

Figure 9.1   Transmission time: one black and white image at 200 dpi

3 UTP (unshielded twisted-pair). It is very similar to that used by telcos for voice communication. When appropriate hardware and software are used with **Category 3 UTP,** data transfer rates of up to 16 Mbps can be achieved.

Libraries have usually relied on a telephone company for the wiring needed for voice communications, but have had the vendor of the automated library system install wiring within the computer room and have retained an electrical contractor to install special data communications wiring for remote peripherals in the same building as the computer room. Among buildings either existing telco facilities or a parent organization's network has been used.

Beginning in 1995, Category 3 UTP began to be displaced by Category 5 UTP. At only slightly higher cost ($.14 as against $.12 per foot, plus installation), Category 5 UTP provides bandwidth of up to 100 Mbps per standards completed in 1994.

UTP is usually made up into cables with four-pair wires each. All that is needed over short distances between a computer and the remote peripherals are the appropriate connectors at each end. However, as distances increase, **line drivers** are required to offset the signal distortion that would otherwise limit the distance and speed of the transmission. Extended-distance transmission produces pulse-rounding—a condition in which the edges of a square wave pulse are distorted due to the loss of high-frequency elements. Transmission over extended distances also increases signal atten-uation (loss of signal), resulting in marginal reception and lost or erroneous data. To handle transmission over short distances, such as to adjacent build-ings, a **limited-distance modem** (LDM) is required. As a general rule, the greater the distance, the more sophisticated the linkage between a remote peripheral and the computer, and the higher the costs.

Data communications can be further degraded when foreign electro-magnetic signals intrude on the transmission. These signals may be gener-ated by electric motors such as those in elevators. **STP** (shielded twisted-pair), should be used when it is necessary to protect against such interference. Shielded cable, which will accommodate 12 pairs of wires, costs more than unshielded cable.

Coaxial Cable

Coaxial cable—used in the past primarily for video transmission—offers high bandwidth (up to 100 Mbps) and relatively widespread availability. These characteristics also make it suitable for voice and data communica-tions. Coaxial cable can be installed within a building or group of adjacent buildings as a local area network (LAN). It can be used throughout a met-ropolitan area, but then the most cost-effective approach is to piggyback the voice and data communications to an existing service, such as the sys-tems installed for cable television.

Coaxial cable is more difficult to pull than UTP or STP. In older build-ings its thickness may make if difficult to pull through restricted spaces. It is also considerably more expensive ($.60 per foot plus installation). Now that Category 5 UTP can accommodate 100 Mbps bandwidth there is little reason to use it when cabling a building for the first time, or when adding cabling.

Using the coaxial cable of a local cable company for data communication among locations is not always possible. Both voice and data communica-tions require a medium capable of two-way (interactive) communications. At the simplest level, a remote peripheral operator needs to transmit a mes-sage requesting that an item be placed on hold and to receive confirmation that the message has been received. In practical, economic terms such ca-pabilities are only available on coaxial cable systems that have been de-signed as two-way systems. Only a small percentage of communities with cable television have systems with such two-way capabilities. Even in these installations, library use of a cable channel for voice and data communica-tions requires that there be spare channels not currently devoted to other applications. The majority of installed systems do not have spare capacity, although recently awarded franchises do have a number of unused channels.

As cable operators begin to compete with local telcos for local telephone service, the prospect of using this medium may improve.

Fiber-Optic Cable

Fiber optics is a communications medium that transmits light through hair-thin strands of clear plastic or glass. Instead of using conventional copper wire for the interconnection, a plastic or glass fiber is built into a cable, with an optical core and an outside structure called a cladding.

The electrical energy from a voice, data or video device is converted to light energy through a light source, such as light-emitting diode (LED) or laser. Like LED, a laser converts electrical energy into light energy but at a higher light-power output. Once the list is emitted from the light source, it is transmitted through the optical core of the fiber. The common types of optical fibers are graded index fiber and step index fiber. The core of the graded index fiber is made of silica. The cladding is also silica, but it is silica with a different index of refraction, meaning that the light is reflected at a different angle from that of the core. A step index cable has a silica core with a plastic cladding. When the light is transmitted through the optical fiber and approaches the cladding area, the cladding acts like a coated mirror and reflects the light back into the core. Virtually no light escapes through the cladding. At the end of the fiber cable the light is projected onto a light-detecting device which produces an electrical current.

The biggest advantage of fiber-optic cable is its wide bandwidth: 100 Mbps per the current standard and 1.0 Gbps (Gigabytes per second) per an anticipated future standard. The frequency range of the medium is such that a single optical fiber can carry the equivalent of 6,000 voice-grade telephone channels.

In a fiber-optic cable, loss of signal strength over distance is relatively independent of frequency when compared with copper wire or a coaxial cable system. Fiber-optic cables are also essentially immune to electrically generated noise; radio interference from electric motors, relays, power cables, or other inductive fields; and radio or radar transmission sources.

As electromagnetic noise does not affect the fiber-optic cable, the bit-error rate depends only on the signal-to-noise ratio within the fiber-optic system. A typical system using fiber-optic cables has a bit-error rate better than 10^9 (one error in one billion bits transmitted) compared with the 10^6 (one error in one million bits transmitted) bit-error rate usually found in wire-based systems. In addition, because of the higher noise immunity, a system designed with fiber-optic cables does not require as many error checks as a wire-based system. Not only are the overall data transfer rates increased by slashing error checking overhead, but a reduction in retransmission further increases overall system performance.

In addition to noise immunity, fiber-optic cables do not aggravate the electromagnetic environment in which they are installed—a factor that can help simplify system design.

Fiber-optic cable is virtually immune to unauthorized access or tapping. While copper wire can be tapped by either directly connecting to the wire or wrapping a coil around the wire, an optical link can only be tapped by physically breaking the core and fusing a connection to it. This is almost impossible to accomplish because the core and cladding are one piece of silica. In addition, when the cladding is penetrated the power loss can be detected. Since the cable is made of glass or plastic, electrical isolation problems are eliminated and the amount of noise within the system is decreased.

Fiber-optic cables offer substantial size and weight advantages over metallic cables with equivalent bandwidths. The tensile strength of available fiber-optic cable is 90 pounds compared with 40 pounds for a twisted-pair cable. Fiber-optic cable is also useful in applications in which crowded conduits prevent installation of the bulkier metallic cables. A fiber-optic cable can usually be installed in these crowded conduits with little or no difficulty. A 10-fiber cable, for example, has less than a 3/8-inch diameter.

In most cases, fiber-optic cable is less affected by harsh environmental conditions than its metallic counterparts and is not as fragile or brittle as might be expected. Fiber-optic cables can usually be protected in harsh environments by properly jacketing the signal-carrying glass or plastic. The fiber cable is not subject to corrosion because it contains no metallic conductors. The only chemical that can affect optical fiber is hydrofluoric acid. In the case of fire, an optical fiber can withstand greater temperatures than copper wire. Even when the outside jacket of the surrounding fiber has melted, a fiber-optic system, in most cases, can still be operational.

Although fiber-optic cable is subject to less data loss than copper wire, repeater or amplification stages are required to span long distances. Most fiber-optic communications equipment can easily communicate up to 3,000 feet. Many longer-distance communications—up to 20,000 feet—are possible without any repeater or amplification stages. Special interfacing equipment, however, is needed to transmit over these long distances. As a general rule, fiber-optic communications require a repeater every 3,000 to 5,000 feet, unless high-performance equipment is used.

While fiber-optic cable is relatively expensive (up to $1.00 per foot, plus installation), it is a clear choice over coaxial cable because it requires less space, offers higher maximum bandwidth, and is more secure. Its main disadvantage vis-à-vis coaxial cable is that it requires a more skilled installer, thus increasing the cost of installation. The hardware and software associated with fiber optics also is more expensive than that required for coax.

The main reason for not using fiber-optic cable in lieu of Category 5 UTP is cost. Generally cabling an entire building with fiber optic instead of Category 5 UTP more than doubles the cost of materials and labor. For that reason, fiber-optic cable tends to be used as backbone cabling among buildings or the vertical risers within a large building. The rest of the cabling usually is Category 5 UTP. Fiber-optic prices are dropping and the skills of installers are improving; therefore, the gap between fiber optics and Category 5 UTP will close in future years.

Cabling a Library Today

With only a few exceptions, new cabling undertaken by libraries should be with Category 5 UTP because it is inexpensive, easy to pull, and offers bandwidth up to 100 Mbps per standard. In those areas where electrical interference from motors is possible, STP should be used instead. Also, whenever cable is to be through a **plenum**, it should be plenum-rated, meaning that it has a special fire-rated cladding.

Fiber-optic cable should be utilized as backbone cabling whenever a hundred or more remote peripherals are to accommodated on a single cable circuit. This usually is among buildings on an academic or corporate campus, but may also occur in a large building when a **riser** among floors accommodates many remote peripherals.

While it is common to use "**home runs**" of cabling from remote peripherals to the computer room, large systems are better installed using telecommunications rooms or closets throughout the building. Distribution from the computer room to the communications rooms or closets can be either Category 5 UTP or fiber-optic cable, depending on the number of remote peripherals. The cabling from the communications rooms or closets to the remote peripherals should be Category 5 UTP. When additional remote peripherals are installed, it is only necessary to cable to the nearest communications room or closet, rather than all the way to the computer room.

If the cabling is to be run in a plenum—the space between the ceiling and the floor above—the National Electrical Code (NEC) requires that it be run within a conduit. Data cabling should not be run in the same conduit as telephone or electrical cabling; nor should cables be placed adjacent to power cables, or close to fluorescent lamp fixtures. Most local building codes provide detailed instructions.

Unless the vendor of the automated library system specifies differently, eight-pin modular jacks or a punchdown block should be used for UTP; BNC connectors or bayonet lock connectors, as specified in IEEE 802.3, should be used for coaxial cable; and ST or FDDI connectors should be used for fiber optic cable.

Universal 4 port outlets should be provided in all areas to accommodate voice/data/video capability. A duplex computer electrical outlet (3-prong grounded 115 ± 5 percent) should be provided next to each Universal 4 port telecommunications outlet.

LOCAL AREA NETWORKS

Local area networks (LANs) have been available since the late 1970s. Most definitions describe LANs by their attributes: service to a limited geographic area, the use of private or non-telco circuits, moderate to high data transmission rates, easy connectivity of many devices, and independence of the devices connected.

A LAN's geographic span usually is only a few miles. Since wiring or cabling is often pulled specifically for the LAN, it is impractical for most LAN users to negotiate right-of-way to go through, over, or under the property of others. Therefore, most LANs are within a single building or on an academic or corporate campus. When LANs at some distance from one another have to be interconnected, the typical solution is a WAN—a wide area network which connects LANs using common carrier or telco facilities.

The bandwidth of LANs installed in the past few years usually is from 1 to 16 Megabits per second (Mbps). New LANs should be planned to be at least 10 Mbps, upgradable to 100 Mbps.

LANs function at high transmission rates because, with few exceptions, they are "packet-switched," meaning they store data in "packets" of bits and ease them into the network's traffic, subsequently reassembling them at the other end. Depending on the LAN, fewer than ten or more than 1,000 devices can be easily connected at time of initial installation or later. Each device connected to the LAN remains able to function as a stand-alone device or a terminal on a host computer.

Why a LAN?

LANs are primarily installed to allow users with different types of data processing equipment, including terminals and PCs, to plug into the network with no concern for compatibility; thus peripheral devices such as high-speed printers and high-capacity disk drives can be shared, files can be exchanged (often called information sharing), software can be shared, and electronic mail can be sent and received.

The first library LANs date back to the early 1980s. Most were departmental LANs linking a few PCs within the library, often the administration or business office. Printers generally were the first devices to be shared among several machines. Not only were high-speed printers expensive throughout much of the eighties, but they often were idle several hours a day if dedicated to a single PC. Later, accounting, payroll, and personnel files were mounted on large hard-disk drives shared by several devices. Both the high cost of large disk drives and the need for several people to have access to the same information were factors. The subsequent use of LANs throughout the library was more often tied to the sharing of bibliographic information. LAN nodes that support shared access to storage peripherals are called **file servers**.

In the 1990s, various communications devices are increasingly being shared, including high-speed modems and fax modems. LAN nodes that provide access to communications devices are called **communications servers**.

Software sharing provides for multiple users accessing the same application software. When installed on a hard disk drive attached to a file server, applications packages can be accessed by any user on the LAN and transferred to an individual PC for execution, thereby minimizing or eliminating the need for multiple software copies. However, this approach may be constrained by restrictions within the applications software license, or by pricing, thereby eliminating the significantly reduced cost of using an application on a network.

LAN-based library automation is another application. While minicomputers and supermicros have been the popular choice for libraries requiring multiuser, multitasking systems for the past two decades, an increasing number of vendors of PC-based automation products have begun to offer LAN options. While most PC-LAN installations have only two to ten devices, the largest have more than 100.

In the past five years, an increasing number of automated library systems have been connected to an enterprise- or organization-wide LAN so that remote access to the library's database would be available to anyone on the network. When the LAN connection is made, it is common to provide access to the LAN from the directly connected devices on the local library system so that they can be used to access other resources on the LAN. Electronic mail has been particularly popular.

Libraries have also implemented LANs for access to multiple CD-ROM drives from a number of PCs. Called CD-LANs, these networks include a tower containing several CD-ROM drives attached to a PC which functions as a file server.

As client/server technology becomes popular, the importance of LANs increases because the architecture assumes a LAN.

LAN Components

Almost every LAN consists of the following components:

Physical LAN. The cabling, connectors, etc. This includes the choice of topology or wiring pattern, usually Ethernet or IBM Token Ring when large LANs are being implemented. The cabling can be UTP, STP, coaxial cable, or fiber-optic cable.

LAN operating system. Every LAN has an operating system. Novell NetWare is the most widely used, but there are many options.

Server(s). At least one network server is included in most LANs for the loading of the LAN operating system and application software. It can be a high-end PC, a supermicro, a mini, or a mainframe.

Workstations. The workstations usually are 486- or Pentium-based PCs. Memory is typically at least 8MB so that Microsoft Windows can be supported as well as the LAN.

Applications software. Applications range from spreadsheets, word processing, and electronic mail to library applications.

Miscellaneous. One or more high-speed printers or high-capacity disk drives are usually configured on a LAN.

Topologies and LAN Architectures

LANs function as decentralized, distributed, multiple-access data communications systems. Key to the design is the pattern of interconnection between the devices in a LAN—a pattern referred to as the "topology." There are four basic topologies: point-to-point, bus, star, and ring. Point-to-point is not widely used in LANs because it is rather inflexible, but it is used in some popular CD-LANs. Figure 9.2 distinguishes the topologies.

Bus topology was the first to be widely implemented. It is characterized by a linear circuit. Nodes are attached parallel to the transmission medium—a cable or wire—using spurs which are clamped to the cable or wire in such a way as to penetrate the outer covering and contact the signal conductor. This eliminates the need for physically cutting the cable to add a new node. Bus topology requires the least cabling. That is significant since cabling can represent up to half the cost of a LAN. It is the most popular topology, with Ethernet the best known LAN architecture using it. The "access protocol" used in Ethernet is CSMA/CD and is discussed in a later paragraph.

Until quite recently, the maximum data transmission rate using Ethernet was 10 Mbps but 100 Mbps Ethernet is now available. Ethernet is available for coaxial cable, ThinNet (a slim coaxial cable), or twisted-pair wire. Twisted-pair usually uses a star topology, rather than bus topology. The national standard for Ethernet was developed by the Institute of Electrical and Electronic Engineers (IEEE). The IEEE standard designation for Ethernet using a bus is IEEE 802.3.

One of the most important reasons for choosing Ethernet is its superior performance. It is not uncommon to have scores, or even hundreds of users, without significant degradation of performance. Nevertheless, there is some degradation of performance if there are both hundreds of users and a very

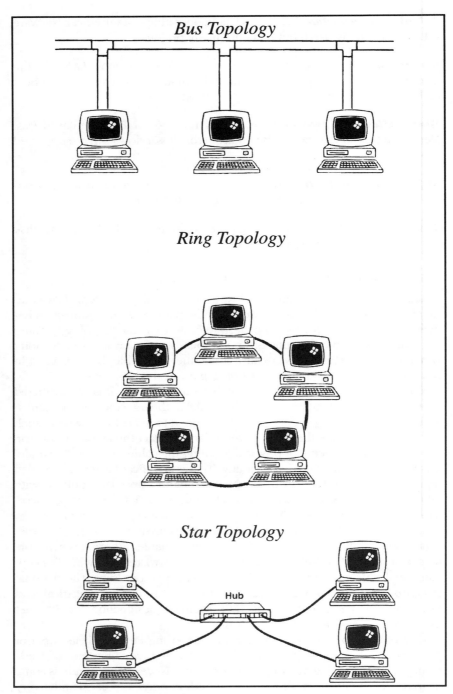

Figure 9.2 Common network topologies

large volume of activity. Under those circumstances multiple LANs connected with bridges are advisable, rather than a single LAN.

An even more important reason for using Ethernet is its ease of inter-connectivity. A wide range of products is available to connect one Ethernet LAN to another Ethernet LAN or to a different LAN. Broadband networks are most often configured as bus networks, or even as a tree or hierarchy of buses.

A well-known product using bus topology is StarLAN, a product of AT&T. The access protocol is CSMA/CD—discussed in a subsequent paragraph. While it is inexpensive and easy to install because it is designed to use two twisted-pair wires, it had been limited to a 1 Mbps data transfer rate; a faster 10 Mbps option is now on the market. Limited interconnectivity is a draw-back however, as is the limited capacity of 50 to 75 users. Nevertheless, StarLAN continues to be a popular choice for small LANs, especially those which involve frequent changes in the number and locations of workstations.

Star topology features a central node or hub to which each network node is directly attached. The hub controls the network functions. The addition of any new workstations must include connection to the hub by installation of a wire or cable.

The best known product using star topology is ARCNET, a product of Datapoint Corporation. It uses a distributed star technology and token ring access. It requires coaxial cable, and has a throughput of 2.5 Mbps. The number of users is generally no more than 75, but there are LANs of up to 255 nodes. It is easy to install and expand, but it has poor interconnectiv-ity. Because ARCNET is a proprietary product, there is no IEEE standard for it, as there is for the other products discussed in this section.

A star topology version of Ethernet is available using twisted-pair wire. The standard for this version of Ethernet is IEEE 802.3i.

In **ring** topology, messages flow unidirectionally from a source node around the ring from node to node until they reach their destination. Each node is connected to two other nodes, with each node functioning as a re-peater, thus a device failure at a node can disable the entire network unless provisions to detect and bypass failures are included in the design. The in-clusion of the word "token" refers to the access protocol. The "token" is a special data packet that includes three 8-bit sequences which denote the start and end of the message and provide access control. The access proto-col is discussed in a subsequent paragraph. IBM's Token Ring product is not a true token ring architecture, but a variation which connects the nodes to hubs using a starlike pattern. There is an IEEE standard for IBM Token Ring networks: IEEE 802.5. The data transfer rate of IBM Token Ring networks has until recently been limited to 16 Mbps, but a 100 Mbps option is now available. IBM Token Ring installations often number hundreds of users, and over 1,000 is not uncommon. The topology is particularly well-suited to very high activity levels and large volumes of data.

ACCESS PROTOCOLS

An access protocol is a set of procedures to be followed to gain access to another device. While there are numerous protocols in use, only three are covered by standards: CSMA/CD, Token Bus, and Token Ring.

CSMA/CD stands for Carrier Sense Multiple Access with Collision Detection. Rather than going into a technical description, it is more important to note that this access method is used by both Ethernet and StarLAN. The base standard is IEEE 802.3. There are associated standards for twisted-pair and coaxial cable at 1 Mbps, 10 Mbps, and 100 Mbps data transfer rates. The protocol works best in small and medium-size LANs.

Token bus is covered by the IEEE 802.4 standard. Most of the implementation is on coaxial cable or fiber optic. The token bus differs from the token ring in that it is a linear bus or cable down which a token passes among the nodes. While ARCNet uses the token bus access protocol, it does not conform to the IEEE 802.4 standard.

Token Ring is covered by the IEEE 802.5 standard. As with the token bus protocol, the token is passed from node to node, but the topology or pattern is a ring. The protocol is particularly well-suited to large LANs, or ones which involve the movement of very large files. Most implementations have used twisted-pair because that is what IBM recommends and provides.

A fourth protocol is emerging: FDDI (Fiber Distributed Data Interface). Because of the expense of implementing it, it tends to be used only for high-speed, high-capacity backbones in large organizations.

NETWORK OPERATING SYSTEMS

Every LAN needs an operating system, just as do individual PCs, minis, and mainframes. An operating system is a set of supervisory programs that regulate the interaction between the hardware and software. A NOS (Network Operating System) is a set of supervisory programs developed specifically for LANs. It works with a workstation's own operating system, rather than replacing it. While small LANs within a single office or department often use a DOS-based operating system, almost all enterprise- or organization-wide LANs use a more powerful operating system as the kernel for the NOS. Novell NetWare, the leader in the market with a 60 percent share, uses a proprietary operating system. Microsoft's LAN manager uses OS/2, and Banyan Vines uses UNIX. These popular NOSes can operate on a number of different topologies.

A PC's operating system has to be interfaced to the I/O bus and to the network. Novell does this with a proprietary product called IPX, but it also supports NetBIOS, a product developed by IBM for its PCs. NetBIOS has become a de facto standard insofar as it is widely supported by the PC industry as a whole. While that works well for connecting PCs with one another, it doesn't overcome the problems associated with interconnecting PCs with minis and mainframes. The most widely used set of network interfacing protocols when dealing with several different hardware platforms is TCP/IP.

A decision about the network operating system involves a careful projection of future activities because it is the key to connectivity between one LAN and another, and between a LAN and a central processor.

NODES, SERVERS, AND WORKSTATIONS

Computers which are attached to a LAN are called **nodes**. Printers or disk drives on a LAN are not properly called nodes; the devices which provide access to them are the nodes. A node may be a "server" or a "workstation." A "server" gives other nodes access to resources such as printers, disk drives, communications, etc.

A server contains the hardware, and, at least part of the software, necessary to provide a service. Whether communications, print, or file server, the device usually operates at a point remote from the end user and is designed for access by several end-users to expensive or infrequently used services. A server usually is at least a high-end Pentium-based PC, and can be a supermicro, mini, or even a mainframe. Workstations are PCs used on desktops to provide applications directly to the user. They usually are 486- or Pentium-based PCs.

As previously mentioned, any size of computer can be a server. The choice depends on the size of the LAN and the amount of activity. In a very small network a single PC can even be both a server and a workstation. Larger computers acting as servers may also support terminals which are external to the LAN. For example, a local library system can have staff terminals and OPAC terminals in the library connected directly to it, and be a server on a LAN for access by users from their offices or dormitory rooms.

NETWORK INTERFACE CARDS

Network interface cards (NICs) are printed circuit boards that occupy an expansion slot on a PC. There are different cards for 8-bit, 16-bit, and 32-bit PCs, and for different LAN protocols. The cards contain programs which format the information into packets for transmission over the LAN, receive information, and support the media access procedures specified by the LAN protocol in use. There is an alternative to a NIC, an adapter that attaches to a parallel printer port.

WANS

A WAN is created whenever LANs are connected to one another through the facilities of a telco or other common carrier. Linking two or more LANs is becoming increasingly common. An organization of any size seldom has just one LAN. A typical Fortune 1000 corporation has hundreds of them, most of them departmental. A multicampus college or university may have several. Some public libraries have multiple LANs in their various branches. In each case, they need to be connected using a LAN.

WANs may connect LANs within the same organization which are at a distance from one another, or they may connect the enterprise LAN of one organization to that of another. An academic or corporate library usually relies on its parent organization to provide access to WANs through the enterprise LAN, but it is not uncommon for a public library to deal directly with a common carrier, usually the local telco, to connect LANs in different buildings.

INTERNETWORKING

In LAN-to-LAN Internetworking, nodes on one LAN can transmit information to, access resources on, or communicate with nodes on another LAN. The two LANs may be in the same building or on the same campus. Linking LANs is more common than extending an existing LAN or reconfiguring existing cabling into a single LAN because LANs acquired for different applications or by different departments are often incompatible. Another is that every LAN is limited as to size. Many corporations and universities have to support thousands of nodes, too much for a single LAN, even an IBM Token Ring LAN.

When it comes time to link LANs, the most widely used approaches for linking a small number are bridges, routers, and gateways.

BRIDGES

Bridges are used to connect similar types of LANs, for example one Ethernet LAN with another, or one Token Ring LAN with another. Bridges are supported by standards which fit into the lowest two layers of the OSI Reference Model, a suite of standards for connecting heterogeneous systems. They are limited to physical and data link connectivity because they are connecting LANs using the same topology. Bridges usually are very fast because they do not need to do any reformatting. Bridges can have different types of cabling interfaces so that one type of Ethernet (broadband/coax) can be bridged to another (twisted-pair).

A LAN bridge creates one logical network from multiple LANs; such LANs are then considered subnetworks. Bridges are normally transparent to users.

ROUTERS (AND BROUTERS)

Routers connect different types of LANs, therefore, they have to resolve incompatibilities among them through the use of network protocols. They also handle the complex routing for Internetwork traffic. Routers are far more sophisticated than bridges, and far more expensive. Increasingly, bridges and routers are being combined in devices called "brouters." Routers and brouters work at the third layer of the OSI Reference Model, the network layer.

GATEWAYS

While routers connect different LANs, they do no protocol conversion. That is why they increasingly are being replaced by gateways. A gateway combines routing and protocol conversion. Gateways can be used not only to connect a LAN to a different LAN, but also to a WAN. The WAN can be a telephone network or a private data communications network.

Gateway servers are an important component of Internetworking. They provide shared access to communication adapters and modems required for devices on one LAN to get out to another LAN or to a remote stand-alone system such as OCLC or Dialog. Gateway software may do more than facilitate access, it may monitor and log activity through the gateway.

Several companies have gateways available that can tie Ethernets into both Digital VAX and IBM mainframe environments with their proprietary DECnet and SNA. In fact, a few companies have introduced products which tie a LAN into both.

INTERNETWORKING PROTOCOLS

If it becomes necessary to link LANs that run different network operating systems using different protocols, routers or brouters have to understand these different protocols so that the "packets" of data can be translated into appropriate format before forwarding them to the destination network. When there are several networks involved, it usually is better to have each of the different LANs use a common protocol—such as TCP/IP—on top of its file server protocol. Then routers that understand TCP/IP would be installed.

When connecting local library systems (hosts) and CD-LANs to enterprise LANs, it is essential that the enterprise network protocol be adopted. TCP/IP is the most widely supported protocol both by automated library system vendors and by CD-LAN vendors.

TCP/IP and OSI

While TCP/IP is currently the most popular Internetworking protocol, OSI (the Open System Interconnection Reference Model) may displace it in the next few years because it is more comprehensive. TCP/IP fits into levels 3 and 4 of the seven level OSI Reference Model. The purpose of both TCP/IP and OSI is to provide a set of communications protocol that are manufacturer independent. While TCP/IP is more widely implemented in the United States, OSI is better established in Europe. An increasing number of gateway and protocol conversion products are now available for interfacing the two products.

Over 20 percent of large corporate and campus networks now combine these protocols, rather than being single protocol implementations. The older proprietary protocols of Digital (DECnet) and IBM (SNA) are beginning to slip in popularity.

IMPLICATIONS FOR FACILITIES

In future years the "computer room" of a library will have to accommodate far more than the central site for the automated library system. It is likely to contain the host or server for the automated library system; disk storage for bibliographic, full-text, and image files; tape back-up; system console; system printer; UPS; and telecommunications devices. It also is likely to contain a number of specialized servers; including CD-ROM, Internet, and special database servers. The room should, therefore, not be sized to accommodate only the central site for the automated library system.

Even more significant is the need to plan at least one communications room or closet on each floor of a multifloor facility to handle communications servers, terminal servers, brouters, and other devices between the remote peripherals (terminals and PCs) and the computer room. When floors are more than 15,000 square feet in size, there should be at least two communications closets on each floor.

There should be provision for cabling not only from the computer room to each of the communications rooms, but also from the communications rooms to all staff and reader areas. If not all the cabling is to be pulled initially, the "pathways" should be planned. These pathways may be open space in the plenum, raceways in the plenum, blank ducts, or grids underneath the floor.

Chapter 10

Connecting Remote Sites

The following paragraphs discuss the various types of connections between a remote site—either a branch library or a library sharing a system—
to the central site. The most common way of doing that is to use the telephone
system. Other options are microwave and satellite communications. Cable
television, an option available to only a few libraries, is also discussed.

TELCO CIRCUITS

The great advantage of the public telephone network for data transmission is its widespread availability. There are telephone circuits virtually
everywhere, and they can always be used for voice or data communications. Computers, computer terminals, telefacsimile machines, or other devices can be linked via the telephone system. However, since the system
was originally designed to transmit the continuous frequencies of the human
voice, it uses an analog signal, necessitating the use of modems or other
devices to convert digital data into analog form. Digital telephone circuits
are increasingly becoming available, however.

There are three common methods of establishing a telephone linkage for
data communications: dial-up access, use of a leased line between two points,
and the sharing of a leased line using multiplexing techniques.

Dial-up Access

Switched service, as telcos refer to it, is the service most widely used
within a LATA or **local calling area**. It is another way of saying dial-up circuits. Most telco circuits are voice-grade analog, thus requiring a modem to
convert the digits of a computer to the analog of the circuits, and back again
at the other end. Higher grades of lines usually are available only by leasing circuits. Most modems used on voice-grade telco circuits communicate
at 9600 bps but adjust to 7200, 4800, or 2400 as necessary if a remote modem
is slower or line conditions are poor. Faster modems, designated V.32bis,
communicate at 14.4 Kbps or 28.8 Kbps. However, many of these faster
modems come with compression software and often can communicate at

up to 57.6 Kbps when the remote modem is compatible and line conditions permit. In a few metropolitan areas telcos are offering switched 56 Kbps circuits making it possible to dial into a remote system which also has a switched service available at 56 Kbps.

Leased circuits or unswitched circuits are circuits leased from a telco to connect specific points and can be voice-grade analog, conditioned analog, or digital. The first usually is limited to 28.8 Kbps, but the other two can support 56 Kbps and higher transmission rates. A leased circuit is open 24 hours a day.

By definition, a digital circuit does not require modems at each end; instead it requires a channel service unit/data service unit (**csu/dsu**) at each end. Digital transmissions are of higher quality, more reliable, and capable of much greater bandwidth than analog circuits. Digital lines are usually available in minimum units of 56 Kbps. The next level up is T-1 service: 24 channels, each with 64 Kbps, for a total bandwidth of 1.44 Mbps (megabits per second). The cost T-1 service is usually no more than four times a 56 Kbps circuit. Fractional T-1 service is available in many areas, usually at 384, 512, and 768 Kbps. It also is possible to increase the bandwidth above T-1, for example, T-3 provides 45 Mbps. There also are many specialized high bandwidth telecommunications services available from telcos, including ISDN, frame relay, and ATM.

ISDN

While ISDN (Integrated Services Digital Network) technology is established, its implementation will take a long time to realize—probably the late 1990s for most potential users. ISDN is an international network architecture for voice and data communications that can provide a number of services over a single transmission path. Instead of separate voice, fax, and data circuits between an organization and a telco's central office, a single circuit would handle all types of transmissions concurrently. Multiple circuits would be required only for organizations with activity levels high enough to require the additional capacity.

Despite its name, ISDN is not a network. Rather, it is a concept built on a series of standards for interconnecting digital equipment. The concept is multilayered and fits within the third (network) layer of the Open Systems Interconnection (OSI) Reference Model. The standards call for two voice and one data circuit over a single wire heretofore used only for a single voice circuit or voice-grade data circuit. Digitizing all of the transmissions eliminates the need to have separate circuits for separate tasks. Not only would the analog switches be replaced with digital switches, but the devices connected to the circuits would be digital. Digitizing voice as well as data transmission will increase the capacity of each circuit and will dramatically improve quality.

Despite the fact that telcos have been replacing analog switches with digital switches, and that they have made a number of installations of ISDN, progress is slow because numerous vendors have to support the standards for ISDN to work and the huge capital investment required to upgrade telephone switches will have to be spread over an entire decade.

While in theory ISDN will simplify the use and management of multiple communication services and reduce communication costs, telephone company rates for ISDN circuits may have to be 50 percent higher than the cost of regular circuits for several years in order to recover the capital investment required. Some telcos, including giant Bell Atlantic, are seeking to recover all of the capital investment very quickly and are charging up to nine times the cost of regular service for ISDN. Users will have to replace existing equipment or install conversion devices to achieve compatibility with ISDN. Nonresidential users which require multiple circuits because of their large transmission requirements will have to install digital PBXs (Private Branch Exchanges).

In the long term ISDN offers greater quality, reliability, and flexibility. It will be a reality by the end of the century for most libraries. However, for the next few years, it will be just one more technology for most of us to watch. Only those planning to make a major investment in customer premises equipment need to investigate further now so that what they install will be able to accommodate ISDN when it becomes a reality.

Frame Relay

Frame relay is a relatively new telecommunication technique extremely well-suited to library transactions, which tend to be short burst of data rather than large file transfers. Frame relay is a less costly alternative to dedicated 56K and/or T1 lines for large libraries and consortia. In many areas of North America a 56K Frame relay line costs no more than the highest speed analog line. It is often half the cost of a dedicated 56K digital line. Pricing is per site, or cloud, rather than based on distance. Typically, the cost is $160 to $200 per month per cloud. Frame relay, therefore, can provide substantial ongoing savings, although the "pay-back period" may be several years because the initial capital outlay is substantial.

Frame relay is a form of statistical multiplexing, through which multiple users or organizations can share bandwidth on a single circuit. Rather than having to match multiplexors with modems at each end of the circuit, the central site equipment remains substantially the same, even as remote sites are reconfigured or new sites are added.

At the central site, a single high-speed circuit from the telco leads to a CSU/DSU (Channel Service Unit/Data Service Unit) and then to a router connected to the host CPU or server. Each remote site is wired with Category 5 unshielded twisted-pair (usually 10Base-T) cable, a CSU/DSU, and a router.

As remote sites are added, they will require similar wiring and equipment, but no changes are required at the central site.

Before specifying frame relay, a library or consortium should determine that frame relay is available in their area. If so, vendors should be asked to offer frame relay as an option. Frame relay should not be mandated, however, because it is not always the best solution.

ATM

Asynchronous Transfer Mode (ATM) is a high-speed connection-oriented switching and multiplexing technology that uses 53-byte cells (5-byte header and 48-byte information) to transmit different types of traffic simultaneously, including data, video, and voice. The data transfer rates on bandwidth ranges from T-1 to 155 Mbps. Very few libraries require that much bandwidth at this time, but as libraries' bandwidth requirements increase and ATM prices drop, it will begin to be used.

Frame Relay to ATM Connectivity

An increasing number of libraries and library consortia are implementing frame relay for linking remote locations to the central site. Those who are looking ahead to high-volume transfer of full-text, image, and multimedia among locations have been concerned that frame relay may not offer enough bandwidth: it may be necessary to have 100 Mbps or more for at least the backbone. At such time it would be desirable to upgrade that part of a network without replacing all of the frame relay components. That is now possible because a standard for frame relay-to-ATM connectivity has recently been adopted by the ATM and Frame Relay Forums.

In late 1995 Sprint was the first company to offer interconnectivity which conforms to the new standard. AT&T, MCI, and LDDS World Com began offering the same service in early 1996. Local telcos also are expected to offer Internetworking using the recently introduced standard. Regardless of the bandwidth of the frame relay circuits, it will be possible to connect with ATM circuits operating at 1.544 to 45 Mbps, or even to OC3 ATM circuits which transmit data at 155 Mbps. Prices per Mbps of ATM service are comparable to prices for frame relay; therefore, the major basis for choosing between the technologies will be the amount of bandwidth needed and the cost of hardware. Prices for ATM hardware and software for ATM to desktop workstations are still extremely high (up to $5,000 per user); therefore, ATM is not expected to become popular for several more years.

MICROWAVE

Microwave communications is a widely used form of terrestrial or earth-based long-distance transmission for voice, data, and video. A single microwave transmission can carry 600 to 1800 voice channels. Using space as the transmission medium, microwaves are beamed from an origination point at which many individual messages have been collected by telephone lines, cable, or other means. Transmission of the microwave beam requires a line-on-sight path (a straight line with no visible obstructions in the path), and therefore the transmitting towers are situated on hills or tall buildings to minimize interference. Usually, towers are placed no more than 30 miles apart. Greater distances are not practical because the curvature of the earth causes the message stream to go into space rather than remain earthbound.

The development of low-cost, low-power, reliable microwave hardware in the last decade has produced a proliferation of applications. One broad category of use is in the communications field where its medium broad bandwidth (potential carrying capacity) and physical path independence make it an attractive alternative to wire and cable systems. Well-suited to video transmission, microwave's typical uses include video surveillance, industrial monitoring, and teleconferencing.

The basic rule governing microwave antennas is that an antenna gets larger as its ability to focus energy in one direction increases. This focusing is called gain, or directivity. In the focusing effect of the microwave, a beam is formed with a width measured in degrees and called the antenna's beamwidth. As one increases antenna size, and therefore gain, the transmission range also increases.

Wave reflection can be a problem when transmitting microwave signals. Objects in a transmitter-to-receiver path can cause wave reflection to occur in a random, undesirable manner. Multiple reflectors can be used to create multiple transmission paths, but when these multiple signals compete with one another at the receiver, "multipath" distortion results. Judicious placement and steering of a receiver antenna can minimize these effects.

In addition, changes in the path characteristics—for example, rain—can cause further attenuation of the signal. In borderline situations (in which communication is not very good to begin with), changes can cause complete loss of communications. To accommodate for these occurrences, an excess of signal level is usually built into systems and is termed the "fade margin."

The simplest receiver is the detector, or crystal, which uses a diode to detect the incoming microwave energy and create a corresponding AC (alternating current) signal. This receiving method is similar in many ways to the old crystal radio sets and, like those radios, it has the same lack of sensitivity.

Another class of receiver, the super hetrodyne type, is much more sensitive and is usually used for communications systems. This receiver also uses a diode, but rather than using the signal itself, it converts the signal to a much lower-frequency band (baseband) that is termed the intermediate frequency (IF). Information is not only transmitted at baseband on the carrier itself, but can also be transmitted on a subcarrier that essentially rides along with the carrier. At the receiver the subcarrier is removed from the received signal and demodulated separately.

When transmission volume is high and distances exceed 25 miles, microwave is usually less expensive than telecommunications options that require the laying of special cables. The cost of constructing a single line-of-sight microwave tower is approximately $50,000. Maintenance costs are approximately $250 per channel per year. It is usually not practical to construct a microwave network for a group of libraries because the transaction levels are not high enough to offset the high start-up costs. It is sometimes possible to utilize excess capacity in existing fire, police, or educational microwave systems. The major risk is that the excess capacity may eventually be claimed by the original users and service to libraries may be discontinued. It must also be kept in mind that telephone lines and other linkages between the libraries and the microwave facilities will represent a major ongoing cost.

Commercial and private uses of microwave are coordinated by the Federal Communications Commission (FCC). Under FCC rules and regulations, equipment is classified in several ways including licensed vs. unlicensed operation. When required, licensing is necessary to prevent interference. When not required, it is assumed that for that particular use, interference is a remote possibility. For example, burglar alarms do not require licenses, but most communications applications do.

SATELLITE COMMUNICATIONS

Satellite data transmission allows high data rates between sending and receiving stations, is insensitive to the distance between stations, and allows one station to broadcast transmission to several other receiving stations.

In order to use a satellite for voice, data, or video communications, the user must have a connection to the central office of the satellite communications vendor. The communications channel starts at a video device or at a host computer. This, in turn, is connected to the central office of the satellite communications vendor by a local communications loop using traditional telephone company facilities, coaxial cable, or microwave. Data from the local loop are then combined with data received from separate sources into a microwave signal that is sent to the satellite vendor's earth station. This signal becomes part of the composite signal that is sent by the earth station to the satellite and is transmitted by the satellite to the receiving earth stations.

The satellite uses a transponder (a device that receives radio frequency signals at one frequency and converts them to another frequency for transmission) to transfer the composite signal from one earth station to another. At the receiving earth station, data are transferred by a microwave link to the satellite vendor's central office. From there, the data are broken down into separate communications channel sand transmitted over the local loop to the receiving device.

The distance between the sending and receiving devices is essentially the same for all points within the area serviced by the satellite, since the satellite is about 23,000 miles above the earth stations. Thus, satellite transmission costs are distance-independent. The cost of a satellite channel connecting Washington, DC and Atlanta, for example, is equivalent to the cost of a satellite channel connecting Washington, DC and Los Angeles.

Satellite communications is most cost-effective with distances of more than 2,500 miles. For example, in 1996 a satellite channel was nearly $800 per month cheaper than the voice-grade channel offered by AT&T for a Los Angeles to Washington, DC connection.

The composite signal between the satellite earth stations and the satellite is assigned a frequency in the gigahertz or billion-cycle-per-second range. As the amount of information transferred over a communications channel is directly proportional to the available frequency bandwidth of the channel, satellite channels operating in the high end of the radio frequency spectrum have large transmission bandwidths and can easily accommodate data transfers up to millions of bits per second.

Satellite channels also provide lower error rates. One reason for their high-quality performance compared with terrestrial microwave links is their protection from atmospheric interference. The composite signal from the terrestrial stations runs up and through the earth's atmosphere directly to the satellite. It proceeds down from the satellite to the receiving earth station, traveling through the atmosphere for 10 miles at the most. Although normal terrestrial communications channels use similar microwave circuits for long-distance transmission, these circuits run through the power atmosphere for hundreds of miles, more or less parallel to the ground. The terrestrial microwave circuits are therefore more subject to atmospheric interference than the satellite microwave channels.

Terrestrial links typically have higher error rates than satellite channels. For example, a satellite channel may achieve a bit-error performance in the range of 10^9, while terrestrial circuits experience bit-error rates of 10^5 (one error in 100,000 bits transmitted). Digital terrestrial channels, however (e.g., AT&T's Digital Dataphone Service), have transmission error rates equivalent to those of satellite channels.

Although satellites offer the advantages of insensitivity to distance, point-to-multipoint communications capability, and improved transmission quality over long distances, there are some limiting characteristics.

Satellite channels are inherently point to point. A terrestrial communications channel running from Washington, DC to Los Angeles could, at very little additional expense, be connected to other cities between the two points. A satellite channel covering a similar route could not service intermediate points unless each one were connected to an earth station. Because of the cost of earth stations and associated electronics needed to perform the communications functions, satellite communications links are economical only with a significant volume of telecommunications over terrestrial distances of more than 500 miles, and become truly attractive at even greater distances.

All communications satellites currently in use orbit the equator at an altitude of 23,000 miles; the satellite appears stationary to all sending and receiving earth stations. This synchronous orbit relieves the earth stations of the need to track the satellite. It does, however, make the satellite channel about 47,000 miles in length compared to a coast-to-coast terrestrial channel length of about 3,000 miles. Although communications signals travel at the speed of light, there is a one-way transmission delay time of approximately 250 milliseconds for the satellite channel. This is about 15 times longer than the one-way transmission delay for a terrestrial channel. Thus, the length of satellite channels causes a propagation delay of more than half a second in data transmission from the transmitting earth station to the receiving earth station and back again.

Rain in the earth's atmosphere absorbs microwave signals; this absorption is currently of little concern in satellite communications because of the frequency now in use by satellite transponders. The frequencies used are 4 and 6 gHz, and rain and clouds are all but transparent to microwave signals in those frequencies. This is not the case, however, with the higher frequencies that will be used in future communications satellite systems. In the higher frequencies, very heavy rain can absorb almost all the signal power going from the satellite to the earth station.

The major costs in establishing a satellite circuit are the terrestrial stations that exchange signals with the satellite, the central office facilities, and the satellite itself. The cost of an earth station capable of both transmitting and receiving is approximately $50,000. Each satellite costs millions of dollars to build and place into orbit. Because capacity is limited, there is great competition for access to the facilities. Lease costs for a transponder on the satellite—capable of supporting the equivalent of 1,000 telephone lines—begin at about $5 million per year. A single 56 K-bit (56,000 bits per second) circuit costs at least $1,000 per month.

For libraries, the development of small earth stations that can be installed at user facilities with large communications loads, and of low-cost mechanisms to connect user facilities with light communications loads to common carrier central earth stations, will be the most important factors in the future use of satellite communications. A number of satellite companies are developing small earth stations and associated communications hardware for installation at customer sties. The hardware will communicate directly with the satellite. To make such installations economical, the supplier will expand the satellite services to include video transmission, facsimile, data communications, and digital voice communications. Since satellite transmission techniques are all digital, analog telephone and facsimile communications must be converted into digital form before transmission is possible over the satellite links.

The point-to-point nature of satellite communications channels makes them useful primarily as backbone circuits carrying a heavy data communications load over long distances. Satellite vendors are developing new techniques for connecting local sites and the satellite system, to form overall telecommunications networks.

HYBRID SYSTEMS

Telecommunications system design is beginning to change. Telecommunications networks no longer have to be composed of only one communications medium. Increasingly systems are being put together using a combination of technologies because of complex requirements which are a combination of cost, capacity, speed, distance, and number of points to be connected.

Network development is moving toward a hybrid approach that combines telephone with one or more other media such as satellites, cost-effective for distances in excess of 500 miles; microwave and coaxial cable (cable TV) for medium-distance transmission; wide area networks (WANs) for metropolitan areas; local area networks (LANs) of fiber-optic or coaxial cable for short distances; and copper wire for linkages within a computer room. However, the implementation of multimedia data linkages is likely to be hampered by high start-up costs, and by FCC regulations which require that data communications applications using media other than the telephone lines be licensed.

THE INTERNET

Libraries are increasingly using the Internet to access other library systems and remote databases. The Internet does not support OSI standards, but it does TCP/IP, a layered set of standards which fits within the OSI. The extensive international network is extremely cost-effective, costing an average of $300 per year per user. Its major drawback is that it is not centrally administered or controlled. It can take a considerable amount of time to address issues of system saturation and downtime. There have been numerous complaints about "traffic jams on the electronic highway." The Internet is best used for accessing other organization's resources, rather than the system which supports one's own.

Chapter 11

Planning, Procuring, and Implementing Systems

A library automation program involves more complex, time-consuming, and costly planning processes than any other library program (except a library building) because the impact of automation is so pervasive. In addition to significant budgetary implications, there may be facilities alterations, organizational changes, revisions in library policies and procedures, and an impact on the attitudes of both staff and patrons. Automation is too complex and costly to undertake without first engaging in extensive investigation, discussion, and decision-making.

RISKS IN AUTOMATING

Automation also involves taking chances, even if the library has identified all the possible outcomes and made a careful estimate of the probability of each outcome. It is not possible to predict what will happen in every case. The most common causes of failure can usually be attributed to a loss of commitment to the project, but there are several others. Part of the planning process entails identifying and addressing these risks.

Vendor Failure or Withdrawal

A minority of the vendors in the library automation marketplace can be considered financially viable. There is, therefore, a risk that the vendor selected by a library will fail or that its parent organizations will withdraw from the automated library system market. More than a score of vendors have failed in the past 25 years and three major companies have withdrawn from the automated library system market because it was not profitable enough: IBM, 3M, and UNISYS. Several other large companies sold their library divisions because of disappointing profits. In many of these instances libraries were left with static systems: systems for which no new enhancements were forthcoming.

The vendors which the author deems viable are capable of delivering fully developed software for acquisitions, serials control, cataloging, circulation, and online patron access catalog. They have a minimum of $5 million a year in sales, have installed at least 100 systems, sold at least 20 systems in the past year, and have at least 15 full-time programmers, and a support staff to customer ratio of at least 1 to 15. These criteria have been chosen because it takes at least a year to develop each function, a minimum of $5 million in sales is necessary for a company to support both significant development and marketing efforts, a customer base of 100 is sufficient to support ongoing software maintenance even if the vendor experiences a downturn in system sales, and 20 sales a year generate enough income to underwrite a basic software enhancement program. A ratio of 1 to 15 in customer support is the approximate borderline between responsive and unresponsive post-sale support.

In any one year only six or seven vendors meet all of these criteria. A core group of five multiuser vendors met the criteria every year between 1990 and 1996: Ameritech Library Services, DRA, Gaylord, Innovative Interfaces, and Sirsi.

The criteria for micro-based products are comparable, but the minimum number of installations is 2,500, the annual sales minimum is 500, and the ratio of support staff to customers is changed to 1 to 200. The two vendors which have met the criteria every year between 1990 and 1996 are Follett and Winnebago.

Lack of Institutional Commitment

While automation is now generally accepted as an appropriate undertaking for libraries, there is often an expectation that automating a library will save money. That is rarely the case. While automating circulation in a large library with a score of staff behind the circulation desk will save money, most libraries operate with one or two staff behind the circulation desk. In over 900 consulting engagements the author was able to document significant potential savings in fewer than one percent of the cases. In all cases it was possible to identify a number of significant service benefits. The decision then was whether the benefits justified the cost of automation.

The temptation to understate potential costs is great when it may improve the chances of gaining support from a library's governing authority. However, there can be serious adverse repercussions later when the actual costs become apparent. Therefore, the best course of action is to emphasize benefits. When necessary, the impact of the cost can be spread out by phasing the project. That should be done in such a way that the initial phases bring substantial benefits.

Facilities Alterations

Most multiuser automated library systems require a controlled environment. While claims are made about the ability of multiuser computer systems to operate in office environments, it is difficult to obtain a vendor's commitment to long-term 98 percent system reliability unless stringent site preparation requirements are met. The electrical power has to be stable, static electricity has to be controlled, the temperature has to be cool, humidity has to be moderate and stable, and dust has to be kept to a minimum. In most buildings that means alterations to an existing room or construction of a new room with dedicated electrical circuits, separate HVAC controls or a supplementary unit, and installation of a no-wax floor.

Micro-based systems require "clean" electrical power and protection against static electricity. While no computer room is required, stable temperature and humidity are desirable if a server is utilized.

Remote peripherals require electrical power and data cabling. There seldom are enough electrical outlets; therefore, electrical cabling will have to be undertaken. Ideally terminals and PCs are provided with **conditioned** electrical power. That usually is practical only when constructing new facilities. In existing buildings, the installation of a **surge protector** between the electrical outlet and the remote peripheral is more practical.

Data cabling presents a greater challenge because most buildings lack it. While relatively straightforward in buildings with **plenums** (dropped ceilings), most library facilities are in older buildings which are difficult to retrofit.

As a percentage of total project costs, facilities alterations are not major, but an extra $10,000 or more which has not been anticipated is almost always a problem.

Organizational Changes

One of the least frequently mentioned risks of automation is the impact on a library's organization. The traditional library's organizational structure is built around files; without the files, units may begin to disappear and the organization chart may shrink.

In a traditional library the departments are relatively independent of one another. The establishment and modification of work processes usually affect merely the department in which such changes are to be carried out. The tying of all departments in a library into a single automated system results in considerably stronger interrelatedness among the departments with the effect that, in the interest of reducing friction, the sphere of action of the department heads must be more limited than in traditional libraries. In an integrated automated system, organizational decisions, which up to now could be handled on the departmental level, will become the responsibility of higher levels of administration or groups of department heads working together.

Staff Attitudes

There is little evidence that libraries have reduced the sizes of their staffs as the result of automation. A few reassignments have apparently occurred, but no layoffs can be documented except for a dramatic reduction in the number of electronic data processing specialists on the staffs of some libraries when an in-house developed system was replaced by a turnkey system. Nonetheless, staff fears continue to be mentioned by library administrators as a significant if unmeasurable factor in the automation of a library. It is the author's opinion that it is not fear of loss of job, but fear of reduced personal performance as the result of the changes which will be occurring that worries most staff.

Worries about automation can often be overcome by carefully outlining the perceived benefits of the automation program and by reassuring people regularly. Visits to libraries that have successfully automated appear to be another effective way of dealing with psychological obstacles to automation. It is reassuring to see people with similar backgrounds to one's own comfortably and successfully using an automated library system.

Patron Attitudes

A number of libraries have experienced system reliability problems when first beginning to operate an automated library system and thus received sharp criticisms from the patrons. The problem is often affected by the rush of most libraries to deploy an online patron access catalog as quickly as possible, rather than limiting system use to staff for a few weeks until the system is stable and the staff are sufficiently knowledgeable to deal with patron questions and frustrations.

The risks and failures experienced by libraries in undertaking automation in the past could have been avoided or lessened by more careful planning.

THE VALUE OF PLANNING

Planning is time-consuming, but it is usually cost-effective because time spent planning will reduce the time required later for system implementation. Even when several people participate in planning for a number of months, the total number of hours they work will be less than the amount of time a much larger number of people will commit to implementing and operating a new system in the first few months after installation.

Planning is an effort to formulate a proposal for future activity. The key to the success of any automation program is the systematic selecting and relating of facts to a number of assumptions about the future. The futuristic aspect of planning is what makes it an uncomfortable undertaking. People are hesitant to predict future events given only limited data.

Good planning is usually formal and recorded in writing, but not always. The essential ingredient in planning is a systematic procedure that has several components: problem definition, analysis, synthesis, evaluation, and iteration. The alternative to planning is random movement or a series of reactions to external influences. Without planning it is difficult to maintain control after implementation has begun.

THE PLANNING PROCESS

Defining the Problem or Need

In this first step, the role of the library administrator is critical. It is the administrator who should spell out the purpose of this particular planning phase: its scope, the amount of time available for the study, the budget, and who is to be in charge. Some expert advice will be needed at this stage. An in-house systems analyst or an outside consultant can provide some guidance about what is feasible and the time required to plan and implement a system. The analyst or consultant can also be charged with actually writing the problem statement or definition of needs. If, however, a draft is written by someone who has limited training in analysis, it should be subjected to a critique by an analyst or consultant. Key staff should be involved in extensive discussion of the statement so that errors can be corrected and differences of opinion reconciled. The outcome of this first step should be a clear statement of the problem or need.

The library administrator should seek the approval of the next higher level of management when he or she is satisfied that the definition of the problem or task has been adequately formulated; however, this is often not done after the initial "go-ahead." Management commitment—both financial and personal—is essential to automating, and should be sought again whenever there is a significant change in direction or scope of planning. The library administrator should be particularly careful to repeat the review of this step with new presidents, provosts, library boards, or superintendents who may be appointed during the life of the project. Commitments are both personal and institutional, and the latter are often shaped by the former.

It is important to stress at this stage that approval may not be sought to automate, but to address an identified problem or need: cost reduction, service improvement, records control, resource sharing with other institutions, or a combination of these.

As soon as approval has been secured, the library administrator should appoint a senior staff member as project coordinator—someone who has the time to do the job properly. It is more important that the individual have a good management record, rather than a great deal of knowledge about automation and other information technologies. It is far easier to acquire information than it is to learn good management skills and attitudes.

Analyzing Operations

The next step is to analyze the library's current operations. It is this process that is usually short-cut by those who are already convinced that the present manual procedures or automated systems are not working and that automation or a new system is the answer. The lack of detailed information about manual operations is also responsible for the lack of cost comparisons between manual and automated library systems. Care must be taken to identify the problem, not the symptoms.

The library literature is filled with articles detailing techniques for analysis of library operations and costs, but there have been very few cost studies.

The price for a good cost study can be very high—up to $15,000 for a whole library and up to $3,500 for the study of a single function. There is no point in undertaking such a study if the decision to proceed with automation is going to be based substantially on other factors, such as service improvements and the availability of better management information. A library may use published cost data to develop its conclusions, rather than data drawn from an analysis of its own specific operations.

Synthesis

An examination of all the alternatives quickly reveals options that go beyond the automation of existing activities. It is not just a matter of performing the same tasks more quickly or more economically. Significant service and management improvements can be realized by automating. An automated library system can be used as a gateway to remote information sources and can provide vital management information for collection development.

At this point in the study, the library should go back to the beginning. It is likely that the original problem definition was not formulated in terms as broad as those the available options allow. The advantage of a formal, systematic planning process is that it may keep a library from rushing ahead before the first step has been reexamined. Successful planning is more likely if the library administrator and the project coordinator keep the process clearly in mind and are not overwhelmed by a voluminous report. It is the library administrator who must decide, in consultation with higher management and staff, whether to adhere to the problem statement as originally formulated, to constrict or expand it.

The most common example of a change in the problem or needs statement occurs when a library administrator has authorized planning for a system to automate circulation and the patron access catalog and is told that the vendors of turnkey online systems offer integrated systems which include acquisition, serials control, and other modules for only slightly more than for a circulation/OPAC system. While the benefits to technical services of adding these modules may be limited, having current on order and serials check-in data available online may be very useful to public services staff and patrons. The budgetary constraints and current library needs may suggest adherence to the initial plan, but a review may result in a longer-term view and a broader mandate.

Evaluation and Iteration

At this stage in the planning process the library should develop detailed specifications or requirements, which will enable it to evaluate all alternatives for automation. The specifications should outline expected performance, rather than specifying how something is to be done. Ideally, the library should write its own specifications, rather than relying on a consultant or on specifications obtained from another library. Although more time consuming, this approach is the surest way to reflect the needs of the library accurately and to get the interest and commitment of the staff who must later work with the system. It is worthwhile to retain a consultant to review the specifications for possible inconsistencies and oversights. If time is limited, a consultant might be asked to write the first draft of the specifications, but with detailed review by library staff.

Comparison of vendor proposals will be aided if elements in the specifications are weighted or labeled "essential," "highly desirable," and "desirable" at the outset. Again, these priorities should reflect the decisions made at step 1. If they do not, the first step should be repeated.

COOPERATIVE VENTURES

An alternative to planning for automation by individual libraries is co-operative planning among several libraries. Such planning may be done by a multitype library group or by libraries that are all of the same type. Cooperative planning may or may not involve cooperative implementation. Much data gathering, analysis, and specification development can be shared, yet separate systems purchased.

Joint Planning

The advantages of cooperation can include less risk, more systematic planning, the ability to draw on a number of people with a wide range of expertise, lower planning cost per institution and greater sensitivity to the future linking or networking of the computer systems in the various libraries. The principal drawbacks of cooperative planning are that a longer time period is required for planning and implementation and that it may be an uncomfortable experience because a participating institution is likely to be challenged on many of its policies and procedures by other libraries in a planning group.

The amount of cooperative planning appears to be declining as libraries realize that there is less need to share automated library systems in order to share resources than before. With Z39.50 automated library systems can be linked and the resources of neighboring libraries determined even when on a system supplied by a different vendor. Nevertheless, if one assumes that joint planning need not result in joint procurement or the sharing of a system, it continues to be useful.

SYSTEM PROCUREMENT

There are more options today than ever before. Despite the fact that more than 90 percent of all libraries automating internal operations with multiuser library systems have chosen turnkey systems—those which include in the price all hardware, software, installation, training, and ongoing support—any automation study should consider all of the available options. Even if the turnkey option appears clearly to be the most appropriate, the others should be at least briefly examined.

There are five major options available to the library seeking to automate:

- Acquiring a turnkey system
- Purchasing a software package and mounting it on a separately procured computer system
- In-house development
- Contracting with a service bureau
- Sharing a system with one or more other libraries

The Turnkey System

The turnkey system is generally the most cost-effective and reliable approach for the automation of multiple internal operations. With this system, the vendor supplies the hardware, software, installation, training and ongoing support of both hardware and software. The software maintenance program also includes enhancements or improvements in capabilities. No electronic data processing expertise is required on the part of the library staff. There is usually a firm contract price and predictable delivery date. As the system has frequently been installed and tested elsewhere, performance is usually highly reliable.

Software Packages

Rather than purchasing hardware and software from a single source, it is possible to purchase them separately. A library might choose this approach because it can obtain hardware at a discount or because it already has hardware available to it. The greatest risk with purchasing a software package is that no one assumes responsibility for the hardware and software working together. The buyer runs a real risk that the hardware vendor will claim that problems in system performance are attributable to the software and that the software supplier will claim that it is a hardware problem.

In the mid-1990s most of the vendors selling multiuser software also sell turnkey systems. Most prefer to sell software only because it is more profitable. Margins on hardware are very small and turnkey sales involve systems performance guarantees which may cost the vendor money to honor. Nevertheless, most vendors sell primarily turnkey systems because that is what libraries appear to prefer.

Micro-based products are almost always sold software only because the cost of turnkey sales cannot be recovered from the margins on hardware and software.

A library may wish to consider requiring the vendor of the software to develop system configuration requirements and stipulating that the vendor is liable for under-configuration. In other words, if the library installs the hardware recommended by the vendor and the system then requires upgrading in order to effectively utilize the software, the vendor is liable. Most vendors refuse to accept this requirement, but some will do so upon payment of a configuration fee of several thousand dollars.

In-House Development

The great benefit of in-house development is substantial control over the design of the system; all the functions the library wants can be included. The library must, however, have electronic data processing expertise on the staff. It is particularly important that a library not rely on a single individual, since the project could bog down if that person were to leave.

The central site hardware for a supermicro-based system supporting 100 concurrent users can cost as little as $50,000, but the development of the software or instructions to operate the system can cost ten times that much. By 1980, more than 80 percent of a typical system's cost was for software, and by 1990, it was 90 percent. Why? Because software technologies are not keeping up with hardware in improving productivity. The Rand Corporation forecast this trend as early as 1972, when it reported that software costs, which represented 15 percent of total costs in 1955, had risen to 70 percent by 1970, and would rise to 85 percent by the late-1980s.

Unless a library has unique requirements which no vendor will meet, it is most unwise to pursue in-house development. It should not be assumed that no vendor will be willing to accommodate a library's perceived unique needs. All of a library's requirements should be incorporated into a complete set of specifications and circulated to vendors for responses. If vendors believe that the cost of additional development is justified by the potential revenue from the entire contract, they may agree to providing the desired functionality.

Contracting with a Service Bureau

A library may avoid making a capital investment in computer hardware and software by contracting with a vendor to supply automation support services. The contract may be for an integrated system or for the support of a single function—usually acquisitions or serials.

The most successful commercially offered service bureau systems have been those of the book and serial jobbers. Baker & Taylor's LIBRIS II and Faxon's LINX have provided hundreds of libraries not only hardware and software, but also access to the vendors's databases and electronic messaging systems. In each case the vendor developed the service to promote its principal book or serials jobbing business. Pricing is generally by the month and favors users who do a large amount of ordering. Neither of these vendors appears to be making money on their automation services, but they are of the opinion that accounts which use a vendor's automated system send a larger percentage of the orders to the vendor. There is also the expectation that order fulfillment costs will be reduced as more orders are received online. There is constant reexamination of these services, however, because the primary motivation of most of these firms is the sale of library materials, rather than supplying automation support.

While Avatar, Gaylord, and OCLC have all offered service bureau support to libraries seeking access to a multifunction library system, none appear to have found it a profitable undertaking. In the 1990s, only Ameritech appears to be committed to continuing this option.

Sharing a System

The capacity restrictions on all but mainframe computers until the late seventies was responsible for most libraries choosing to acquire a standalone system that served only the one library. By 1978, a number of public libraries began to share automated circulation systems. In less than a decade, several hundred public libraries in Illinois, Connecticut, Michigan, and several other states installed shared systems. Academic libraries generally did not participate in shared systems until the mid-1980s, partly because before that time, consortia emphasized circulation control without provision for the addition of other functions at a later time and also because of concerns about governance in systems dominated by public libraries.

Until the mid-1980s, those academic library consortia which were developed to sponsor library automation used mainframe computers. The costs were high and flexibility limited because of the large number of participants needed to justify the investment. However, beginning in the mid-1980s, several academic library groups set up consortia to procure and manage automated library systems configured around turnkey minicomputer systems. Among the largest of these is the Pioneer Valley Cooperative of Massachusetts which ties together five institutions with combined resources of more than 3.7 million volumes.

Multitype library consortia are becoming more common. Two of the oldest, the Capitol Region (CT) and Southwestern Connecticut Regional Systems include several academic and public libraries. The parameterized or table-driven nature of most library automation software permits libraries to meet their individual needs with regard to specific operational functions and screen and report formats. The major issue in the case of multitype systems has not been system design, but governance: bringing libraries with only limited cooperative experience together in a joint program.

In most cases, there are only limited economic benefits in two or more libraries sharing a computer system—unless the libraries are quite small. Now that hardware is highly modular and most applications software licenses are based on the number of concurrent users to be supported, the cost per concurrent user (total cost divided by the number of concurrent users for which the system is licensed) tends to be approximately the same whether 30, 130, or 230 concurrent users are supported by a single system. However, the costs are dramatically higher when a system supports fewer than thirty concurrent users.

Small systems—those supporting fewer than 30 concurrent users—cost more per concurrent user because the cost of selling, installing and training staff to use a system are substantially the same for systems of different sizes. When these costs are spread over fewer than 30 concurrent users, the cost per concurrent user will rise substantially.

Libraries which require fewer than 30 concurrent users should seriously consider sharing a system for economic reasons; those which require more should base their decision on other than economic factors.

If libraries which decide to share a system have complementary collections and already have a history of interlibrary lending and reciprocal borrowing, the sharing of a system can facilitate and strengthen these services. Some libraries which have shared computer systems report a doubling of interlibrary loan within the first twelve months. Increased movement of patrons among libraries has also been observed. Libraries should consider sharing systems only if they are prepared to substantially increase the flow of materials and patrons among themselves.

Now that Z39.50 linkages among library systems provide patrons with a relatively easy-to-use means of searching multiple library systems, the sharing of a system is not the only way to share resources. The shared system option should be compared with the Z39.50 linking option before making a decision to base a system sharing decision on the desire to share library resources.

There are important governance issues to be addressed when libraries share a system. A decision must first be made whether the libraries are equal partners or whether one institution owns the system and sells services to the others. If they are equal partners, committees will have to be established to determine such answers as what bibliographic standards shall prevail, what rates shall be charged to the participants, and how decisions about expansion of system capabilities shall be reached. The decision-making process is likely to be time-consuming—often two or more years to select, procure, and implement a system when six or more institutions are involved. The length and complexity of the process has prompted some libraries to plan systems for themselves, but with capacities large enough to bring in other libraries at a later date. While this is technologically feasible, it may be a politically delicate matter to plan without involving potential participants.

USING CONSULTANTS

Both individual and cooperative planning efforts can often be improved by using outside consultants to assure objective, formal planning in a short time and at a known and moderate cost. Consulting services cost from $500 to $1,000 per day plus expenses, but when used effectively they will save several times that amount for the library.

Consultants provide objectivity, a source of new ideas and/or fresh approaches, analytical ability, specialized skills and experience, ability to work on a specific problem with all of his/her resources at one time, and more up-to-date knowledge than that of library staff.

The American Library Association and state library agencies are good sources of names of consultants. It is important to check the references of a consultant, ideally by contacting past clients with similar requirements. Also, possible bias should be investigated by seeing whether the consultant has consistently recommended the products of a single vendor or has his or her clients using the products of several vendors.

But using consultants also has the possible disadvantage of insufficiently involving the library administrator and staff in the consultation process. A responsible consultant will insist on such involvement, but since consultants charge by the hour, most libraries are forced to place strict limits on the number of days devoted to staff-consultant meetings. A consultant will normally seek to formalize the planning process and gain prior agreement on the role of the library administrator and the appointment of a project coordinator.

A library or group of libraries has the option of appointing its own planning team and foregoing the services of a consultant. Usually such a team will devote only part of its time to the planning process and may have to spend a great deal of that time gathering information already available to an experienced consultant. The time required to complete planning thus becomes longer. The true cost is seldom calculated because people's salaries are existing line items in the general library budget. The greatest advantage of this approach is that a nucleus of knowledgeable people develops within the library itself.

An in-house team studying automation may not insist on the formality usually associated with a contracted outside study. The group may go to work with a vague responsibility and fail in its mission; even the most competent team can be handicapped by a problem statement that fails to make the objective clear. Therefore, it is a good idea for the library administrator to meet with the planners, have them restate the objective(s), and then have some discussion.

PROCUREMENT

Once the decision has been made to automate the library, an appropriate computer system must be procured. To do this, the normal process is the release of **specifications** (or "specs"). As recommended previously, a library should extensively involve its staff in the development of specifications in order to have them accurately reflect its needs and to assume broad support for the project.

Several people should participate in preparing and/or reviewing the specifications—this is a way of encouraging the interest and commitment of the library staff members who will have to operate the system after it is installed.

Preparing a set of specifications and the related instructions to bidders, which together make up the **RFP** (Request for Proposals), is fundamental to implementing automation. Even the very largest institutions have been known to generate deplorable documents that make evaluation difficult and bidding a game of roulette for the vendors. There are some simple rules for preparing the specifications and related RFP documents:

- Explain what is to be automated in simple, everyday language.
- Describe the library's present holdings, service points, volume of activities, and related details so that the vendor can determine what size computer system is required.
- Estimate the probable growth of the library over the anticipated life of the system, so the vendor can determine the probable maximum size of the computer system.
- Specify any standards that are important to the library, such as conformity to Z39.2 and the capability to load, retain, and output full-MARC bibliographic records.
- Define any related services the vendor is to supply, either of a basic or optional nature, such as training, staff manuals, labels, etc.
- Stipulate how the price or prices should be quoted.
- Set forth the rules or regulations for bidders.

Although this is a very simplified list for a document which can run hundreds of pages, these elements are basic to any RFP.

Performance Specifications

The specifications need not be detailed nuts-and-bolts statements that spell out how the computer system shall be designed. A performance specification that outlines what the system must be capable of doing is preferable. It usually assures competitive bidding, because there is greater similarity in the functioning of various systems than in their hardware/software design.

A performance specification may not protect a library against a system design that lacks flexibility for future growth or modification or one which may be costly to expand. The vendor may bid the smallest system capable of meeting the requirements, forcing the library into premature upgrades. The library should, therefore, specify the minimum initial capacity and expandability of the central processor or include in the performance specifications a requirement that the initial system be capable of supporting a specified number of concurrent users and level of activity. The same should be done for secondary storage. It is far more costly to expand a system designed around small disk drives than one which uses the largest disk drives justified by the size of the library's collection.

Libraries should decide which features are essential before seeking bids and should seek to adhere to the requirements. The essential elements can be identified in the specification or retained as a checklist. A library should avoid "mandatory" requirements: requirements, which if not met, lend to automatic disqualification of a vendor. Some libraries have developed weighted criteria to assist them in evaluating vendor's bids, sample criteria to be used for awarding the contract follow; compliance usually represents half the weight and the other criteria 10 percent each, except as much as 20 points may be shifted from compliance to cost, making those two equal:

- Compliance with the specifications
- Hardware configuration
- Software design
- Conformity to standards, including interfaces
- Delivery schedule
- Vendor viability and past performance
- Total cost of the system over five years

A library should consider disqualifying any vendor which ranks last in two or more categories, regardless of the overall rating. Point counting—a counting of each of hundreds of features and requirements in an RFP—is not recommended because the best choice is usually one that involves a good balance of all elements, rather than high scores on a few points and poor scores on others resulting in a high overall score but, potentially, the procurement of a system which is basically unattractive.

Contracting with a Vendor

Responses to requests for bids are seldom so complete and clear that a library is left with no unanswered questions. A small team should represent the library in discussions or negotiations with the bidders to determine the answers to these remaining questions. Representations made in these conferences or other oral communications often are not enforceable, however, unless subsequently put into writing.

The written contract, and a limited number of other written documents identified in the contract, usually represent the entire agreement between the parties. Consequently, a library should consider retaining an experienced consultant during the evaluation and post-bid negotiation. The vendors are experienced in bidding and in the discussion or negotiations that follow. Few librarians are. A good consultant can provide both technical expertise and observations on the deficiencies of a vendor's standard contract.

The contract should reflect the substantive agreements reached in the negotiation. It should also include a detailed hardware and software schedule. The library's RFP and vendor's response should be part of the contract. The delivery schedule should also be included. This means not only the date for the initial delivery of the hardware, but also the timing of the delivery of all software and the demonstration that all contracted functions can be performed. The library should recognize that delivery, installation, and training may take several months.

Site preparation for the automated system is usually the library's responsibility and should begin as soon as the contract with the vendor is signed. The library must obtain detailed, written requirements for the site from the vendor during the negotiation process and to seek a guarantee that a site meeting these characteristics will be acceptable to the vendor. Any future site modifications made necessary because of an error by the vendor, or a change in the requirements of the vendor, should be the responsibility of the vendor.

The terms of payment should also be included in the contract. A vendor may want a substantial payment upon signing because up to 40 percent of the cost of the contract may represent hardware the vendor has to purchase from manufacturers some time before delivery and installation. Typically, libraries pay only ten percent on signing, another 40 percent on delivery, and 25 percent on completion of installation and training. Payment of too much, may weaken the future negotiating position of the library. The final payment to be made on acceptance of the system should be significant, ideally 25 percent.

An acceptance test plan should be included in the contract. It should have three components: functionality, response time, and reliability. The acceptance test should be a record of consistent performance for a period of at least 30 days. Although 100 percent performance is rarely achieved, the system should be functioning at least 98 percent of the time.

The contract also should clearly spell out the terms of the maintenance program for both hardware and software. Multiuser system vendors will manage both hardware and software maintenance when a turnkey system is purchased. Hardware maintenance is usually done by the manufacturer(s), although at least one major turnkey system vendor (Geac) has sought to do all maintenance itself. The important questions are to determine that a service representative is available nearby and that this representative has access to a local stock of parts. Vendors of micro-based products rarely manage hardware maintenance.

Software maintenance may be limited to remedying any defects that are discovered after the system has been installed and accepted, or it may include software improvements made to the vendor's standard system. The latter benefits the library by providing a dynamic system that can accommodate the constantly changing improvements in library automation. The vendor also benefits because it has to support only a single standard system rather than many different systems.

SYSTEM MANAGEMENT

Every system requires a system manager and system operators. The system manager should be appointed no later than the day of contract signing as this individual will liaise with the vendor, monitor contract compliance, coordinate implementation and training, and handle the many other details involved. The system manager need not have data processing expertise, but must have a good knowledge of the library and have good communication skills. The system manager will need to spend at least one-quarter time on these tasks. Systems supporting more than 60 concurrent users usually require a half-time system manager, and those supporting more than 100 concurrent users usually require a full-time manager.

The primary responsibility of system operators are the start-up and end-of-day routines, contacting the vendor when there is a system or component failure, and maintaining logs of system performance. This requires a minimum of two hours a day for a small multiuser system. The demands gradually increase as the system gets larger. Systems supporting more than 200 concurrent users require that an operator be on duty all of the hours the library is open.

A micro-based system usually requires five hours a week of system management and operation if a stand-alone; a LAN-based system requires at least one-fourth time.

Staff Training

Preliminary training should begin shortly after the contract is signed, when curiosity is usually high. It should be on-site. The training itself has several components. Initially, training should consist of a basic orientation to the system, as well as demonstrations of what the system will do and how it will affect the duties of the staff and services to library users. Good publicity at this stage can play an important role in winning staff acceptance of the new system.

Most initial training in the use of turnkey systems is done by representatives of the vendors. Most libraries now choose to have a small number of people trained by the vendor and to have these people, in turn, train the rest of the staff. Libraries that have done this appear to have better ongoing training programs. Turnover in libraries can be high. Also, there are usually a few new people who must be familiarized with the equipment.

Few vendors of micro-based systems offer training; when available, it is seldom on-site.

Records Conversion

Converting the library's collection of old manual or machine-readable records, or both, should be undertaken as early as possible because it is usually a time-consuming task. There are strong differences of opinion on how much of a library's database must be developed before a system can be effectively used. In the case of circulation systems, converting 50 percent of the data is considered a minimum for most public libraries if the active parts of the collection are converted. The figure is usually higher for special libraries and lower for academic libraries.

For an online catalog, 100 percent conversion beginning with a specific imprint date is essential because patrons will generally ignore the card catalog once an online catalog becomes available.

Competitive bidding is strongly recommended for large conversion projects because prices do vary. A rule-of-thumb for planning is to budget $1.00 per bibliographic record, including authorities processing.

Before contacting conversion vendors, a library should know the following:

1. *Mix of type of material*—Serials, AV materials manuscripts, and maps cost more than monographs.
2. *Number of titles in foreign languages*—Operators can process English language records more quickly than foreign language records.
3. *Percentage of titles requiring original input*—This is the percentage of titles for which no usable match can be found in the database, normally 15 percent or less. A library can determine the "hit rate" by searching the first 50 cards of each shelf list drawer against the OCLC database.
4. *Percentage having LCCN or ISBN*—The fastest searching of the database is by these unique search keys. Sampling for this element can be done at the same time that the sample for number 3 is being done.
5. *Amount of editing of matching records*—It is least expensive to accept contributed records "as is."
6. *Amount of local data to be entered*—This includes call number, holding symbols, copy number, accession number, etc.

A contract conversion service can convert from the shelf list cards, card catalog, or official catalog. It will accept photocopies or microfilm of cards.

Selling the Program

Investing in a technologically sound system does not assure success. Similar libraries, installing identical automation systems, can have widely differing results—depending on staff and user reactions. The library that is constantly encountering problems with staff and users is usually the one that lacks a planned program of promoting the new system. Furthermore, the library that carefully identifies all of the groups that are, or should be, interested in the new automated system and informs them of what is happening has greater acceptance and apparently fewer problems.

A single promotional technique is not sufficient. Moreover, different "audiences" may require different information or emphases. Staff members are probably most interested in knowing how an automated system can relieve them of routine chores. Patrons, on the other hand, may be more concerned about how the system will save them time or improve access to information. Finally, administrators should learn the ways in which improved management information will result in more effective use of library resources.

Promotional Techniques

Although a library administrator's personal contacts may be the most effective way to sell the new automated system, those contacts will be limited by the time available. Libraries have employed a variety of other techniques, both to announce plans to automate and to report progress on installation and operation.

Newspaper Articles

Articles in a community, campus, or company newspaper describing the library's automation program have been the most common promotion technique used with large groups, but success has been mixed. Several libraries "lost control" over the stories because the newspaper reporter took the initiative and developed a story on the basis of a few telephone interviews. Unplanned interviews can produce the wrong emphasis or, sometimes, actual misinformation. To avoid these problems, a press release that carefully describes what the library wishes to say is essential. The release should be interesting, even at the risk of leaving out details; the expository material may be covered by a manual or leaflet.

Leaflet

A handout describing the why, when, and how of a new library automation system is inexpensive yet very effective. It can be aimed at those who most use the library. Although the leaflet should emphasize the prospective benefits to the library user, it should also set forth any possible disadvantages. It is tempting to "oversell" when a library feels its audience may be unsure or skeptical about an innovation; but the problems created if the automation timetable is delayed may be fatal to the entire program. For example, when one public library had to discontinue use of its new system for several weeks to iron out some reliability problems, it reportedly had significant difficulties explaining the delay to a public that had come to expect great things from the heavily promoted system.

Staff Newsletter

A staff bulletin can be the most common and important single regular publication of a library with more than five employees. It need not be elaborate but it does need to be an honest and thorough report of what is going on in the library. The bulletin can have an effect beyond that of helping employees to formulate their own opinions—its influence can be transmitted, in turn, to the hundreds of users with whom the staff is in daily contact. The newsletter is an effective ongoing way of telling the story of a new automated system.

Radio

A few libraries have arranged interviews on campus or community radio stations. This somewhat more personal identification with the interviewee can result in greater acceptance and more response than with a printed story.

Displays

Public libraries have made the greatest use of promotional displays. Simple explanations of how the computer system works are of particular interest. Photographs of the various components of the system in use are inexpensive and can also be used for newspaper and newsletter stories.

Demonstrations

Demonstrations of the computer system for the staff should be done even before the system is installed. A good demonstration is more convincing that the best of prose. Also, rehearsing with the staff is essential to avoid damaging mistakes. First, everyone should be able to see clearly. CRT displays can be presented on a large screen television monitor borrowed or rented for the occasion. An RF interface is needed to make the connection. If no large screen display is available, only very small groups, ideally six people or fewer, are advisable.

Public demonstrations can also be scheduled. An academic library placed a patron record conversion station in the main lobby outside the circulation desk and found that the terminal operator drew a curious and appreciative crowd all day long.

Support Groups

The friends of the public library, or the campus or company library committee, can be an important supporting group from the earliest planning stage through implementation of a computer system, even when the statutory responsibility is limited. The people composing such groups usually have quite diverse interests and, thus, will pose the questions on the minds of many library users. They can also be a source of sympathetic support when the computer system malfunctions.

Contacts with Opinion Leaders

The library's administrator and staff have usually identified the people who most influence opinion in their community, company, or academic organization. A letter to each of these people describing the new program can be very effective. Personal contacts, when possible, are even better. The approach should be informational rather than promotional and ideally should be made just before a newspaper story is scheduled to appear. People who influence the opinions of others do so because they usually have news before everyone else.

Remedial Activity

At times, even the best of automation systems will frustrate some library users. For example, a record may be temporarily lost, or two different records may be tied together. A phone call to someone who has had difficulty with the library's new system can keep the library administrator and immediate staff alert to progress and might prevent the individual from broadcasting the problem. Staff should be instructed to record the names of patrons who were inconvenienced so that the follow-up can be made.

These techniques are used by many public libraries as part of their ongoing efforts to promote the library as a whole. They are less common in academic and special libraries. The higher risks associated with introducing automated systems make such efforts particularly important.

SYSTEM CARE

Backing Up a System

The library should have a plan for backing up the system, not just the equipment, but also the procedures. The typical system is 98 percent reliable, meaning that during normal operations, all transactions can be conducted. Up to two percent of the time, one or more essential components will not be functioning and a library will have to resort to some type of back-up system. In the case of a library open 100 hours per week, that can be more than two hours each week during the time that patrons are using the library. Virtually all of the back-up devices for stand-alone systems acquired to date are intended to keep circulation operations going during the time that an automated system is down.

The most cost effective back-up for an online patron access catalog is a union catalog or CD-ROM (if the library participates in a union catalog, or patron access to a bibliographic utility which has the library's holdings in its database).

Humidity

Computer users are accustomed to humidifying air to avoid static electricity around computers, but few realize that high humidity can also cause problems. Most computer manufacturers specify that air entering computer equipment must not exceed 80 percent relative humidity. Too high humidity causes physical changes in metal contacts and circuits. The results are intermittent and chaotic operation. Computer users who are aware of high humidity conditions or who are experiencing poor computer performance should take readings not only in the computer room, but also inside the computer cabinets. If the humidity is near 80 percent, dehumidification should be undertaken.

Third-Party Maintenance

When a turnkey computer system incorporating hardware from several vendors is installed, no single manufacturer may be willing to assume maintenance responsibility for all of the system hardware. In choosing equipment from multiple manufacturers, the system owner faces the prospect that each manufacturer will blame the other's components when something goes wrong. In order to avoid this situation, some turnkey vendors obtain all of the hardware from a single source, others do their own maintenance, and some rely on "third-party" maintenance by an organization which will maintain a site with components from several manufacturers.

A third-party maintenance firm is usually one which has service as its primary business, is licensed to service each of the components of a system, and emphasizes rapid response time by virtue of maintaining offices near its clients. Several computer manufacturers, realizing that "open systems" means components from several manufacturers, now will act as third-party maintenance providers for components not manufactured by them.

Electrical Power Requirements

The following requirements are common to many of the supermicro-based systems and should, with only minor modifications, be suitable for all but the largest systems.

- *Central Processing Unit (CPU)*—Voltage 120 or 208 (± 15%), 30 amp dedicated circuit
- *Disk Drives*—Voltage 120 or 208 (± 10–15%), 15 amp dedicated circuit per drive
- *Tape Drives*—Voltage 115 or 230 (± 10%), 2.8 amps to 5 amps on shared circuit
- *System Console*—Voltage 110 or 220 (± 10%), 7.5 amps on shared circuit.

Ideally, all of this equipment would be contained in a single room of 150 to 300 square feet. The room should be secured so that only authorized system operators will have access. These figures should be used for preliminary planning only, as the specific requirements vary from vendor to vendor.

Typically the cost for revamping the electrical and air conditioning systems of a building to adequately accommodate a multiuser supermicro is $5,000 to $7,000. The costs for a building more than 20 years old may be twice as high.

A micro-based system will require a central site only if a LAN server is involved. In that case, it is a good idea to locate the server in an environmentally controlled room and install an **UPS** (uninterruptable power supply) to protect the system against surges, spikes, brownouts, and blackouts.

Chapter 12

The Costs of Automation

One of the major considerations in automation is the cost of implementing and operating a system. The multiuser automated library system industry offers systems in a wide range of sizes and prices. The smallest installed systems support three or four concurrent users; the largest support 1,000 or more concurrent users and bibliographic databases of several million records. Micro-based systems are available in both stand-alone and networked versions, with the typical network supporting four to 20 devices.

It is difficult to be precise about prices for automated library systems because there are so many variables. Foremost among them is the fact that vendors are continually changing their pricing in response to changes in their costs and competitive pressures. Hardware costs change particularly rapidly. Many vendors routinely extend discounts, but the amount of the discount varies with perceptions of the competition and the desirability of a particular account. Vendors generally do not discount software-only sales. Vendors of micro-based systems rarely discount.

There are several general guidelines that can be applied to the total hardware and software costs of multiuser library systems mounted on supermicro, mini, or mainframe computers:

- System purchase price ranges between $4,000 and $13,000 for each concurrent user the system is licensed to support.
- Monthly maintenance costs for hardware and software average one percent per month of the system purchase price.
- Over five years, total operating costs—including hardware and software maintenance, telecommunications, supplies, and system personnel—will equal or exceed the system purchase price.

The simple formula is to budget $5,000 per concurrent user for the purchase of a multiuser automated library system with "dumb" terminals as remote peripherals. There is one exception: libraries which plan multiuser systems supporting fewer than 30 concurrent users should expect the costs per concurrent user to be higher; much higher if there are fewer than ten concurrent users. The suggested formula usually does not change if a library "unbundles" the procurement and purchases hardware and software from different sources.

Using PCs or Macs as remote peripherals may increase the cost per concurrent user by as much as $2,000.

The purchase price of micro-based systems typically is $4,000 per concurrent user. There is one exception: libraries which plan to network more than 30 micros should budget $5,000 per concurrent user. Most micro-based systems are purchased software-only.

The purchase price and operating costs for the system do not constitute all of the costs which will be incurred. The following cost components typically are encountered with most systems:

Start-up Costs

Site preparation
Central site hardware
System software
Applications software
Telecommunications
Remote peripherals
Shipping and installation
Database preparation
Database load
Staff planning and implementation

Ongoing Costs

Central site hardware maintenance (5 years)
System software maintenance (5 years)
Applications software maintenance/enhancement (5 years)
Telecommunications (5 years)
Supplies (5 years)
System manager (5 years)
System operators (5 years)

Each of these costs is discussed in the following pages.

START-UP COSTS

Site Preparation

A minimum of $10,000 should be budgeted for preparation of the central site for a multiuser system. Typically, a library will spend up to $5,000 for HVAC modifications, $3,000 for electrical modifications, and $2,000 for carpentry and related work. If remodeling is necessary to create a room, the cost may double or triple. A network server for a micro-based system usually requires no more than $1,000 in site preparation if the server is a 486 or Pentium.

An additional $200 per remote peripheral should be budgeted for electrical and data cabling in buildings which have plenums and $400 in older buildings. The cost usually is no more than $75 for stand-alone micro-based systems—almost always for electrical work.

Central Site Hardware, System Software, and Applications Software

Central site hardware, system software, and applications software are almost always purchased as a turnkey product. As vendor practices differ with regard to margins on hardware and software, the best way to budget for these components is to bundle them together and budget $2,500 per concurrent user. In other words, multiply the number of concurrent users the system is to support by $2,500 to determine how much to budget. For a networked micro-based system, these components usually cost only $1,500 per concurrent user for up to 30 users.

Telecommunications

Telecommunications hardware and software are increasingly purchased from specialist telecommunications vendors, rather than from the automated library system vendor; therefore, it is wise to budget separately for it. The cost of telecommunications will vary dramatically, not only because libraries differ with regard to the number of branches, but also because they require different bandwidths. At a minimum one should budget $500 per remote concurrent user for telecommunications hardware and software. Micro-based systems usually are not networked among multiple sites, but were they to be, the costs would be comparable to those for multiuser systems.

Remote Peripherals

This is the most rapidly changing area of library automation. Libraries are increasingly using PCs or Macs, rather than "dumb" terminals so that they can use GUIs (graphical user interfaces) and can access remote information sources from the same devices as used to access the local system. "Dumb" terminals usually cost $500–600 each, but PCs or Macs cost approximately $2,500. Most libraries have some micros which can be used with a new automated library system and many opt to configure their system with a mix of micros and "dumb" terminals. That is why the typical per concurrent user price for a complete system with micros as remote peripherals is $6,000. Were a library to configure a system with all new high-end micros, the price would rise to $7,000 per concurrent user.

Shipping and Installation

While the size of the system is a major factor in shipping and installation, the typical range for these services is $6,000–10,000 for a multiuser system. Vendors of micro-based systems usually do not supply and install hardware. It is usually purchased locally.

Database Preparation

If a library has not completed retrospective conversion, it should antici-pate spending $.65 per English-language and $1.00 per foreign-language bibliographic record to be converted.

If the library decides to subject its database to authorities processing, in-cluding the creation of cross references, before loading into the new sys-tem, it should budget $.15 per bibliographic record for this service.

These costs are the same regardless of whether a multiuser or micro-based system is being implemented.

Database Load

A vendor of a multiuser automated library system will typically charge from $4,500 to $9,500 to load the library's database into the new system. This typically is done before the system is shipped to the library. Vendors of micro-based systems usually do not offer this service.

Staff Planning and Implementation

Staff costs vary a great deal because some libraries choose to involve many more staff than others. A minimum which should be budgeted is $100 per concurrent user which the system is to support. This figure usually is the same whether a multiuser or micro-based system is involved. The key is how much staff participation in planning a library administrator seeks.

ONGOING COSTS

Central Site Hardware and System Software Maintenance

Maintenance of hardware and maintenance/enhancement of software for a multiuser system will cost approximately one percent per month of the initial purchase price before discount: approximately $500 to $600 per con-current user per year. This amount is payable to the vendor of the auto-mated library system if a turnkey procurement has been made. The amount will be reduced somewhat if hardware and software have been purchased from separate sources, but that will mean that there is no single vendor li-able for total system performance. Vendors of micro-based systems offer much more limited support. For that reason their charges are much lower, but no single rule-of-thumb can be articulated for estimating the cost.

Telecommunications

The most common types of circuits used to connect libraries remote from the central site to the host or server are voice-grade telco circuits. These are usually leased at rates of $7.00–14.00 per mile per month. However, such circuits are limited as to bandwidth. Libraries increasingly are leasing digi-tal circuits which support data transfer rates of 56 Kbps and faster. Most tel-cos charge 10 to 50 percent more for such circuits. When many of the remote locations are more than ten miles distant from the central site, frame relay is often more cost-effective because its pricing is not distance-sensitive. Each node typically costs $160 to $200 per month. Unfortunately, frame relay is not yet widely available. The most important thing to remember is that there usually are several options available, often at significantly different costs.

Supplies

Supplies include not only computer supplies such as magnetic tape cartridges, but also paper and ink or toner for printers. A good rule-of-thumb is $50 per concurrent user per year.

System Manager and Operators

The personnel costs incurred by libraries with systems of comparable size vary a great deal because expectations vary a great deal. Some library administrators only ask that system staff deal with the vendor and keep the central site operational; others expect that a great deal of assistance will be given to system users in learning how to use the system, making configuration changes in PCs, and discussing the exploiting of the system's capabilities. System management usually costs at least $300 per concurrent user per year. The cost of operators is at least $200 per concurrent user per year. Micro-based systems do not require operators unless they are networked. Their cost of operation usually is no more than $100 per device each year; at least three times that if networked.

Glossary

The following brief definitions are offered to facilitate the reading of this book. Only those terms used in this book and those most commonly used in the vendors' general literature are included.

8088. The original processor or "CPU" for the IBM PC and IBM XT class of computers.

80286. The first upgrade in the processor designed for the IBM AT class of computer. The IBM AT and compatibles have 16-bit "slots" on the mother board.

80386. It is the next upgrade in processor. The 80386 comes in two configurations, the 80386DX and the 80386SX. The 80386DX is the original 80386 processor. It runs at clock speeds of 16, 20, 25, and 33 MHz. The 80386 is a 32-bit processor, and can handle "boards" designed for the 32-bit architecture. The 80386SX is a cheaper processor. It runs at clock speeds of 16 and 20 MHz. The 80386SX uses a 16-bit "AT" architecture.

80486. The next upgrade in processor is the 80486. The 80486 comes in two configurations, the 80486DX and the 80486SX. The 80486DX runs at clock speeds of 25, 33, and 50 MHz. A major advantage of the 80486DX has over the 80486SX or the 80386 is a math coprocessor. A math coprocessor speeds up calculations, and it is helpful for scientific or mathematical applications.

AACR (**A**nglo-**A**merican **C**ataloging **R**ules). A widely accepted set of rules for describing and establishing name headings for books and other library materials. The second edition (AACR 2) was published in 1978.

access control. The operating system feature which categorizes users in order to control their access to files and to functions.

access time. A term that describes two types of activities: (1) *memory access time* is the time required to get an instruction or a unit of data from computer memory to the processing unit of a computer. (2) *data access time* is the time required to get a unit of data from a direct access storage device to computer memory.

acoustic modem. A type of modem that uses the handset of an ordinary telephone to transmit signals from the computer to the distant computer and back again.

ad hoc interface. An interface developed between two systems which does not conform to any standards.

address. The specific location in computer memory or on a drive where a particular file or piece of information can be found.

algorithm. A method of problem solving by which solutions are derived from a prescribed set of well-defined steps of a finite number. Any step-by-step procedure for arriving at a solution to a specific problem.

alphanumeric. A character system consisting of both letters and numbers.

analog. A representation of an object which bears some physical relationship to the original. That which is continuously available (often expressed as a wave), as opposed to that which is discretely variable (often expressed as pulses). Analog data are often graphically represented as a sine curve. Voice-grade telephone lines are analog as distinguished from the *digital* representation used in computer systems.

analog monitor. One that displays an unlimited range of brightness for each primary color.

analog signal. Signal that is formed by a continuous range of amplitudes or frequencies, for example, a continuously varying current or the human voice.

anonymous FTP (File Transfer Protocol). The procedure of connecting to a remote computer as an anonymous or guest user in order to transfer public files back to your local computers. See also **FTP** and **protocol**.

ANSI. The American National Standards Institute, a body that has established voluntary industry standards for business equipment manufacturers. It has accepted many programming languages as ANSI standards, which can be taken as evidence that they are well-established and generally sound. ANSI standard languages used in automated library systems include "C", COBOL, FORTRAN and MUMPS.

APL (A Programming Language). A high-level programming language which uses unique characters to represent functions to be performed; APL is well-suited for interactive problem solving.

application. Software designed to perform a specific function such as word processing, cataloging, or accounting.

application package. A set of computer programs or software used to solve problems in a particular application.

application program. One that performs useful work not related to the computer itself; a sequence of instructions written to solve a specific problem facing organizational management.

applications layer. The top layer of the seven-layer Open System Interconnection Reference Model at which standards specific to an application reside.

applications software. Programs designed to perform a user specific task. Examples of application software include full-text search and retrieval packages and word processing.

Archie. Acronym for ARCHIve sErver, an Internet searching tool that acts as a global card catalog for public computer files. Given a keyword, it automatically searches an index of registered worldwide archives of the Internet and provides pathway information that then can be used in conjunction with FTP.

architecture. The basic design of a computer or computer system.

archive. To back up data onto a disc or tape. A filing system for information designed to be kept for a long time.

ASCII. (pronounced "ask-ee") A standard code that assigns specific bit patterns to each letter, number, and symbol. Stands for American Standard Code for Information Interchange.

ASCII file. A data or text file on a machine that uses the ASCII character set.

assembler. A computer program that translates the symbolic coding that a programmer wrote into machine language.

assembly language. Similar to machine language but made up of convenient abbreviations rather than groupings of "0"s and "1"s; intermediate-level language in terms of user orientation.

asynchronous communication. A method of data transmission dependent on the condition of the transmitting line at that time and not related to anything at either end.

audio jack. A connection for stereo headphones or speakers, usually located on the front of a CD-ROM drive.

authority control. Control over records so that the headings are consistent with those which have been established in a library's authority file.

authority file. A record of the correct headings to be used for names, subjects, or series. Its purpose is to provide consistency.

AUTOEXEC. In MS-DOS (PC-DOS), AUTOEXEC.BAT is the name of a file that contains commands to be executed whenever the computer boots up.

auxiliary storage. See **secondary storage**.

background. The execution of lower priority programs at the same time as the higher priority ones but without interfering with them. The other major option is processing the lower priority work overnight.

backup. Alternate procedures, equipment, or systems used in case of destruction of the original.

bandwidth. The capacity of a communications channel, usually measured in millions of bits.

bar coded labels. Machine-readable identification symbols printed on paper strips for attachment to library materials and patron identification cards. Bar code symbols represent binary numbers by using height, width, distance between vertical bars, or relationship among bars to express characters. Codabar labels developed by Pitney Bowes and marketed by Monarch are the most widely used in library applications.

bar codes. Identification symbols which use vertical bars to express characters.

BASIC. Beginners' All-purpose Symbolic Instruction Code; a programming language commonly used for interactive problem solving by users who may not be professional programmers.

BAT FILE. In MS-DOS (PC-DOS), a BAT (batch) file is a file whose name ends with ".BAT" and which contains a list of commands.

batch processing. Processing of data after it has been accumulated over a period as opposed to doing it immediately or **online**.

baud. A unit of signaling speed. One baud most commonly means that one **bit** moves through a line every second. Common low baud rates are 300 bits per second (bps) and 1200 bps; common high baud rates are 2400, 4800, and 9600 bits per second.

BAUD rate. A unit of measurement used to indicate the speed with which data is transferred from one device to another by communications systems. The term usually refers to modem-to-modem transmission and customarily will be at the rate of 300, 1200, 2400, or 9600 bauds or bps (bits per second).

benchmark test. Test used in the measurement of computer equipment performance under typical conditions of use, such as a computer program run on several different computers for the purpose of comparing execution speed, throughput, etc.

bibliographic file. A file of records which consist of pointers to books and other library materials.

BIOS (Basic **I**nput/**O**utput **S**ystem**).** Software programs built into an IBM PC's ROM. They make it possible for the CPU to interact with its input/output devices such as the monitor, printer, disk drives, and keyboard.

BIT (BInary digi**T).** A unit of information that is in the smallest unit in the binary system used in the computer systems discussed herein. A bit is a representation of one or zero. It is the combination of these that represent the data of interest to libraries.

bit-mapped. Method by which the electronic signals on a video screen are controlled. Each position on the screen is represented by a "bit" in a two-dimensional matrix. A "1" bit indicates that the screen should be "on" at this location; a "0" bit indicates the screen should be "off" at the position.

BITNET. A cooperative computer network interconnecting over 2,300 academic and research institutions in 32 countries. Originally based on IBM's RSCS networking protocol, BITNET supports mail, mailing lists, and file transfer. Now merging with CSNET and running the RSCS protocol over TCP/IP protocol (BITNET II), the network is now called Computer Research and Education Network (CREN).

block size. The number of logical data records included in one physical record, usually on a medium such as magnetic tape or magnetic disk.

board. A printed circuit.

Boolean search. A search strategy for selected information that uses AND, OR, and NOT functions.

boot. To start a computer. Maybe done as a cold boot, when the computer is initially switched on, or as a warm boot, which is used to reset the computer after it has been operating.

buffers. An area used to hold data during transfer from one device to another, e.g., from the CPU to a terminal, or from the disk to a line printer.

buffer device. Device which provides temporary storage. Used to balance unequal operating speeds of different devices.

bug. A malfunction or error.

bus. The main communication avenue in a computer. If the computer did not have a bus, it would require separate wires for all possible connections between components.

byte. The common unit of computer storage from PC to mainframe. It is the amount of memory space needed to store one character, normally made up of eight bits.

C. A high-level programming language widely used with the UNIX operating system.

cache. See **cache memory**.

cache memory. Pronounced "cash." Very high speed storage area which acts as a buffer between the processor and main memory. Cache memory increases computer system performance by eliminating the need to access main memory when the data needed are stored in the cache memory.

CAM. See **content addressable memory**.

carrier. Electrical current on an analog transmission medium which can be modulated to carry data.

catalog. A list of the contents of a disk.

Category 3 UTP. Unshielded twisted pair wire used in voice communication.

Category 5 UTP. Unshielded twisted pair wire suitable for data communication at bandwidths of 10 to 100 Mbps.

cathode ray tube. Electron tube in which electrons strike a phosphor-coated screen to form an image. Used as a means of input and output to computer.

CBX. See **computer private branch exchange**.

CCD. See **charge coupled device**.

CD/I (Compact Disc/Interactive). A technical specification proposed jointly by Philips and Sony for a consumer product based on CD-ROM technology. It holds data, audio, still video pictures, and animated graphics.

CD-LAN (**CD**-ROM **L**ocal **A**rea **N**etwork). A local area network to connect multiple PCs to multiple CD-ROM drives using a network operating system.

CD-ROM (**C**ompact **D**isk-**R**ead **O**nly **M**emory). Refers to the use of compact discs as a computer storage medium. CDs can store 680 megabytes (MB) of information on a single disc.

CD-ROM drive. The device that reads the CD-ROM disc. The drive, or player, "reads" the information with a laser beam. It can be housed and used as a stand-alone "external" device or installed directly into the computer as an "internal" device.

CD-ROM server. A computer which controls access to multiple CD-ROM drives.

CD-ROM tower. A cabinet containing several CD-ROM drives which are accessible through a server.

Central Processing Unit. See **CPU**.

CGA (**C**olor/**G**raphics **A**dapter). A video card for the IBM computer. Software written for the CGA will usually run on the EGA and VGA modes. It provides low resolution text and graphics.

channel. A path or circuit along which information flows; any physical path over which signals may be transmitted.

character. May be a number, letter, punctuation mark, or other symbol that is uniquely expressed in computer code.

character string. Any group of characters acted on by a computer system as though it were a single unit.

charge coupled device. A memory device in which stored data circulate rather than stay in one fixed location.

check digit. A digit added to a string of digits which will make the total add up to a predetermined number so that a faulty reading of a digital will cause the total to vary from what it should be.

chip. An integrated circuit; a small slice of silicon containing one or more electronic circuits. Chips are made of highly refined silicon (sand). Chips are usually to store memory or to control the types of chips. One type of chip, a PROM, is programmable and cannot be changed. Another type, an EPROM, is programmable but also erasable.

circuit switching. Channel allocation technique in which connection is made to the destination prior to the start of the message transmission. Message routing is completed before the message is sent.

CISC (**C**omplex **I**nstruction **S**et **C**omputing). A long established way of handling instruction sets in computers until **RISC** was developed.

client/server. See **client/server architecture**.

client/server architecture. In a communications network, the client is the requesting machine and the server is the supplying machine. It implies that software is specialized at each end. For example, in a network-ready database system, the user interface would reside in the workstation (client) and the storage and retrieval functions would reside in the server.

client/server interface. A program that provides an interface to remote programs (called clients), most commonly across a network, so these clients can access some service such as databases, printing, etc. In general, the clients act (indirectly) on behalf of a human end-user.

clip art. Artwork that can be freely reproduced, usually stored in TIFF, GI, EPS, or PCX formats.

clock. A circuit that generates a series of evenly spaced pulses.

clone. A computer that is an exact imitation of another or a software product that exactly imitates another.

closed (proprietary) system. system composed of hardware and software that is specific to one company, which is responsible for additions or improvements to the system.

coaxial cable. Cable consisting of one conductor placed concentrically within an outer conductor of larger diameter.

COBOL (COmmon Business Oriented Language). a higher level programming language generally used for accounting and business data processing.

collateral archive. Historical data that can be collected and retrieved online.

COM (computer output microfilm). Microfilm produced from magnetic tape generated on a computer.

command. An instruction in machine language such as from a terminal to the computer to execute a particular program.

command language. The search syntax used by a system to retrieve information.

compatibility. Ability of a computer system to run programs, share data, or share peripherals on other systems without modification: (1) two devices are compatible if they can work together; (2) two computers are said to be compatible if they can run the same programs.

compiler. A computer program used to translate other computer programs (in a high-level language) into machine language.

complementary metal oxide semiconductor. Semiconductor that will perform many functions on a single die at fast speeds with low power and heat dissipation requirements.

composite terminal. One which offers lightpen or OCR wand and keyboard functions in one unit.

compression. The reduction or gain of a signal with respect to the reduction or gain at another level of the same signal.

computer architecture. See **architecture**.

Computer output microform. See **COM**.

computerized private branch exchange. Exchange established by the communications common carrier for transmission of digitized messages, including digitized voice.

conditioned electrical power. Electrical power which has a conditioner to control surges and spikes in voltage.

CONFIG.SYS. in MS-DOS (PC-DOS), a configuration file that customizes a particular hardware environment. It contains information about the type of keyboard and the amount of memory to be set aside for disk buffers.

configure. To set up a computer or program for a particular use.

content addressable memory. Storage device in which storage locations are identified by their contents rather than by addresses. Data are retrieved from a memory cell when it matches the content of the data at the input.

contention. Technique of channel control in which the device raises an electrical signal in order to seize the channel when needed.

control unit. The section of the **CPU** that directs the sequence of operations by electrical signals and governs the actions of the various units which make up the computer.

controller. Device in a data processing system which controls the operation of input/output devices usually multiple devices of the same kind, e.g., line printers).

conversion. The process of changing from one method of recording and manipulating data to another, manual to computerized, or one computerized system to another. For example, paper to microform, or microform to electronic information.

coprocessor. A separate circuit inside a computer that adds additional functions to the CPU or handles extra work while the CPU is doing something else.

Core memory. Main memories made of iron cores, which could be magnetized in either of two directions. These memories are quickly being replaced by memories using semiconductors.

CPU (**C**entral **P**rocessing **U**nit). The part of the computer which actually performs the computations; part of a computer where arithmetic and logical operations are performed and instructions are decoded and executed. CPU controls the operation of the computer.

CPU gateway. A gateway in a CPU which allows remote peripherals on the CPU to go out through it to remote information sources, rather than having a modem and a telephone line for each remote peripheral.

crash. When a hardware failure or program error causes the computer to become inoperable.

CREN. Computer Research and Education Network is the new name for the merged computer networks, BITNET and Computer Science Network (CSNET). It supports electronic mail and file transfer.

CRT. See **cathode ray tube**.

cursor. A solid underscore that appears under a character or space on a CRT or VDU to show the location where the next character entered will appear. In the IBM, the cursor is a blinking underline (_).

custom interface. An interface between two systems which does not conform to any standard.

daisy chain. Running two or more CD-ROM drives from the same CD-ROM interface card and connecting the drives together with a cable.

daisywheel printer. Uses a rotating plastic wheel as a type element.

data communication. Electronic transmission of encoded data from one location to another.

data compression. The reduction of storage space by eliminating gaps or redundancies not essential to an intelligible record.

data integrity. The accuracy, consistency, and completeness of data that are maintained by the computer system.

data link layer. Level two of the Open System Interconnection Reference Model at which the Ethernet, FDDI, or other controller resides.

data management. The organizing, locating, storing, maintaining, and recovering of data and the programs developed to accomplish that.

data processing. A sequence of operations that manipulates data according to a previously developed plan.

data set. See **modem**.

database. The entire collection of files maintained in the computer system.

database management system (DBMS). A set of programs which serves as an interface between the database and three principal users—the computer programmer, the operating system, and the manager or other information user; provides the following. a method of arranging data to limit duplication, an ability to make changes easily, and the capability to handle direct inquiries; a method of storing, organizing, retrieving and calculating data in database files.

database server. Software and hardware that operates as the designed "hub" of a local area network. This "hub" stores the network's shared database files. In addition to managing the distribution and retrieval of files among users or applications, a database server offers additional manipulation and protection capabilities.

DBMS. See **database management systems**.

debug. To identify, locate, analyze, and correct a malfunction or error in the computer.

decoder. Device for reversing a coding process, e.g., demodulation in a modem (modulation = encode; demodulation = decode).

dedicated computer. A computer devoted to exclusive use as opposed to one which is shared with other users who maintain different files and may control them differently.

default. An assumption a computer makes unless it is given specific instructions to the contrary.

default drive. When a computer is operated under MS-DOS, one of the disk drives is designated as the default drive. The computer will use this drive unless instructed otherwise.

diagnostic routine. A program that is run periodically to detect malfunctions or errors.

dial access. A switched connection made each time it is needed by dialing the target host or server.

digital. (1) A function which operates in discrete steps. (2) Digital computers manipulate numbers encoded into binary (on/off) forms, while analog computers sum continuously varying forms. (3) Digital communication is the transmission of information using discontinuous, discrete, electronic, or electromagnetic signals that change in frequency, polarity, or amplitude. Analog intelligence may be encoded for transmission on digital communication systems.

digital audio. The storage of sound and music on a compact disc or digital audio tape.

digital signal. Signal which is formed by discrete electrical pulses using a two-state or binary system.

direct access. Any method of accessing data in which the time necessary for accessing the data is independent of the storage location. Also known as random access.

directory. An area where the names and locations of files are stored.

disc. A data storage device that contains "read-only" information. The user cannot write on or add to the information on a disc.

disk. A data storage device that not only stores information but can also be written on or erased at the user's discretion. The principal means of storing information in a computer system. The capacity of disk storage is usually measured in megabytes. See also **disk pack** and **megabyte**.

disk drive. A direct access device which is used to read from and record data on a magnetic disk. A peripheral storage device that enables a computer to read and write data on disks.

disk pack. A package containing several individual platters (five or more commonly), each one of which has hundreds of tracks of information. The tracks are subdivided into several dozen sectors. It is these sectors that are "accessed" when entering or reading information.

diskette. The popular name for a 3.5 or 5.25 inch disk used in a PC or Mac.

distributed database management systems (DDBMS). A database management system which is physically spread over the sites of a computer network and is connected via a communication network.

distributed processing system. An in-library system that does not stand alone, but relies on a host computer, outside the library to do part of the processing. The host usually has a greater storage capacity and faster printing capability.

directory. Any named file which contains within it the addresses of other files.

document. A file containing a text or a drawing.

documentation. The detailed record of decisions made in developing a computerized system that is necessary to replicate, repair, or enhance the system. The written, narrative, or graphical description of a computer program.

Domain Name System (DNS). The Internet naming scheme, which consists of a hierarchical sequence of names from the most specific to the most general (left to right), separated by dots; for example, nic.ddn.mil. See also **IP address**.

DOS (**D**isk **O**perating **S**ystem). A generic term for various operating system.

dot-matrix printer. A printer that forms images out of dots. It creates characters on paper by striking an inked ribbon with needle-like hammers.

download. A process during which data is transferred from one computer or peripheral device to another. Especially refers to downloading files from a mainframe computer or an electronic messaging system to a personal workstation.

downloading. The electronic transfer of information from one computer to another, generally from a larger computer to a smaller one, such as a microcomputer.

down-time. The time during which a system or a part thereof is not functioning.

dumb terminal. Terminal which can do input/output but no data processing.

dump. To transfer (or print out) memory from one area to another within a computer system.

e-mail. Electronically distributed mail, from one-to-one or one-to-many.

EBCDIC (**E**xtended **B**inary-**C**oded **D**ecimal **I**nterchange **C**ode). A standard code which assigns specific bit patterns to each letter, number, and symbol.

EDI (**E**lectronic **D**ata **I**nterchange). The standards for business communication, including online ordering and claiming.

EGA (**E**nhanced **G**raphics **A**dapter). Provides all of the graphics modes of the CGA as well as additional high-resolution modes and sharper text.

EISA (**E**xtended **I**ndustry **S**tandard **A**rchitecture). Pronounced "eesa." A PC bus standard that extends the AT buss architecture to 32 bits and allows more than one CPU to share the bus.

electronic bulletin board. A shared file where users can enter information for other users to read or download. Many bulletin boards are set up according to general topics and are accessible throughout a network.

electronic data interchange. See **EDI**.

electronic messaging. An older term for e-mail. See **e-mail**.

EMS (**E**xpanded **M**emory **S**pecifications). The MS-DOS (or PC-DOS) operating system only allows 640K of RAM memory to be used by the operating system and application programs. To get around this barrier, Lotus, Intel, and Microsoft agreed on a standard method of expanding memory beyond the DOS limit. EMS allows applications to allocate memory beyond the DOS limit by breaking this memory use. Expanded memory on an 8088 computer is added in the form of a separate memory card. 80286 and 80386 computers have the added capability of allowing their extended memory to emulate expanded memory by using special device drivers or memory manager.

emulation. Imitation of a computing function by a system not originally designed to perform that function.

end user. The person ultimately intended to use a program or system.

environment. Mode of operation for hardware and software systems.

erasable programmable read only memory. PROMs which can be erased and reused.

EXE File. In MS-DOS (PC-DOS), OS/2 and VAX/VMS, a file that contains a relocatable machine code program and has a name ending with ".EXE."

execute. To follow instructions in a program. Same as run.

extended memory. The 8088 processors used in the IBM PCs, XTs, and compatibles only have the capability of directly addressing 1 MB of RAM. This limit was greatly increased when the 80286 was built with the ability to address 16 MB of RAM. The memory above the first MB in an 80286 and 80386 computer is referred to as "extended" memory. Unfortunately, the 640K limit still exists for most MS-DOS programs. A few programs have the capability of using extended memory; however, a more common option is to use a memory manager or device driver to allow the extended memory to emulate expanded memory.

extension. A file name in some computer operating systems can be followed by a three-letter file extension that often indicates the nature of the file. When typing the file name, a period is used to separate the name from the extension.

external storage. See **secondary storage**.

facsimile. Method of transmitting paper documents, pictures, etc. by telephone. The document is scanned at the transmitter and reconstructed at the receiver.

failsafe. Procedure by which the computer can store certain data from its own main memory when it detects that it is failing, e.g., through a loss of power. This enables a more rapid recovery than a simple "crash."

fax. See **facsimile**.

fiber optics. Cables composed of glass fibers which carry data via pulses of a laser beam.

field. Part of a record. The specific area used for a particular category of data such as title, call number; a single piece of information and smallest unit of information in a record. A record is made up of one or more fields.

filtering. The removal of "noise" signals during the process of imaging.

file. A grouping of related records; a collection of information stored as records.

file layout. The arrangements of the elements of the file including the order and size of the elements.

File Transfer Protocol. See **FTP**.

firmware. "Halfway" between hardware (the machine) and software (programs written in a programming language). Firmware consists of programs (instructions and/or data) that are implemented in read only memory (ROM) or memory that is programmable in a less flexible manner than writing in a programming language, e.g., programmable read only memory (PROM) or erasable programmable read only memory (EPROM).

fixed length record. A record that has the length fixed in advance rather than being varied according to the actual extent of the contents. See also **variable-length record**.

floppy disk. See **diskette**.

font. A collection of characters with a consistent size and style.

format. Any method of arranging information that is to be stored or displayed.

FORTRAN (FORmula **TRAN**slator). A language used primarily for performing mathematical or scientific operations.

frequency division multiplexing. Technique whereby total bandwidth of a communication channel is divided into smaller bands which can transmit different signals simultaneously. Each device sharing the channel is assigned to a given subchannel.

frequency shift keying. Modulation of the frequency of a carrier signal by a digital modulating signal. The frequency of the carrier is raised by a specified amount to represent a "1" bit and lowered by a specified amount to represent the "0" bit.

front-end systems. A form of **distributed processing**. The computer in a library, usually a micro, is used only for only minor processing and the bulk of the work and the files are handled on a **host computer**.

FTP. File Transfer Protocol allows a user to transfer files electronically from remote computers back to the user's computer. The feature is part of the TCP/IP/TELNET software suite.

full-duplex channel. Channel which transmits data in both directions simultaneously. This is accomplished by the use of four separate transmission paths.

full-text. A database that contains, word for word, all of the information of the original document, book, etc.

function. A specific machine action that may be initiated by a function key or by an internal instruction. A number of predefined functions can be initiated by a **terminal** operator.

function keys. Special numbered keys used to perform a predesignated task. May perform a different function in different application programs or operating systems. Function keys may either be preprogrammed by the manufacturer or by the computer user. Generally labeled F1, F2, etc.

gate. An integrated circuit which produces an output only when certain specified conditions are present.

gate array. Integrated circuits consisting of a series of logic gates that the manufacturer can link together to perform any function desired by the customer.

gateway. Used in different senses (e.g., Mail Gateway, IP Gateway), but most generally, a computer that forwards and routes data between two or more networks of any size.

gigabyte (GB). One billion bytes or 1,000 megabytes.

glitch. A burst of line noise that can cause a computer to fail or crash; an erroneous response that occurs inside a computer because signals that are supposed to be simultaneous actually arrive at slightly different times. It is a temporary or random situation.

gopher. A network retrieval tool that presents hierarchical menus of information across the Net, which may be linked to other gopher servers or local data. Collectively called gopherspace, gophers are based on client/server distributed databases.

graphical user interface (GUI). A user interface which use graphics, including icons to make a screen more intuitive for users.

graphics. Displays on the screen that are pictorial in nature, such as graphs, artwork, or charts.

graphics card. A video card that can display graphics as well as text.

Grosch's Law. An early theory that assumed that the larger the computer system, the more cost effective it would be. It is no longer valid.

GUI. See **graphical user interface**.

half-duplex channel. Channel that transmits data in both directions but not simultaneously.

hard card. A type of hard disk built into a card that can be plugged in to a slot inside the computer.

hard copy. A printed copy of machine output as opposed to temporary display on **CRT** or VDU; a paper printout of a computer's output.

hard disk. A storage medium using rigid aluminum disks coated with iron oxide. It has a much larger storage capacity than floppy disks.

hardware. All of the tangible components of the computer system, including the **central processing unit, disks drives, terminals**, etc.—as distinguished from the programs that operate the system.

Hayes compatible. A modem that responds to the same set of auto-dialing commands as the Hayes Smartmodem.

Hercules graphics card. Provides all of the functions of the IBM MDA (Monochrome Display Adapter) with the same type of monitor plus a high-resolution graphics mode.

heterogeneous. Two or more computer systems with different operating systems.

hierarchical. A system architecture which has a host on which the presentation on remote peripherals is controlled.

High Sierra. A standard established by CD-ROM producers for volume and file format of CD-ROM discs. This has since evolved into the ISO 9660 standard.

higher-level languages. English-like coding schemes which are procedure-, problem-, and user-oriented.

hit. A successful matching of two items. In conversion, one may seek to utilize another library's records by search key to minimize the time and cost of data entry. The hit rate is the percentage of successful matches.

hologram. Image recorded by causing interference between a laser reference beam and a beam reflected from the object. Three-dimensional images are possible. Holograms can be used for data storage and have the advantage that extremely high recording densities can be achieved.

home runs. Running cabling from remote peripherals all the way to the computer room, rather than to intermediate terminal servers or data concentrators.

homogeneous. Two or more systems which are fully compatible with regard to operating systems and applications programs.

host. The controlling or principal computer in a system that ties two or more computers together.

host computer. In the context of networks, a computer that directly provides service to a user. In contrast, a network server provides services to a user through an intermediary host computer.

housekeeping. Operations that prepare or maintain the computer to do the processing a library needs done.

image files. Files of images of pages, photographs, etc., as opposed to files of characters.

imaging. The transformation of video signals into a digital form of storage.

index or **index search.** An index is used to locate the contents of a file together with the pointers to access the data. In an index search, the system matches the **search key** with an index entry which points to the physical location. If a file is very large, there will be several levels of indices. The index entries are arranged sequentially so it is therefore possible to search by partial keys when one does not have full author or title.

information & referral files. A common name for the software module which includes the names of agencies, whom they serve, and on what terms. Also known as community information files.

injection logic. Method by which electronic charges are stored in a memory cell. This type of storage is referred to as charge injection transistor memory (CITM).

input. The term used to describe data that is submitted to the computer for processing.

Input/Output (I/O). (1) Signifies the transfer of data between computer storage and peripheral devices. (2) The equipment or processes which transmit data into or out of a computer's central processing unit (CPU).

inquiry. A request for information from storage.

integrated. A computer system in which applications share a common database and a common command language.

integrated chip. Thin wafers of silicon on which integrated circuits are built.

integrated circuit. Entire circuit, including active and passive components built on a chip. Integrated circuits offer small size and high reliability, low cost and high speed.

intelligence. Having memory. A PC has intelligence because it has memory, but a terminal does not.

intelligent terminal. Has logic circuitry internally, so that some functions such as editing for syntax errors can be done at the terminal rather than at the CPU.

interactive. A back-and-forth dialog between the user and a computer.

interactive computer graphics. The use of a computer terminal for drawing lines and images.

interface. The linking of two or more computers or the storage of a computer being accessed by two or more computer programs, such as acquisitions or circulation; point of meeting between a computer and an external entity, such as an operator, a peripheral device, or a communications medium.

internal memory. Another name for the primary storage unit of the **CPU**.

Internet. The series of interconnected networks that includes local area, regional, and national backbone networks. Networks on the Internet use the same telecommunications protocol (TCP/IP) and provide electronic mail, remote login, and file transfer services.

interpreter. A computer program which controls the execution of another program which has not been previously compiled or assembled.

interrupt. Temporary suspension of a sequence of operations.

I/O. See **Input/Output**.

inverted file. A file created from another by altering the sequence or a cross index to another file so that a key word identifies a record. Call number access often involves inverting a file.

IP (Internet Protocol). The Internet standard protocol that provides a common layer over dissimilar networks and is used to move packets among host computers and through gateways if necessary.

IP address. The numeric address of a computer connected to the Internet; it is also called Internet address.

ISBN (International Standard Book Number). A distinctive and unique number assigned to a book. It is hoped that eventually the system will cover all of the publishers in the world.

ISSN (International Standard Serial Number). A distinctive and unique number assigned to a serial.

ISO 9660. A standard established by the International Standards Organization (ISO) for volume and file format of CD-ROM discs. This standard has evolved from the work of the original high Sierra Group. See also **High Sierra**.

in print. Currently available from the publisher.

JAVA. A relatively new programming language which provides for the creation of "applets" or small bundles of applications software which can be downloaded as needed by remote peripherals.

jobber. A wholesaler who stocks or supplies the books of many publishers for resale to bookstores and libraries.

journal citation files. An applications module which provides for a periodical index on the automated library system, usually with a link to a library's serials control module so that a user can determine whether the cited serial titles are in the collection.

K. 1,024 **bytes.** Each byte is a character or number.

KB. A term used to describe the primary storage capacity of a computer. See also **MB**.

key. A unique identifier for a record; used to sort records for processing or to locate a particular record within a file.

keyboard. A device for entering data by pressing keys as opposed to badge reading or scanning with a **lightpen** or **OCR** wand.

labeling. Affixing barcode or OCR labels to books and other library materials.

LAN. See **local area network**.

language. A set of software representations and rules used to convey information to the computer. It is the way we communicate with computers. Examples of computers languages are BASIC, COBOL, LOGO, or APL.

language processor. Computer program that compiles, assembles, or translates a specific programming language into a form the computer can operate on.

laser printer. Uses a laser beam to generate an image, then transfers it to paper electrostatically. They are quieter and faster than printers that mechanically strike the paper. They print graphics and are commonly used in desktop publishing.

LC MARC. The Library of Congress' implementation of the MARC format for bibliographic records.

LDM. See **limited-distance modem**.

leader. In the context of MARC formats and other formats based on ISO 2709, a leader (or record leader) is a 24-character string at the beginning of a record which defines fundamental machine-processing aspects of that record, including its length, status, and makeup of directory.

LED (**L**ight **E**mitting **D**iode). A type of semiconductor frequently used in computers to signal on/off conditions in toggle keys. For example, a Caps Lock or Num Lock key may be fitted with a LED so that electrical current will pass through it and light it up when the key is pressed for an "on" condition, until it is pressed into the "off" position.

letter quality. Produces print equal in quality to that of the best typewriters.

level of detail. The extent to which all of the tags in the MARC format are included in a bibliographic record.

lightpen. The pen-shaped device with a photo cell at its end; used to read **barcoded labels**.

limited-distance modem (LDM). A modem used for connecting remote peripherals over short distances.

line drivers. Devices which boost an electronic signal.

line printer. A device that prints all of the characters of a line as a unit as contrasted with one character at a time.

linking. The affixing of barcode labels to library materials, calling up the associated bibliographic record, and scanning the barcode into the record.

listserv lists. Electronic discussion of technical and nontechnical issues conducted by electronic mail over BITNET using LISTSERV protocols. Similar lists, often using the UNIX readnews or rn facility, are available exclusively on the Internet. Internet users may subscribe to BITNET listservers. Participants subscribe via a central service, and lists often have a moderator who manages the information flow and content.

Local Area Network (LAN). A interconnected set of computer equipment and peripherals which allows data and resource sharing among the members of the LAN; a communications network that serves several users within a confined geographical area or a network of personal computers within a confined area made up of servers and workstations.

Mac-based. A micro configured on a Macintosh computer.

machine language. The only set of instructions that a computer can execute directly; code that designates the proper electrical states of the computer as combinations of "0"s and "1"s.

magnetic bubble memory. Very high capacity chips which use small cylindrical magnetic domains ("bubbles") which move over the surface of a magnetic film. The presence of a bubble corresponds to a "1" bit and the absence of a bubble to a "0" bit.

magnetic disk. Flat circular plate with a magnetic surface on which data can be stored by magnetization of parts of the surface.

magnetic disk. A storage medium consisting of a metal platter coated on both sides with a magnetic recording material upon which data is stored in the form of magnetized spots; suitable for direct-access processing.

magnetic drum. A cylinder with a magnetic outer surface on which data can be read or stored by magnetizing specific portions of the surface.

magnetic tape. A tape with magnetic surface on which machine-readable data can be stored.

magnetic tape transfer. Interfacing two computer systems by taking data off one computer by magnetic tape and loading it into another computer.

main storage. That which is directly accessed as opposed to that which is in auxiliary storage or secondary storage such as that on magnetic tape. See also **storage**.

mainframe. The **central processing unit** (CPU). Normally used to describe a large computer of the type operated by a municipality, academic institution, or other parent organization.

maintenance. Any activity to keep computer hardware or software running, including not only repairs, but also tests, adjustments and scheduled replacements.

management information. The data organized in such a way as to aid in the management of an enterprise. It usually consists of statistical cumulations.

management reports. The reports which a computer system can generate to provide management with information about a library's pattern and level of activity.

MARC (**MA**chine **R**eadable **C**ataloging). Initially a program of the Library of Congress in which machine-readable cataloging is distributed in LC format, but now a de facto standard for formatting and tagging bibliographic information in machine-readable form.

MARC compatibility. The ability to accept records in the MARC format. It does not necessarily mean the ability to retain and output records in the MARC format.

mass storage devices. Devices used to store large amounts of data; retrieval time is measured in seconds; offers cost advantages over disk storage, but is much slower than magnetic disk.

material types. Books, documents, periodicals, microforms, and phonodiscs are all material types.

MB (**M**ega**B**yte). A term normally used to describe the secondary **storage** capacity of a computer such as disks. Each megabyte is one million characters or numbers, or 1,048,576 bytes (1,024 x 1,024).

MCA (**M**icro **C**hannel **A**rchitecture). Made popular by IBM. The IBM PS/2 family of computers, based on a 386 processor, all have a Micro Channel Architecture. MCA "boards" will not fit or run in ISA computers.

MDA (**M**onochrome **D**isplay **A**dapter). Provides very sharp, readable text, but no graphics, on a monochrome screen.

media booking. An applications module which makes it possible to schedule the loan of audiovisual material days to months in advance.

megabyte. See **MB**.

memory. Same as **storage**. The location in the computer where data and programs may be stored. Memory may be considered to be internal (ROM), in memory chips or may be external or add-on and contained on floppy or hard disks.

memory controller. Device that regulates the reading of data from or to the main memory of a computer system.

menu. A list of choices that appears on the screen while a particular program is being executed.

metal oxide semiconductor. Process used to make LSI chips. MOS memories are slower than bipolar, but cost less to manufacture and have low power and heat dissipation requirements.

microcomputer. See **microprocessor**.

microprocessor. A complete computer processor on a single integrated-circuit chip approximately the size of a dime. (1) An integral piece of hardware, a microchip, which performs the logic functions of a digital computer. (2) A piece of hardware that houses the computing parts of a computer on one circuit board and in one set of integrated circuits. The microprocessor does not contain the 1/0 interfaces and memory unit.

microsecond. One-millionth of a second.

microwave. A telecommunications technology which uses radio signals to send data from one station to another along a line of sight; highly sensitive to weather and other environmental influence.

migration path. Ability to move applications to the next level of computer (faster, bigger) without modification.

MIIS/MUMPS. A higher level programming language and database management system developed for medical records and used in some automated library systems in the past.

millisecond. One-thousandth of a second.

minicomputer. A physically compact digital device that has a **central processing unit**, at least one input/output device and a primary storage capacity of at least 4,000 characters.

Mode 1. CD-ROM using error correction. This will result in less information being stored on the CD-ROM disc, usually around 540 megabytes.

Mode 2. CD-ROM using no correction. This results in greater storage capacities, 640–680 megabytes.

modem. An abbreviation for modulator-demodulator. A device that allows one computer to communicate with another over telephone lines.

modular approach. A method used in structured programming which emphasizes working from a general structure of a program to smaller logical sections (called modules) which perform the required functions of the program.

monitor. The screen display device of a computer. Sometimes also called a **CRT**.

MOS. See **Metal oxide semiconductor**.

mouse. A special kind of peripheral device for CPU data manipulation purposes. It is so called because it is shaped something like a mouse and may have two switches on top resembling eyes. Some application programs from the IBM use mouse technology, although it has become popularized primarily by its use in the Macintosh computer.

MPC—Multimedia (PC). MPC is a trademark of the Multimedia Personal Computer Council. It is used to identify software and computer systems compatible with the MPC specifications. A multimedia PC consists of five basic components. a PC (80386), a CD-ROM drive, an audio or sound board, Microsoft Windows with Multimedia Extensions, and a set of speakers or headphones for audio output. Note. Microsoft Windows version 3.1 has the multimedia extensions built-in.

MS-DOS (**M**icrosoft **D**isk **O**perating **S**ystem). An operating system for computers that use the 8088 or higher microprocessor.

MS-DOS CD-ROM extensions. A software program developed by Microsoft that allows CD-ROM discs that adhere to the High Sierra or ISO 9660 standards to be accessed as if they were a very large DOS drive. CD-ROM applications that require MS-DOS CD-ROM Extensions are generally compatible with any CD-ROM drive. This program is usually supplied with the CD-ROM drive.

multidrop channel. Single communications line shared by several devices. One end of the line is connected to a communications controller. The line may be used by only one device at a time.

multifunction. An applications software package which includes several modules, usually acquisitions, serials control, circulation, and online patron access catalog.

multimedia. Multimedia CD-ROM applications include a minimum of three elements. text, still pictures, or drawings and sound. Moving pictures, animation, and computer sounds are other elements of multimedia. Note. some multimedia applications export sound through the audio jack on the CD-ROM drive and therefore do not require a sound card.

multiplexor. Device used in data communications which permits several devices to share a single transmission line.

multiprocessor system. A computer which has more than one processor.

multitasking. Procedures in which several separate but interrelated computer tasks (i.e., creating a word processing document and updating a database) operate under a single program identity.

multiuser. A system which supports several users at the same time.

nanosecond. 1/1,000,000,000 of a second.

near letter quality. Produces output that resembles the print of a cloth-ribbon typewriter.

network. A number of communication lines connecting a computer with remote terminals or with other computers; a set of computers connected together.

network layer. Layer three of the seven layer Open System Interconnection Reference Model. One of the two layers at which TCP/IP operates.

NIC (**Network Information Center**). A NIC provides administrative support, user support, and information services for a network.

nodes. Every point on a network at which there is a computer.

NREN. The National Research and Education Network is a proposed national computer network to be built upon the foundation of the NSF backbone network, NSFnet. NREN would provide high speed interconnection between other national and regional networks. SB 1067 is the legislative bill proposing NREN.

OCLC MARC. OCLC's implementation of the MARC format.

OCR. Optical character recognition or a type font that can be read by both humans and machines. The best known is OCR-A, the type approved by the National Retail Merchants Association. An OCR wand is a device, when passed over the special type font, "reads" the data into the machine.

off-line. Equipment or storage not under control of the **central processing unit**.

online. Equipment or storage under the control of the **central processing unit** so that a use can interact directly with the computer.

online database services. A service bureau such as Dialog which provides access to databases.

online reference services. An online database service which offers a service suitable for end users to access without a skilled intermediary.

OPAC. An acronym for Online Patron Access Catalog, which is a computerized library catalog.

open operating systems. An operating system which is supported on a wide range of hardware platforms, rather than on only one manufacturer's.

open system. System that is not dependent on a specific hardware platform so that applications from different vendors will work on the system.

Open Systems Interconnection (OSI). This is the evolving international standard under development at ISO (International Standards Organization) for the interconnection of cooperative computer systems. An open system is one that conforms to OSI standards in its communications with other systems.

Open Systems Interconnection (OSI) Reference Model. Networking interface model developed by the International Standards Organization which allows disparate computer systems to communicate.

OpenVMS. Digital's proprietary operating system, but with POSIX compliance so that it looks like an open system on a network.

operating system. A collection of programs (software) designed to permit a computer system to manage itself and to avoid idle CPU time while increasing utilization of computer facilities; software that controls the basic internal functions of a computer and enables it to run a variety of applications (examples. UNIX, MS-DOS, MVS).

optical disc. A high-density storage device that uses lasers to create patterns to represent information. A CD-ROM disc.

OSI. See **Operating Systems Interconnection**.

output. The term used to describe information that comes out of a computer as a result of processing; the information that a computer generates as a result of its calculations.

parallel. A connection of different wires to reach the same destination. This type of connection is faster than serial.

parallel processing. Concurrent or simultaneous execution of two or more processes in multiple devices.

parameterization. The use of parameters or tables in applications software so libraries can adapt the software to their use by setting parameters or selecting from tables.

PASCAL. A computer language developed by Niklaus Wirth. PASCAL is touted as a modern, structured, standard, and transportable language. It is structured, but neither as standard nor transportable as adherents would claim. A standard PASCAL does exist, but lacks sufficient power for most uses.

password. A symbol a person gives when first beginning to use the system to identify him/her or to provide access to restricted functions.

patron file. The file of names and addresses in a computer.

PC-based. A micro configured around a PC.

PC-DOS. DOS distributed by IBM with its computers. Now better known as MS-DOS.

peripheral equipment. Anything other than the **central processing unit** that provides the system with external communication.

personal computer (PC). A computer with a single processor board.

Photo CD. A consumer CD product which allows camera photos to be stored on a single CD. It requires a special Photo CD drive that can be hooked up to a TV to display the photos.

physical layer. The lowest layer of the seven-layer Open Systems Interconnection Reference Model. The level at which physical connectivity is detailed.

PICK. Proprietary operating system which incorporates a database facility.

pipelining. In RISC-type computers the ability to separate a problem into several components so that each goes through a separate pipe so they can be worked on concurrently.

PIXEL. A picture element within a monitor which is made up of single dots of light. They are grouped together to create images or graphics. The higher the resolution of the monitor, the greater the number of pixels it will contain.

PL/1. Program Language One; a general-purpose language used for both business and scientific functions.

plenum. The space between the ceiling and the floor above it.

pointer. An **address** or other way of indicating location.

polling. A technique by which each of the **terminals** or computers sharing a communications line is queried to get information.

port. That part of the central processing unit which provides a channel for receiving or sending data from or to a remote device. More than one such device may be put on a port.

portability. Ability to transfer a computer program or application from one computer environment or hardware platform to another.

presentation layer. The sixth layer of the seven-layer Open System Interconnection Reference Model. The layer at which the standards for control of the user interface are detailed.

primary memory. The main memory of a computer.

primary storage unit. Also known as internal memory, this section of the CPU holds instructions, data, and intermediate as well as final results during processing.

printer. An output device that converts machine code into readable impressions on paper or microform.

printer port interface. The port on a computer at which a printer is attached.

process. A single computer task.

program. A series of instructions for computer actions to perform a task or series of tasks.

programmer. The individual who writes step-by-step instructions for the computer to carry out.

programming language. The language in which the applications software is written, such as COBOL or "C."

prompting or **prompts.** A function that tells a **terminal** user what to do next or asks what he or she wants to do next.

proprietary operating system. A computer operating system developed by a computer manufacturer and usually unique to its machines.

protocol. A mutually determined set of formats and procedures governing the exchange of information between systems.

public domain. A computer program not covered by any kind of copyright.

public domain. A repository of material that is not protected by copyright and so is free to be used without permission.

query. A specific request for data or instructions in a computerized DBMS.

queue. A waiting line under either in the order received or in another order previously determined.

RAM. See **Random Access Memory**.

Random Access Memory (RAM). Storage technique in which time required to retrieve data is independent of location. Random access memory can be read from and written into by the user.

RDBMS. See **Relational database management systems**.

read. Process of transferring data from an input device or an auxiliary storage device to a computer.

Read Only Memory (ROM). Storage technique in which instructions or data in memory can be accessed but not altered by the user. Used to store interpreters, monitors, etc. Semiconductor memory that contain prewritten programs or data. The content of ROM circuits is permanent, while the content of random access memory (RAM) is volatile.

real-time processing. Provision of data at the time a user is at a terminal so those responses may be used in further queries.

reboot. To restart a computer, that is, turn it off and then on again or by pressing a special key sequence such as Ctrl+Alt+Del on MS-DOS computers.

record. A collection of related items of data treated as a unit. The author, title, and call number fields may constitute the item record in a circulation system; a group of related fields of information treated as a single unit.

record length. A measure of the size of a record, usually in characters.

record structure. The way records are stored in a system.

recording density. Number of bits per inch or number of bits per cubic inch.

register. High speed memory used for arithmetic and logical operations, address indexing, subroutine linkage and, in some cases, as a program counter and stack pointer.

Relational Database Management Systems (RDMS). Database management system that allows data to be accessed based on relationship set up among several database files.

release. A periodic revision of software that is distributed to all customers of a circulation system vendor.

remote access. The ability to access a computer from outside a building in which it is housed, or outside the library. Remote access requires communications hardware, software, and actual physical links, although this can be as simple as common carrier (telephone) lines or as complex as a TELNET login to another computer across the Internet.

remote database. A database which is accessible from a library, but retained outside it.

remote peripheral. A device such as a terminal, micro, lightpen, or printer which is connected to a computer remote from it using an RS-232 interface.

report generator. Applications software which facilitates the designing of reports which have not already been coded into the software package.

resist. Photographic-type emulsion, sensitive to ultraviolet light, which is used as a coating in the production of integrated chips.

resolution. A measure of the sharpness of the images a printer or screen can produce. The higher the resolution, the sharper the image or graphic.

response time. The time between the entry of a query and the beginning of the response on the screen, printer or other output device.

ring topology. A local area network structure which looks like a ring as opposed to a bus (straight line) or a star.

RISC (**R**educed **I**nstruction **S**et **C**omputing). A simplified computer design which uses pipelining and many registers to facilitate throughput.

riser. The vertical network cabling in a building.

RLIN MARC. RLIN's implementation of the MARC format.

ROM. See **Read Only Memory**.

root directory. The main directory of a disk containing files and/or sub-directories.

scanners. A device which can read barcode or other labels without actually touching the label. Most use infrared light beams or a laser.

SCSI (**S**mall **C**omputer **S**ystems **I**nterface). Pronounced "scuzzy." A standard bus for connecting devices such as disk drives to computers.

SCSI-2. Pronounced "scuzzy two." SCSI-2 is a 16-bit implementation of the original eight-bit SCSI bus. SCSI-2 uses a superset of the SCSI commands. SCSI-2 has a "disconnect-reconnect" feature which increases performance with networked CD-ROM drives.

search. To examine a number of items in order to find one or more that meet the characteristics or properties specified.

search key. The data entered in for the conducting of the **search**.

secondary storage. Also known as external or auxiliary storage; supplements primary storage but operates at slower speeds.

sector. Data on a CD-ROM disc is stored in sectors of 2,352 bytes. Every sector contains its own error detection and correction coding, and has its own unique address on the disk. The smallest addressable unit of a disc's track.

seek. To seek is to read back data from a CD-ROM disc in an attempt to find a particular file or piece of information. Because seeking on a CD-ROM is time-consuming when compared to magnetic disks, the number of seeks required to find the desired information is an important determinant of overall CD-ROM system performance.

semiconductor. A material which has low resistance in one direction and high resistance in the opposite direction. This difference in resistance makes possible the use of semiconductors for computer logic circuits and memory.

sequential search. The examination of each item in the order in which the items are arranged on the **disk** or other **storage** medium. The method is most suitable for such **records** as patron names and addresses.

serial. A single wire connection used to carry data. This is slower than a parallel connection.

serial transmission. Data transmission in which individual bits of a character or word are transmitted one after the other over the same channel.

session layer. The fifth layer of the seven-layer Open System Interconnection Reference Model.

shared logic. Situation in which a control facility supplies the logic and utilizes dumb or intelligent terminals to access the central computing facility.

shareware. (1) A software that is copyrighted but can be distributed free of charge to anyone. (2) Microcomputer software, distributed through public domain channels, for which the author expects to receive compensation.

shift register. Register in which stored data can be shifted to the right or left.

side printers. A printer which is attached to a PC or terminal and prints that which is on the screen.

simplex channel. Channel that transmits data in one direction only.

simulate. To represent features of the behavior of one system by another, such as using a large computer to simulate the behavior of a minicomputer for the purpose of testing **software** or the effect of a specific number of **terminals**.

single processor system. A computer which contains only one processor. Usually a PC or a Mac.

site license. A software license that allows unlimited copying of a computer program for use by a single organization at a specified site.

slaves. Remote peripherals which have no control over the presentation or user interface, but rely on the host computer.

SMTP (**s**imple **m**ail **t**ransmission **p**rotocol). The electronic mail protocol used on the Internet.

Software. A set of programs, procedures and documentation concerned with the operation of a computer system.

software package. A set of standardized computer programs, procedures, and related documentation necessary to solve problems of a specific application (e.g., an inventory control package).

SOS. Silicon-on-Sapphire. Refers to layers of material that achieve high speeds using MOS technology; this is done by insulating circuit components from each other.

sound card. A special sound board installed in a computer that adds sound capability to the computer. This is usually done to comply with the MPC specifications for running multimedia CD-ROMs.

spell-check. A software program which compares words against a stored dictionary and highlights potential spelling errors.

spike. A temporary, sharp increase in signal or voltage.

SQL. See **Structured Query Language**.

stand-alone. A computer system that is capable of performing all the specified functions without the help of another computer, such as is necessary in a **distributed processing system**.

standard. Rule established to improve the quality of various aspects of information system development and operation. A standard may be laid down by a statutory body or created by a major manufacturer's practice.

standing order. An order for all works in a series, all volumes of a set, or all editions of a work.

star topology. A local area network cabling structure which looks like a star.

static memory. Memory that retains its values in the event of power failure. Also termed "nonvolatile" memory. Volatile memory loses its values in the event of a power failure. Core memory, based on magnetism, is an example of nonvolatile memory; semiconductor memory, based on electrical current, is volatile.

storage. The memory of a computer. The device in which data is held for later retrieval and use. See also **main storage**.

store-and-forward switching. Channel allocation technique in which the whole message is transmitted to the next node and stored there in a queue until the proper outgoing circuit is available, then transmitted to the next node.

STP (**s**hielded **t**wisted **p**air). Wiring which has a cladding around it to protect it against adverse environmental conditions.

streaming. Process by which data are written on magnetic tape, interjecting inter-record gaps after each data block is written without starting and stopping the tape drive between blocks of data.

Structured Query Language (SQL). A nonprocedural language, developed by IBM, designed for the creation, maintenance, and manipulation of relational databases. SQL statements allow the easy manipulation of data in large groups as well as by individual elements. In 1987, SQL became an ANSI standard and was adopted by IBM as the database language standard for its System Application Architecture (SAA).

sub directory. A disk directory that is stored in another directory.

subfield. The subdivision of a field in a record.

super VGA (SVGA). The next step above VGA, capable of displaying 256 colors at resolutions of 640X480 or greater.

supermicro. A powerful micro which has more than one processor. Almost always one which uses an multiuser operating system.

supported software. Applications software which the vendor continues to maintain and enhance for a fee.

surge. A dramatic AC power line change that can damage computer circuitry.

surge protector. Absorbs brief bursts of excess voltage coming in from an AC power line.

synchronous transmission. Block transmission wherein blocks of characters are sent in a continuous stream without each character being framed between start and stop bits. An internal clocking mechanism within the modem is required to synchronize sender and receiver.

system. A set of interrelated parts that work together to achieve an overall objective.

systems analyst. The communication link or interface between users and technical persons (such as computer programmers and operators).

system console. A terminal or micro which has access to the computer's system software and to system parameters.

system program. A sequence of instructions written to coordinate the operation of all computer circuitry and to help the computer run fast and efficiently.

system software. The software which controls the operation of the computer, including the operating system, program utilities, and database management system.

tag. A numeric or alphanumeric label which identifies a field and allows software to retrieve records which contain the tag.

tagging conventions. The rules for assigning tags to fields.

target market. The specific market a vendor has chosen to which to market a product.

TCP/IP (Transmission Control Protocol/Internet Protocol). A combined set of protocols that performs the transfer of data between two computers. TCP monitors and ensures correct transfer of data. IP receives the data from TCP, breaks it up into packets, and ships it off to a network within the Internet. TCP/IP is also used as a name for a protocol suite that incorporates these functions and others.

telnet. A portion of the TCP/IP suite of software protocols that handles terminals. Among other functions, it allows a user to log in to a remote computer from the user's local computers.

teleprocessing monitors. Programs which manage telecommunications traffic over a network of communications channels.

terminal. A point in the computer system at which data can be entered or withdrawn.

terminal emulation. Most communications software packages will permit your personal computer or workstation to communicate with another computer or network as if it were a specific type of terminal directly connected to that computer or network.

terminal server. A machine that connects terminals to a network by providing host TELNET service.

throughput. The total amount of work a computer system performs in a specified time period.

time-division multiplexing. Technique in which two or more signals are sent on the same channel using different time intervals.

time sharing. A method of using a computer system to allow a number of users to execute programs at the same time, with the system servicing them in such rapid sequence that the users appear to be handled simultaneously.

TN3270. A version of TELNET providing IBM full-screen support.

tracks. A term used to describe the concentric circles on the surface of a magnetic disk upon which data is represented by magnetized spots (bits). A storage channel on a disk or tape. The track on a CD-ROM disc is actually one continuous three-mile-long spiral beginning in the center of the disc and traveling outward. Adjacent turns of the track are 1.6 microns apart.

transaction processing. The running of a sequence of database operations as a single unit of work.

transfer time. Amount of time required to transmit data from one storage device to another storage or display device.

transistor. Semiconductor with three electrodes. The current between one pair of electrodes is a function of the current between the other pair. Transistors are used for switching or amplification of a signal.

Transmission Control Protocol/Internet Protocol. See **TCP/IP**.

transparent. Something which is not visible or apparent to a user.

transport layer. The fourth layer of the seven-layer Open System Interconnection Reference Model. One of the two layers at which TCP/IP functions.

truncate. To terminate a process or to shorten **fields** according to previously established rules.

turnkey. The provision of a complete system by a vendor, including equipment, software and training.

turnkey system. A system which is offered by a vendor which bundles hardware, software, installation, and training at a single price.

UNIX. Operating system developed by AT&T Bell Laboratories which is portable to a wide variety of computers, including mainframes, minicomputers, and microcomputers. There are different versions of UNIX, developed by different manufacturers. These include. XENIX (Microsoft Corp.), ULTRIX (Digital Equipment Corporation), and DYNIX (Sequent Computer Systems).

update. To modify a file with current information.

UPS (uninterruptable power supply). Hardware which protects a system against power problems, including surges, spikes, brownouts, and blackouts.

USMARC. Generic name for MARC bibliographic formats in the United States, principally LC MARC from the Library of Congress, but also OCLC MARC, RLIN MARC, and WLN MARC (among others).

utilities. Programs that assist in the operations of a computer but do not do the main work.

utility programs. Programs, often supplied by the manufacturer, for executing standard operations such as sorting, merging, reformatting data, renaming files, comparing files.

variable-length record. A file in which the **records** need not be uniform in length but are only as long as the amount of data warrants.

VDU (**v**isual **d**isplay **u**nit). See **CRT**.

Veronica. The full-text search engine for searching Gopherspace.

VGA (**V**ideo **G**ate **A**rray). The video circuit built into the PS/2 model 50 and higher. It provides high-resolution graphics modes and crisp text as well as emulation of the CGA, EGA, and MDA. Many new CD-ROM programs require VGA capability to access the graphics. A VGA monitor and VGA card must be used in these instances.

video card. A plug-in circuit board that enables a computer to display information on a particular type of monitor.

videodisk. Disk on which optical images may be stored. Videodisks are often written and read using laser beams.

virtual memory. Space on secondary storage devices that appears to the computer user as main storage. The instructions and data required by a program are divided into segments and only the necessary segments are brought into main memory at any one time.

volatile. Becoming erased or destroyed when power is cut off.

WAIS (**W**ide **A**rea **I**nformation **S**ervers). A system of fully-indexed client/server distributed databases on the Net, using a system called relevance feedback for using successful searches as a model for additional searches.

WAN (**W**ide **A**rea **N**etwork). In communications, a network that interconnects users regardless of geographical boundaries, such as cities and states.

Web server. A server which stores records in the HTML protocol for access from Web browsers such as Netscape.

WebPAC. A patron access catalog device which has a Web browser such as Netscape built into it.

Wide Area Network. See **WAN**.

Winchester Disk. Large capacity, high density, magnetic disk with sealed head-to-disk assembly that is nonremovable. These disks are highly reliable.

World Wide Web. See **WWW**.

word. The number of bits a computer's control unit can retrieve from the primary memory at one time.

workstation. A powerful single processor computer which can perform applications which require a great deal of memory.

WORM (Write Once, Read Many). This is an optical disk where a computer can save information once, then read that information, but cannot change it. In contrast, with a CD-ROM disc the computer can only read information that has been provided by the supplier of the disc.

write. Process of transferring data from a computer to an output device or to auxiliary storage devices.

Write Once, Read Many. See **WORM**.

write protect. To prevent a floppy disk from accidentally being written over. The process of applying a covering (these are metallic strips that are usually provided in a box of floppy disks) over the notch located on the upper right side of a disk.

WWW (World Wide Web). A system of client/server distributed databases using hypertext links to navigate from one information server to another.

Z39. American National Standards Committee Z39, formed in 1940. The standards committee devoted to libraries, information science, and publishing. ANSC Z39 became NISO (Z39), the National Information Standards Organization, in 1984.

Z39.50. A United States-based protocol (with international OSI counterparts) that provides for the exchange of information, such as full-text or catalog records, between dissimilar computer systems.

Z39.50 protocol. Name of the national standard developed by the National Information Standards Organization (NISO) that defines an applications level protocol by which one computer can query another computer and transfer result records, using a canonical format. This protocol provides the framework for OPAC users to search remote catalogs on the Internet using the commands of their own local systems. Projects are now in development to provide Z39.50 support for catalogs on the Internet. SR (Search and Retrieval), ISO Draft International Standard 10162/10163 is the international version of Z39.50.

Z39.50 server. A computer which has the server side of the Z39.50 interface software loaded on it.

Bibliography

Advances in Library Automation and Networking, Volume 1, 1987; a research annual; editor: Joe A. Hewitt. JAI Press, 1987.

American National Standards Institute. *Volume and File Structure of CD-ROM for Information Exchange.* Approved January 16, 1990 by the American National Standards Institute/developed by the National Information Standards Organization. New Brunswick, NJ: Transaction Publishers, 1993.

American National Standards Institute, Accredited Standards Committee, X12. *X12/DISA Information Manual.* Alexandria, VA: Data Interchange Standards Association, Inc. (DISA). Summer 1994.

Anders, Vicki. *Automated Information Retrieval in Libraries: a Management Handbook.* New York: Greenwood Press, 1992.

Association of Research Libraries, Office of Management Studies. *Barcoding of Collections in ARL Libraries.* Association of Research Libraries, Office of Management Studies, 1986.

Aumente, Jerome. *New Electronic Pathways; Videotex, Teletext, and Online Databases.* Sage Publications, 1987.

Avedon, Don M., *Computer Output Microfilm.* 2nd ed., N.M.A. Reference Series, no. 4. Silver Spring, MD: National Microfilm Association, 1971.

Barber, David. "Electronic Commerce in Library Acquisitions with a Survey of Bookseller and Subscription Agency Services." *Library Technology Reports* 31(5), September–October 1995.

Benson, Peter. "EDI and the Internet," *Internet Systems*, May, 1996, pp. 29–32.

Bernstein, Judith, ed. *Turnkey Automated Circulation Systems: Aids to Libraries in the Marketplace.* Chicago: American Library Association, LAMA, 1980.

Berst, Jesse. "10 Pitfalls to Avoid in Buying a Small Computer System." *Interactive Computing*, May/June 1981, pp. 4–9.

Besser, Howard. "Adding an Image Database to an Existing Library and Computer Environment: Design and Technical Considerations." pp. 31–45 in *Studies in Multimedia: State-of-the-Art Solutions in Multimedia and Hypertext*, edited by Susan Stone and Michael Buckland. Medford, NJ: Learned Information, 1992.

205

Bierman, Kenneth John. *Alternatives to Card Catalogs for Large Libraries: The Current State of Planning and Implementation.* Final Report to the Council on Library Resources Fellowship Project, June 1975. Washington, DC: Council on Library Resources, 1975.

Boss, Richard W. "Accessing Electronic Publications in Complex LAN Environments," *Library Technology Reports* 28(3), May/June 1992.

————. *Automating Library Acquisitions: Issues and Outlook.* White Plains, NY: Knowledge Industry Publications, Inc., 1982.

————. "Automated Circulation Control Systems." *Library Technology Reports* 18, March/April 1982.

————. "Client/Server Technology for Libraries with a Survey of Current Vendor Offerings," *Library Technology Reports* 30(6), November/December 1994.

————. "Facilities Planning for Technology," *Library Technology Reports*, 31(4), July/August 1995.

————. "Imaging for Libraries and Information Centers," *Library Technology Reports*, 28(6), November/December 1992.

————. *Information Technology and Space Planning for Libraries and Information Centers.* Boston: G.K. Hall & Co., 1990.

————. "Interfacing Automated Library Systems." *Library Technology Reports* 20, September–October 1984: 615–703.

————. *The Library Manager's Guide to Automation, 3rd Edition.* White Plains, NY: Knowledge Industry Publications, Inc., 1990.

————. "Online Catalog Functionality in the 90s: Vendor Responses to a Model RFP," *Library Technology Reports* 29(5), September/October 1993.

————. "The Procurement of Library Automated Systems," *Library Technology Reports*, 26(5), September/October 1990.

————. "The Procurement of an Automated Library System with a Model RFP." *Library Technology Reports*, 30(3), May/June 1994.

————. "Technical Services Functionality in Integrated Library Systems." *Library Technology Reports*, 28(1), January/February 1992.

————. "Technical Services Functionality in Integrated Library Systems." *Library Technology Reports*, 31(6), November/December 1995.

Boss, Richard W. and M. Casey. "Operating Systems for Automated Library Systems," *Library Technology Reports*, 27(2), March/April 1991.

Boss, Richard W. and S. Harrison. "The Online Patron Access Catalog: The Keystone to Library Automation." *Library Technology Reports* 25(5), September/October 1989.

Boss, Richard W. and J. McQueen. "The Uses of Automation and Related Technologies by Domestic Books and Serials Jobbers." *Library Technology Reports*, 25(2), March/April 1989.

Brownrigg, Edward B. and J. Michael Bruer. "Automated Turnkey Systems in the Library: Prospects and Perils." *Library Trends* 24: 727–36 (April, 1976).

Bruer, J. Michael. "The Public Relations Component of Circulation System Implementation." *Journal of Library Automation* 12 (September 1979): 214–218.

Bruntjen, S. and Hall, S.D. "Attempting to Automate: Lessons Learned over Five Years at the Pittsburgh Regional Library Center." *Advances in Library Administration and Organization*, volume 4, 1985. JAI Press,1985, pp. 177–92.

Buckland, M. 1992. *Redesigning Library Services: A Manifesto*. Chicago: American Library Association. (ERIC ED367317XSP)

Burton, P.F. and Petrie, J.H. *The Librarian's Guide to Microcomputers for Information Management*. Van Nostrand Reinhold, 1986.

Cage, Mary Crystal. "The Virtual Library." *Chronical of Higher Education* 41(4):A23+, Sept 21, 1994.

Cawkell, A. E. "Selected Aspects of Image Processing and Management: Review and Future Prospects." *Journal of Information Science* 18:179–92, 1992.

CD-ROM Local Area Networks: A User's Guide. Edited by Norman Desmarais. (Supplements to Computers in Libraries; 24.) Westport, CT: Meckler, 1991.

Chachra, V. "A Perspective on Linking Multimedia Digital Libraries." *Information Technology and Libraries* 11(1):41–42, March, 1992.

Changing Technology and Education for Librarianship and Information Science. Edited by Basil Stuart-Stubbs. JAI Press, 1985.

Clarke, A. *The British Library's Compact Disc Experiment*. British Library, 1986.

Clayton, M. *Managing Library Automation*. Gower, 1987. Clinic on Library Applications of Data Processing, Urbana, IL, 1972. Proceedings: Applications of Minicomputers to Library and Related Problems. Edited by F. Wilfrid Lancaster. Urbana, IL: University of Illinois Graduate School of Library Science, 1974.

Cohen, E. and Cohen A. *Automation, Space Management, and Productivity; A Guide for Libraries*. Bowker, 1982.

Corbin, J.B. *Developing Computer-Based Library Systems*. Oryx Press, 1981.

Cortez, E.M. *Proposals and Contracts for Library Automation: Guidelines for Preparing RFPs*. Pacific Information; American Library Association, 1987.

Costs and Benefits of Automating Library Processes in Small and Medium-sized Libraries; studies initiated by the Alberta Culture Library Directors' Council and jointly funded by Alberta Advanced Education, Alberta Culture, and Alberta Education; carried out by LMG, the Library Management Group, Inc., New Westminster, BC, 1983.

Cowley, R. *ALS, A Guide for Librarians and Systems Managers*. Gower, 1988.

Crawford, W. *Technical Standards: An Introduction for Librarians*. White Plains, NY: Knowledge Industry Publications, 1986. (ISBN 0-86729-192-3)

Crawford, W. *MARC for Library Use; Understanding the USMARC Formats*. Knowledge Industry Publications Inc., 1984.

Cronin, M.J. and Kirk, J.H. "Bibliographic Database Searching; The Use and Cost of a Free Service." (In Academic Libraries; Myths and Realities. Association of College & Research Libraries, 1984, pp. 352–6).

DeGennaro, Richard. *Libraries, Technology, and the Information Marketplace.*, G.K. Hall & Co., 1987.

DeGennaro, Richard. "Library Automation: Changing Patterns and New Directions." *Library Journal* 101: 175–83 (January 1, 1976).

Divilbiss, J. L., ed. *Negotiating for Computer Services.* Proceedings of the 1977 Clinic on Library Applications of Data Processing. Urbana, IL: University of Illinois, Graduate School of Library Science, 1978. (ERIC Document Reproduction No. ED 167 078).

Dowlin, K.E. *The Electronic Library; the Promise and the Process.* Neal-Schuman, 1984.

Dunlap, Connie R. "Mechanization of Acquisitions Processes." *Advances in Librarianship.* Edited by Melvin John Voight. New York: Academic Press, 1970. vol. 1, pp. 35–57.

Elshami, Ahmed M. *CD-ROM Technology for Information Managers.* Chicago: American Library Association, 1990.

The Emerging Virtual Research Library. Washington, D.C.: Association of Research Libraries, Office of Management Services. (Association of Research Libraries. Systems and Procedures Exchange Center SPEC flyer; no. 186). 1992.

Eyre, J.J. "Uses and Limitations of Computers in Libraries." (In *Aspects of Library Development Planning.* Mansell, 1983.)

Feher, Kamilo. *Digital Communication, Facilities, Networks and System Design.* New York: Wiley, 1978.

Fischer, A. and Swora, T. Library of Congress Optical Disk Pilot Program. Optical Disk Print Pilot Project; print project document preparation and input report, phase 1. September 1984–December 1985. Library of Congress, 1986.

Fundamentals of Computer Output Microfilm. Silver Spring, MD: National Microfilm Association, 1974.

"The Future is NOW: Changing Library Paradigms." *Computers in Libraries,* 14(5), May 1994:43.

Greenberg, Esther. *Innovative Designs for Acquisitions and Cataloging Departments as a Result of Library Automation.* Cleveland: Case Western Reserve University, School of Library Science, 1974. ED 096 993.

Harris, Virginia B.; Frohmberg, Katherine; and Moffett, William A. *Research on the Impact of a Computerized Circulation System on the Performance of a Large College Library.* Oberlin College, Ohio, 1979. (NTIS Report. PB80-137938).

Hildreth, Charles R. *Library Automation and Networking in North America: A Reassessment of the Impact of New Technologies on Networking.* R.R. Bowker, 1988.

Horsnell, Verini. "International Standards." *Library and Information Briefings*, 1988 Cumulation (116–127). London: British Library, 1989. (ISBN 0-9512412-2-2).

Horsnell, Verini. "The State of the Art in the Field of Documentation and Librarianship in Great Britain." *Librarianship and Bibliography Abroad* 115 (1987): 32–49.

Housley, T., *Data Communications and Teleprocessing Systems*. Englewood Cliffs, NJ: Prentice-Hall, 1979.

Hsu, John Y. *Computer Networks: Architecture, Protocols and Software*. Boston, MA: Artech House Publishers, 1996. (ISBN 0-89006-852-6).

Hull, Philip and Porter, S. "Use of COM and OCR in the Guelph Cataloging Systems," *The LARC Reports* (Computerized Cataloging Systems Series) 1: 95–103 (1974).

Hunter, E.J. *Computerized Cataloguing*. Bingley, 1985.

Hunter, Rhonda N. 1991. "Successes and Failures of Patrons Searching the Online Catalog at a Large Academic Library: A Transaction Log Analysis." *RQ* 30(3):395–402.

Hyatt, J.A. and Santiago, A.A. *University Libraries in Transition*. National Association of College & University Business Officers, 1987.

Insider's Guide to Library Automation: Essays of Practical Experience. Edited by John W. Head and Gerard B. McCabe. Westport, CT: Greenwood Press, 1993.

International Organization for Standardization. *Access to Standards Information*. Geneva: International Organization for Standardization, 1986. (ISBN 92-67-10118-8).

International Organization for Standardization. *ISO Catalogue of Standards* (Annual). Geneva: International Organization for Standardization. (ISBN 92-67-01074-3).

International Organization for Standardization. *ISO Standards Handbook: Documentation and Information*, 3rd edition. Geneva: International Organization for Standardization, 1988. (ISBN 92-67-10144-7).

International Organization for Standardization. *ISO/IEC Directives—Part 1 Procedures for the Technical Work*, 2nd edition. Geneva: International Organization for Standardization, 1992. (ISBN 92-67-10173-0).

International Organization for Standardization. *ISO/IEC Directives—Part 2 Methodology for the Development of International Standards*, 2nd edition. Geneva: International Organization for Standardization, 1992. (ISBN 92-67-10174-9).

International Organization for Standardization. *ISO/IEC Directives—Part 3 Drafting and Presentation of International Standards*, 3rd edition. Geneva: International Organization for Standardization, 1993. (ISBN 92-67-10170-0).

International Organization for Standardization. *Standardization and Documentation*. Geneva: International Organization for Standardization, 1983. (ISBN 92-67-10071-8).

Kamilo, F. *Digital Communication*. Englewood Cliffs, NJ: Prentice-Hall, 1981.

Kearney, J.M., and Mitutuinovich, J.S. *A Guide to Successful Computer System Selection*. Park Ridge, IL: Data Processing Management Association, 1976.

Kennedy, James H. and Sokoloski, James S. "Man-Machine Considerations of an Operational On-Line University Library Acquisitions System." American Society for Information Science, Annual Meeting, 33rd, Philadelphia, October 11–15, 1970. Proceedings. Washington, DC, 1970. vol. 7, pp. 65–67.

Kessler, Jack. *Internet Digital Libraries: The International Dimension*. Boston, MA: Artech House Publishers, 1996. (ISBN 0-89006-875-5).

Khoshafian, S. et al. 1988. "Parallel Query Processing of Complex Objects." *Procedings from the Fourth International Conference of Data Engineering*, (February):202–209.

King Research Inc., *Alternatives for Future Library Catalogs: A Cost Model*. Rockville, MD: King Research, 1980.

Kuo, F., ed., *Protocols and Techniques for Data Communication Networks*. Englewood Cliffs, NJ: Prentice-Hall, 1981.

Kwasnik, Barbara H. 1992. "The Functional Components of Browsing." *Annual Review of OCLC Research*, July 1991–July 1992:53–6. Dublin, Ohio: OCLC.

Lancaster, F. Wilfrid, ed. *Problems and Failures in Library Automation*. Proceedings of the 1978 Clinic on Library Applications of Data Processing. Urbana, IL: University of Illinois, Graduate School of Library Science, 1979. (ERIC Document Reproduction No. ED 174 223).

LARC Association. *A Survey of Automated Activities in the Libraries of the World*. Tempe, AZ, 1971- (World Survey Series) Vol. 1 *Survey of Automated Activities in the Libraries of the United States*. Vols. 9–10 Bibliography of Literature on Planned or Implemented Automated Library Projects.

LARC Institute on Acquisitions Systems and Subsystem, Lake Geneva, WI, May 25–26, 1972. Proceedings. Edited by H. William Axford. Tempe, AZ: LARC Association, 1973.

Library LANS: Case Studies in Practice and Application. Edited by Marshall Breeding. (Supplements to Computers in Libraries; 39.) Westport, CT: Meckler, c1992.

The Library Microcomputer Environment; Management Issues. Edited by Sheila S. Intner and Jane Anne Hannigan. Oryx Press, 1988.

Library Technical Services; Operations and Management. Edited by Irene P. Godden. Academic Press, 1984.

Lynch, Clifford A. and C.M. Preston. "Internet Access to Information Resources," *Annual Review of Information Science and Technology (ARIST)*, Vol. 25 (NY 1990): 271–293.

Madden. Mary A. *Minicomputer Applications in Acquisitions and Cataloging*. American Society for Information Science, Annual Meeting, 39th, San Francisco, October 4–9, 1976. Proceedings. Washington, DC: 1976, vol. 13.

Madron, Thomas W. *Local Area Networks: The Next Generation*, 2nd edition. New York: John Wiley & Sons, Inc., 1990. (ISBN 0-471-52250-3).

Malinconico, Michael S. "The Economics of Output Media," a paper presented at the 13th Annual Clinic on Library Applications of Data Processing. April 25–28, 1976. Urbana, IL: University of Illinois, Graduate School of Library Science.

Malinconico, Michael S. and Paul Fasana, *The Future of the Catalog: The Library's Choices*. White Plains, NY: Knowledge Industry Publications Inc., 1980.

Management of Serials Automation; Current Technology & Strategies for Future Planning. Edited by P. Gellatly, Haworth Press, 1982.

Managing Online References Services; edited by Ethel Auster. Neal-Schuman, 1986.

Markey, K. *Subject Access to Visual Resources Collections; a Model for Computer Construction of Thematic Catalogs*. Greenwood Press, 1986.

Marsterson, W.A.J. *Information Technology and the Role of the Librarian*. Croom Helm, 1986.

Matthews, Joseph R. *Guidelines for Selecting Automated Systems*. American Library Association. Lib. & Information Tech. Assn., 1986.

Matthews, Joseph R. "Microcomputer Circulation Control Systems; An Assessment." *Library Technology Reports*, 22:5–152 (January/February, 1986).

Matthews, J.R. and Williams, J.F. "Oh if I'd Only Known; Ten Things You Can Do Today to Prepare for Library Automation Tomorrow." *American Libraries*, 14:408–12 (June, 1983).

McQueen, J. and Boss, R.W. "Serials Control in Libraries; an Update of Automation Options." *Library Technology Reports*, 21:231–343, (May/June 1985).

McQueen, J. and Boss, R.W. "Serials Control in Libraries; Automated Options." *Library Technology Reports*, 20:89–282, (March/April 1984).

McQueen, J. and Boss, R.W. "Sources of Machine-Readable Cataloging and Retrospective Conversion." *Library Technology Reports*, 21:597–732, (November/December 1985).

Microcomputers in Libraries; edited by Mrs. C.C. Chen and S.E. Bressler. Neal-Schuman, 1982.

Miller, I. *Microcomputers in School Library Media Centers*. Neal-Schuman, 1984.

Minicomputers for Library Decision-Making: Issues, Trends, and Applications. Edited by Peter Hernon and Charles R. McClure. Ablex. 1986.

Minoli, Daniel. *Broadband Network Analysis and Design*. Boston, MA: Artech House Publishers, 1993. (ISBN 0-89006-675-2).

National Information Standards Organization. *Scholarly Information and Standardization*, Proceedings of the Twelfth Open Forum on the Study of the International Exchange of Japanese Information and Scholarly Databases in East Asian Scripts 1992/1993. Bethesda, MD: NISO Press, 1992. (ISBN 1-880124-06-8).

Nonbook Media; Collection Management and User Services; John W. Ellison and Patricia Ann Coty, editors. American Library Association, 1987.

Oakeshott, P. *The Impact of New Technology on the Publication Chain*. British National Bibliographic Research Fund, 1983.

Pierce, A. R. *Circulation and Finding System*. Blacksburg, VA: Virginia Polytechnic Institute and State University, 1979. (ERIC Document Reproduction No. ED 183 141).

Professional Librarian's Reader in Library Automation and Technology. Knowledge Industry Publications, 1980.

Projects and Procedures for Serials Administration. Compiled and edited by Diane Stine. Pierian Press, 1985.

"Public Libraries and the Internet." *Library Journal*, 119, No. 15 (September 15, 1994): 50.

Reed-Scott, J. *Issues in Retrospective Conversion*; report of a study conducted for the Council on Library Resources. Council on Library Resources. Bibliographic Services Development Program, 1984.

Ritchey, Tim. *Programming with Java*. Indianapolis, IN: New Riders, 1995.

Rockman, Ilene F. "The Potential of On-Line Circulation Systems as Public Catalogs: An Introduction." *RQ* 20 (Fall 1980): 39–58.

Roden, M. S. *Analog and Digital Communication Systems*. Englewood Cliffs, NJ: Prentice-Hall, 1979.

Rogers, Kenneth A. "Cost Benefits of Computer Output Microfilm Library Catalogs." American Society for Information Science. *Proceedings 10: Innovative Development in Information Systems: Their Benefits and Costs*. October 21–25, 1973.

Rohrbach, P.T. *FIND; Automation at the Library of Congress, The First Twenty-Five Years and Beyond*. Library of Congress, 1985.

Role of Computers in Sci-Tech Libraries; Edited by Ellis Mount, Haworth Press. 1986.

Rowley, J.E. *Computers for Libraries, 2nd Edition*. Bingley, 1985.

Saffady, William. *Computer-Output Microfilm: Its Library Applications*. Chicago, IL: American Library Association, 1978.

Saffady, William. *Introduction to Automation for Librarians*. American Library Association, 1983.

Salmon, Stephen R. *Library Automation Systems*. New York: M. Dekker, 1975.

Santosuosso, Joseph. "Electronic Data Interchange (EDI) for Libraries and Publishers," *Bulletin of the American Society for Information Science*, 19(1) (October/November 1992):15–17.

Savage, N. "LAMA Spotlights Pitfalls in Automated Circulation." *Library Journal* 105 (August 1980): 1570+.

Schatt, Stan. *Understanding Local Area Networks*, 3rd edition. Carmel, IN: SAMS, a Division of Prentice Hall Computer Publishing, 1992. (ISBN 672-30115-6)

Schultheiss, Louis A. "Data Processing Aids in Acquisitions Work." *Library Resources and Technical Services* 9: 66–72 (Winter 1965).

Scientific Journals; Issues in Library Selection and Management Edited by Tony Stankus. Haworth Press, 1987.

Serials Librarianship in Transition; Issues and Developments. Haworth Press, 1986.

Shammugan, K.S. *Digital and Analog Communication Systems.* New York: Wiley, 1979.

Stueart, R.D. "Libraries: A New Role?" In *Books, Libraries and Electronics.* Knowledge Industry Publications, 1982.

Swanson, Don R. "Requirements Study for Future Catalogs." *Library Quarterly* 42: 302–315 (July, 1972).

Taylor, Gerry M.; Hansard, James W.; and Anderson, James F. "Cut to Fit." *Library Resources and Technical Services* 14: 31–35 (Winter 1970).

Tedd, L.A. *An Introduction to Computer-Based Library Systems, 2nd Edition.* Wiley, 1984.

Tracy, J.I. *Library Automation for Library Technicians, an Introduction.* Scarecrow Press, 1986.

The Unicode Standard, Version 2.0. Reading, MA: Addison-Wesley Developers Press, 1996. (ISBN 0-201-48345-9)

Veaner, Allen B. "Major Decision Points in Library Automation." *College and Research Libraries.* 31: 299–312 (September 1970).

Video to Online: Reference Services and the New Technology, edited by W.A. Katz and R.A. Fraley, Haworth Press, 1983.

Viterbi, Andrew J., and Jim K., Omura, *Principles of Digital Communication and coding.* New York: McGraw-Hill, 1979.

Webb, T. *The In-House Option; Professional Issues of Library Automation.* Haworth Press, 1987.

Weber, David C. "Personnel Aspects of Library Automation." *Journal of Library Automation* 4:27–37 (March 1971).

Whitney, Gretchen and Stuart Glogoff. "Automation for the Nineties: A Review Article," *Library Quarterly,* 64(3), 1994:319–331.

Wilder, Floyd. *Guide to the TCP/IP Protocol Suite.* Boston, MA: Artech House Publishers, 1993. (ISBN 0-89006-693-0).

Willard, P. and Teece, V. *Public Libraries and Automation; Four Case Studies.* University of N.S.W. School of Librarianship, 1983.

ABOUT THE AUTHOR

Richard W. Boss is Senior Management Consultant, Information Systems Consultants Inc., Kensington, Maryland. He has served as a consultant to more than 1,000 libraries and library consortia on the selection and procurement of automated library systems or other information technologies. He has drafted over 100 information technology plans.

Mr. Boss was formerly University Librarian at Princeton University and Director of Libraries at the University of Tennessee at Knoxville. He is the author of *The Library Manager's Guide to Automation. 3rd Edition* (1990), *Automating Library Acquisitions: Issues and Outlook* (1982), and *Telecommunications for Library Management* (1984). His many other publications include *Information Technology and Space Planning* (1987), *Grant Money and How to Get It* (1980), *Fee-Based Information Services* (1980), *Developing Microform Reading Facilities* (1981), "Automation and Approval Plans," *Advances in Understanding Approval and Gathering Plans in Academic Libraries* (1970), and a score of studies for *Library Technology Reports*, a publication of the American Library Association. He is the contributing editor for *Library Systems Newsletter*.

Mr. Boss is a graduate of the University of Utah and holds an M.A. in Library Science from the University of Washington.

Index

217